IMAGES
of America

AROUND HILLSBORO

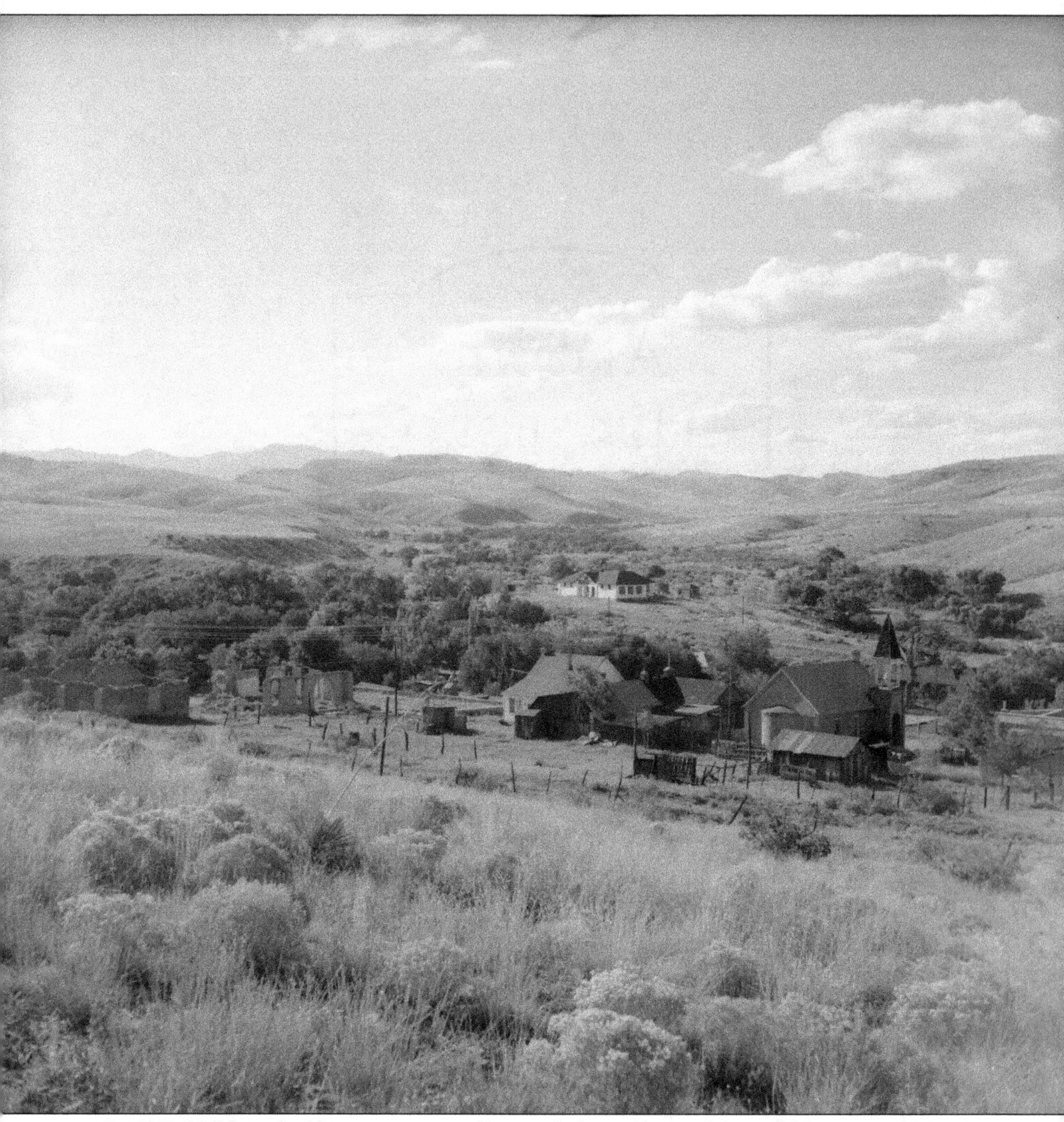

By 1959, Hillsboro had become a quiet village with descendants of the early Gringo and Mexican miners and ranchers and a few retirees seeking a quiet place to live. It has changed little since. Karl Kernberger took this photograph that year for the book *Ghost Towns of New Mexico: Playthings in the Wind*, but Hillsboro has never been a ghost town. (New Mexico History Museum)

ON THE COVER: William D. Slease appears in the 1920 census for Hillsboro. He was 46, and his occupation is listed as auto stage owner. In the 1930 census, he is shown as a merchant and owner of a general store. His garage was a popular gathering place. Slease died as a result of falling off of a cliff at a remote mine that he owned. (Tom Sullivan)

IMAGES
of America

Around Hillsboro

Hillsboro Historical Society
Foreword by Max Evans

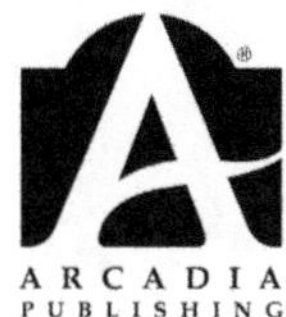

ISBN 9781531652470

Published by Arcadia Publishing
Charleston, South Carolina

Library of Congress Control Number: 2011923572

For all general information, please contact Arcadia Publishing:
Telephone 843-853-2070
Fax 843-853-0044
E-mail sales@arcadiapublishing.com
For customer service and orders:
Toll-Free 1-888-313-2665

Visit us on the Internet at www.arcadiapublishing.com

This book is dedicated to Lydia Keyes and June Anders, who have owned and maintained the Black Range Museum and cared for the important artifacts and photographs that represent the earliest days in Hillsboro, Kingston, and Lake Valley. Our community owes them deep appreciation.

Contents

Foreword

. . . and the world's most varied short drives are a few miles west of I-25 South. The slightly rolling road through high-desert terrain first passes a tiny settlement of seven high-end mobile homes. The smooth, two-lane blacktop goes past the cattle-guard entrance to Ted Turner's vast Ladder Ranch, where he raises hundreds of buffalo.

Now it begins. The terrain changes unpredictably like the world's weather. The earth is undulating more and more in a totally different mixture of shapes and shadows. If the rains have come, and the grass has grown and cured, the whole landscape will seem coated in waving gold—except where the rocks push out as a reminder that the Earth is held together by stone.

With luck, off to the right a mile or two, a building can be seen—the first of a planned mining mill, and the traveler's vision has just swept across millions of tons of copper. Because of water concerns, the ore remains securely hidden underneath the virgin soil and stones just as it was when formed millions of years ago.

Now the landscape suddenly appears so wide and high it stretches the eyes as the easy curves of rounded hills descend towards the village of Hillsboro, New Mexico. To the right, the view sweeps across a valley of stones and up to the Black Range and the vast Gila Wilderness.

Gradually, the nearly-a-mile-high village—inhabited by artists, writers, photographers, ranchers, ex-prospectors, and varied thinkers—starts to appear in a sheltered bowl of mesa-like hills. Drivers going through the village cross a bridge over tiny Percha Creek and soon see the beginning of a block-and-a-half-long business district. Sue's Antiques starts it off, then several small, in-residence shops and art galleries, a tiny motel, and the post office line the quiet thoroughfare. Across the street sits the General Store Café, which serves as a dining/visiting room, museum, and country club—all combined in this one structure.

The city limits end quickly, and the road crosses the Percha again on a much larger bridge with high rocky bluffs on each side. The landscape evolves into seemingly endless formations and foothills that range from massive cones to the two upright stone projections called the Kissing Rocks.

Passing through the F+ Ranch on towards the once-upon-a-time mining village of Kingston, a few scattered cows or horses can be seen, but in the increasingly forest-shrouded formations, the mind must imagine the truth of countless elk, deer, Mearn's quail, wild turkeys, coyotes, cougars, and bobcats and numberless birds hidden there, each one struggling to make a living in whatever manner nature and opportunity provides.

It's no wonder that the Mimbres Indians—and their ancestors the Mogollons—settled and survived in this area hundreds and hundreds of years before, living from, and with, all the aforementioned creatures. In their time, there were also wolves and even jaguars. The tribes imprinted their art and histories on faces of rocks and left behind the remains of now priceless pottery. After the other tribes vanished, Apaches roamed and hunted here, partaking in all the gifts of this ever-changing part of rare earth. The remains of their campsites and *pueblitas* have all but vanished, but the Indians seem to have left behind some ethereal magic still embedded in the rocks, trees, and air.

A short distance up the road above Kingston, in the forests of the Black Range, there is a pull-off with benches and tables where I sat and made the first notes to write a national award–winning story entitled "Super Bull." This symphonic land is inspirational to creative minds. Several of what I consider my best stories have these local settings. The Hillsboro country plays a critical part in my most ambitious novel, *Bluefeather Fellini.*

The short drive from Kingston to Hillsboro is totally different but no less fascinating, as the mighty view is reversed.

Now, back to this unique village populated with more dogs than people, where another side trip is to be experienced. A right turn in front of Sue's Antiques angles the pavement southward through endlessly changing formations of such scope, distance, and undulations that it could be a microcosm of the entire world. The hues of reddish brown, amber earth, turquoise skies, and cloud formations like mighty flying, castle-shaped ships give the feeling that this is indeed a treasure found. Magical.

Off to the right, dozens of little mountains suddenly appear that feel like a huge Chinese painting on silk? No. Real earth and stones, cacti, trees, grass, animals, and talented people in far-scattered, secluded homes live here.

To the left of the road, about the distance of throwing a rock, the earth opens up to what was one of the richest silver mines ever—the Bridal Chamber. The ore was so concentrated that miners used saws to cut it out.

On the other side of the mine, the ghost town of Lake Valley, with its weather-bruised buildings still standing in the sun, leaves a reminder of the Old West and its spirits. Just over the hill from this, the brutal battle of Gavilan Canyon between miners, buffalo soldiers, and Chief Nana's Apaches took place. The bloody contest had no real winner.

As the hills flatten out into a vast prairie on all sides of the road, the golden tan grass waves in countless patterns with the slightest breeze. And in the far distance, hazy blue mesas and mountains cling to the edge of the Earth. The whole easy drive from the turnoff above Kingston to this soothing Lake Valley prairie is only about 30 miles.

Moving upward while leaving Hillsboro and going back to I-25, the easy curves even out for a short spell at the edge of the valley and reveal a view of spectacular scope. The distance of vision is enhanced between mid-morning and mid-afternoon to encompass almost 100 miles across wondrously bent, curving, rolling ground that finally, in the immeasurable distance, becomes a single, hazy lull to the pale blue mesas trying to vanish in the curvature of the Earth.

These unique drives are short—about 10 to 30 miles long, but the visit to Hillsboro country and its residents—two- and four-legged—gives special moments that last forever.

ACKNOWLEDGMENTS

We want to thank everyone who contributed photographs and information for this book. We were not, unfortunately, able to use every photograph submitted, but we are no less appreciative for those pictures not included here. Many of them may be used for future projects. Abbreviations alongside the following individuals and institutes are used to identify sources of the images.

Those who responded to our request included John Luna (JL), Nancy McCauley (NM), Jackie Faulkner (JF), Daisy Wilson (DW), Fred R. "Stretch" Luna (SL), Sonja Rutledge (SR), Don Turner (DT), Donald Graham (DG), Sue Bason (SB), Tommy Sullivan (TS), Jay Lett (JL), Gloria Spellman (GS), Martha Choquetee (MQ), Martha Martin (MM), Sandy Lane (SaL), David Pike (DP), Patricia Heydt (PH), Mark Thompson III (MT), and Gerald Yankee (GY). Photographs with no courtesy line are from the private collection of Matti Nunn Harrison and Patti Nunn.

We especially thank June Anders and the Black Range Museum (BRM) for opening the museum's extensive photographic collection. LaRena Miller of the Geronimo Springs Museum (GSM) provided access to the George Miller Collection, and New Mexico State University Special Collections allowed us to use the Rio Grande Historical Collection (NMSU/RGHC). Mark Nero of the Percha Bank Museum (PBM) in Kingston kindly provided photographs from that collection. Also, we thank Evan Davies and Ann Morgan of the Institute of Historical Survey Foundation (IHSF) at Las Cruces for providing images from the Ed Ostertag Collection. Photographs were also provided by the staff of Gila National Forest (GNF) and the New Mexico History Museum (NMHM).

We have barely scratched the surface of history around Hillsboro. If there are errors or serious omissions, we apologize and accept full responsibility. We hope this book will serve to stimulate more detailed and inclusive research into the history of our area.

Introduction

Starting in 1877 and ending in 1939, Hillsboro was the center of a lively commercial complex that could have been the source for every dime western novel and Hollywood western ever made. The town received its name when Joe Yankie tossed his name into a hat, along with other names submitted by the various founders. Yankie's name was drawn, and he got to name the town. The original spelling was Hillsborough, the same as Yankie's hometown in Ohio. It was shortened to Hillsboro in 1884. Within Sierra County, of which Hillsboro was the seat, lived Apache warriors, Navajo hunters and traders, Mexican farmers and ranchers, Scots-Irish cowmen, wandering rustlers and gunslingers, gentle goat- and sheepherders, grizzled prospectors, expectant mining speculators, adventurous scientists, novelists, circuit preachers, lawyers, engineers, and, amidst it all, shopkeepers seeking stable livelihoods. Surrounding three vital and booming towns—Lake Valley, Hillsboro, and Kingston—was rugged and nearly impenetrable wilderness inhabited by wolves, grizzly bears, black bears, and mountain lions. Mule deer, tiny Coues white-tailed deer, and wild turkey helped feed the rare individual who wandered the timber-covered mountains.

To some extent, a mystery regarding the human history of this landscape resides in the very abruptness of the arrival of European-based civilization. Although the region shows signs of prehistoric human settlement since the beginning of the Holocene, the expanse represented by western Sierra County was virtually empty when Europeans arrived around 1540. The region encompassing the Rio Grande from approximately present-day Hatch to the south boundary of the Bosque del Apache was devoid of villages or farms until about 1830. The history of Pueblo cultures and Navajo incursions into northern New Mexico has been written many times, and the Spanish *entrada* and growth of a Hispanic agricultural society along the major rivers is the subject of a large body of American literature. The settlement of El Paso del Norte and the middle Rio Grande has likewise been told many times over. The major tributaries flowing into the Rio Grande from the Black Range and Mimbres Mountains show only sporadic settlement before 1830, and the region covered by our book lacked European culture until 1877, save for a few remote ranches. Even after farm communities appeared along Alamosa and Cuchillo Negro creeks north of Hillsboro, the middle and lower reaches of Animas, Percha, Trujillo, Berrenda, and Macho Creeks remained a sporadically used province of Apaches. Stated simply, while ruins of prehistoric cultures exist in the area, no evidence exists that the grassy foothills or the watered bottoms of this region held historic human settlements before the discovery of gold and silver created the 1877 boom. Then, almost instantly, three towns appeared that, despite their relative isolation, had nearly all of the modern amenities of their time in the way of transportation, business, communications via printing presses, post offices, and housing. Only when this had happened did modest farming begin along the creeks and ranching expand into the rangelands.

No clear reason exists for why this region was settled so late. A simple explanation says that marauding Apaches and Navajos kept the early Hispanics out. But John Wilson, in *Between the Mountain and the River*, gives evidence that even the Apaches rarely used this region and were, in fact, probably driven into its rough terrain by expanding Anglo miners and the American military. The mining communities created the need for protection, and the military responded, forcing the native tribe to hide in the wilderness and ultimately driving it from the Black Range. But the early settlers would have been no more threatened by Apaches in our region than they were in settled areas to the north and south. Apache presence does not seem to explain the lateness of settlement, although future archaeological and historical evidence may modify this conclusion.

Be that as it may, the result is an opportunity to develop a complete and well-documented history of what we are calling "Perchaland." A local government and legal records of mining claims and homestead claims formed almost instantly along with settlement, relying upon legal systems already in place further east and west. Newspapers also appeared overnight, and daily events began to be recorded. Because of a tremendously diverse mix of people coming to the area, the papers had plenty to report. Ranching and associated brand records and landholding claims, especially around water, also emerged instantly. By 1880 or so, people were present with cameras, in some cases high-quality, large-format models, and documented people, places, and landscapes. Three men in particular made their livings or supplemented their incomes with a camera, and their work appears in this book; they were J.C Burge, George Tambling Miller, and Henry Schmidt. Probably few regions in the United States have such a rich array of photographs available virtually from the day they were settled. In producing a book like this one, the problem lies less in finding enough photographs than in sorting, selecting, and locating original images. It also lies in determining ownership and acquiring permissions for use. And of course, as with any effort, it lies in identifying people, dates, and places that appear in the aged prints.

Perchaland went into decline after the mines played out and the population center shifted to the Rio Grande. The Sierra County seat moved to Hot Springs (now Truth or Consequences), and only a few older families, largely associated with ranching, remain. Lake Valley slowly died and became a true ghost town. Hillsboro became a quiet village occupied mainly by people with outside incomes. No commercial base remained that would support working-age people with families. The stately 1892 Sierra County Courthouse is a mere husk, gravity reducing it to a ruin—but one the Hillsboro Historical Society seeks to save. A good many people—common folk and folk with uncommon ability—walked through its last remaining arch conducting the business of the day. Kingston became more of a playground for people seeking relief from the summer heat of Truth or Consequences, Las Cruces, and El Paso, and its few full-time residents rely upon outside wealth—tourism, mainly.

Of the early commercial bases for the area, only cattle ranching remains. Sheep and goats are gone, and the cattle industry is meager compared with its first 70 years. Use of federal lands has become more restricted, and modern ranchers graze their private lands with a longer look to the future. Stocking rates more nearly reflect the lower end of the carrying capacity of the range, which is determined by periodic droughts rather than the rare wet periods, when grass grows tall.

The founders of Perchaland are gone, but some of their immediate descendants remain, including two of the authors of this book. Some of the founders survived well into the 20th century, and people live today who remember and talked with them. *Around Hillsboro* is an effort to assemble the rich photographic history that documents our region. It asks more questions than it answers, and we hope that it stimulates additional research before the cultural memory of the area dims beyond retrieval.

One

Apache Wars

The Apache wars of the American Southwest were grist for Hollywood westerns. Though often fictionalized, the real war unfolded around Hillsboro from 1879 to 1886. In a seven-year span, Chinese farmers were killed at Lake Valley, woodcutters died on Berrenda Creek, citizens and soldiers walked into an ambush in Gavilan Canyon, and an entire family on Jaralosa Creek was murdered and mutilated on September 11, 1879. A few miles away that day, eight Hillsboro men died at McEver's Ranch. A week later, Maj. A.P. Morrow's buffalo soldiers and Navajo scouts faced a blistering fight in Massacre Canyon against Victorio.

The environs around Hillsboro were raided by the few Apaches who rejected reservation life with a vengeance that exacted a toll of life, property, and public treasury. African American Buffalo Soldiers of the 9th Cavalry were stationed at Camp French at Hillsboro in 1880. Five years later, the 8th Cavalry and 25th Infantry would spend a year at Camp Hillsboro/Camp Boyd. Apache Scouts were detailed to Hillsboro, and army supply stations were set at McEver's Ranch.

The Burt Lancaster movie *Ulzana's Raid* was rooted in a kernel of truth. Only a mere mile or so from Hillsboro, the Apache Ulzana and his band tested the horse soldiers in 1885. The cavalry, manned with the likes of Tom Horn, chased the marauders, who ably melded into the mountains. In a few weeks, 38 people would die by Ulzana's hand.

Decisive battles with the Apaches never occurred, and that frustrated the citizenry and the military. The raids of Victorio's band (1879–1880) were particularly bloody, and as many as 500 citizens in the Southwest died. A Michigan mining engineer, Frank Robinson, working in Hillsboro in October 1880, wrote this to his wife:

> I traveled on a buckboard these last 40 miles. All along the road are the marks sad and savage of Victorio and his band of 300 Apache. From Hillsboro one year ago went out 15 young men to attack them. A few hours later came back eight—all that were left. Ranches are deserted, mining stopped and business unsettled by those terrible raids.

Mrs. Robinson, no doubt, did not hear the last of it. The next year, the elderly Nana would blast by Hillsboro and kill more people on the road to McEver's Ranch as his grand finale. Geronimo raided ranches until 1886, when he and all the Chiricahua Apache became prisoners of war and were exiled to the East.

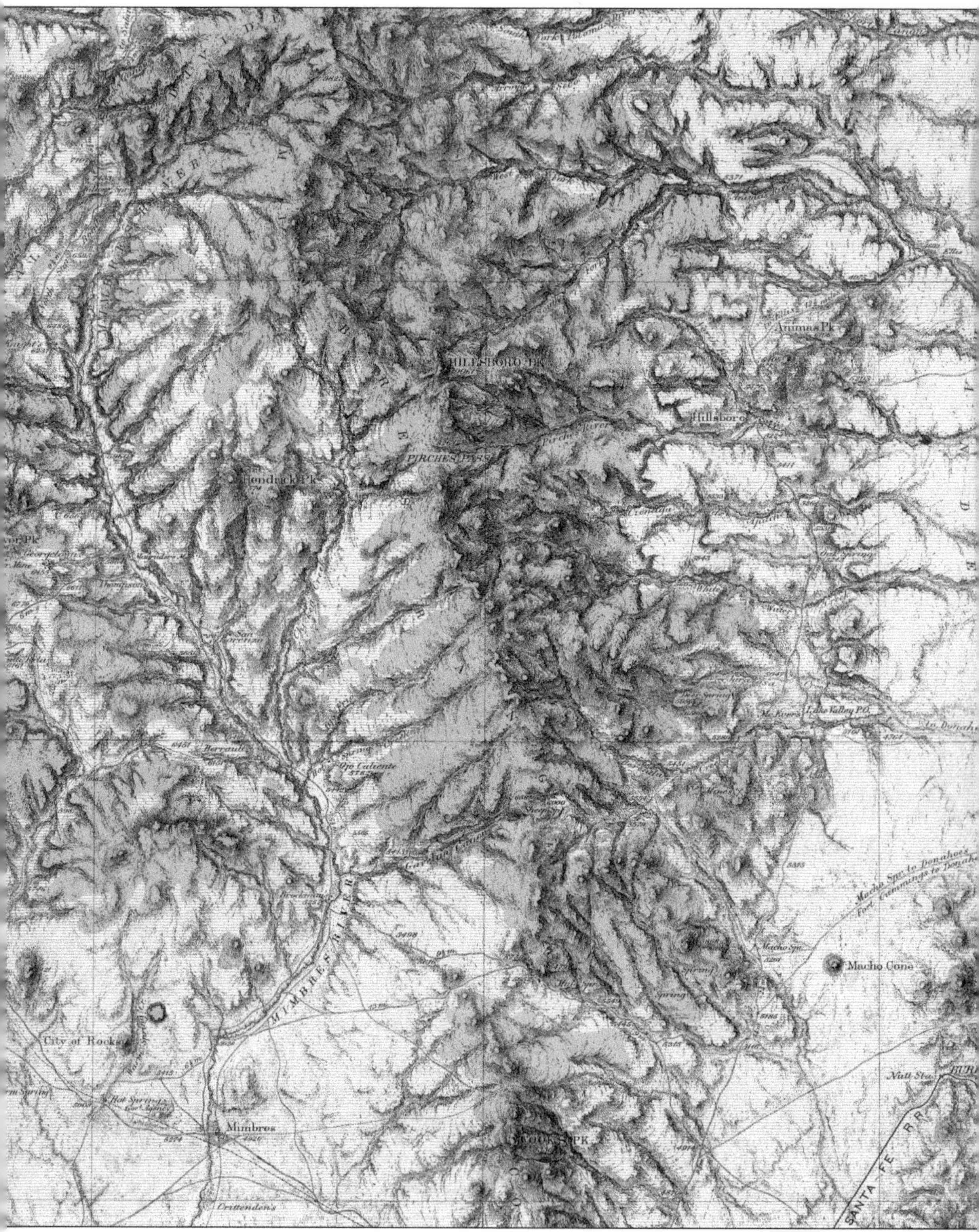

HILLSBORO PK
Animas Pk
Hillsboro
PIRCHES PASS
Hendrick Pk
Georgetown
Ojo Caliente
MIMBRES RIVER
Macho Cone
Macho Spr.
City of Rocks
Hot Springs
Mimbres
Crittenden's
Lake Valley P.O.
Nutt Sta.
SANTA FE R.R.

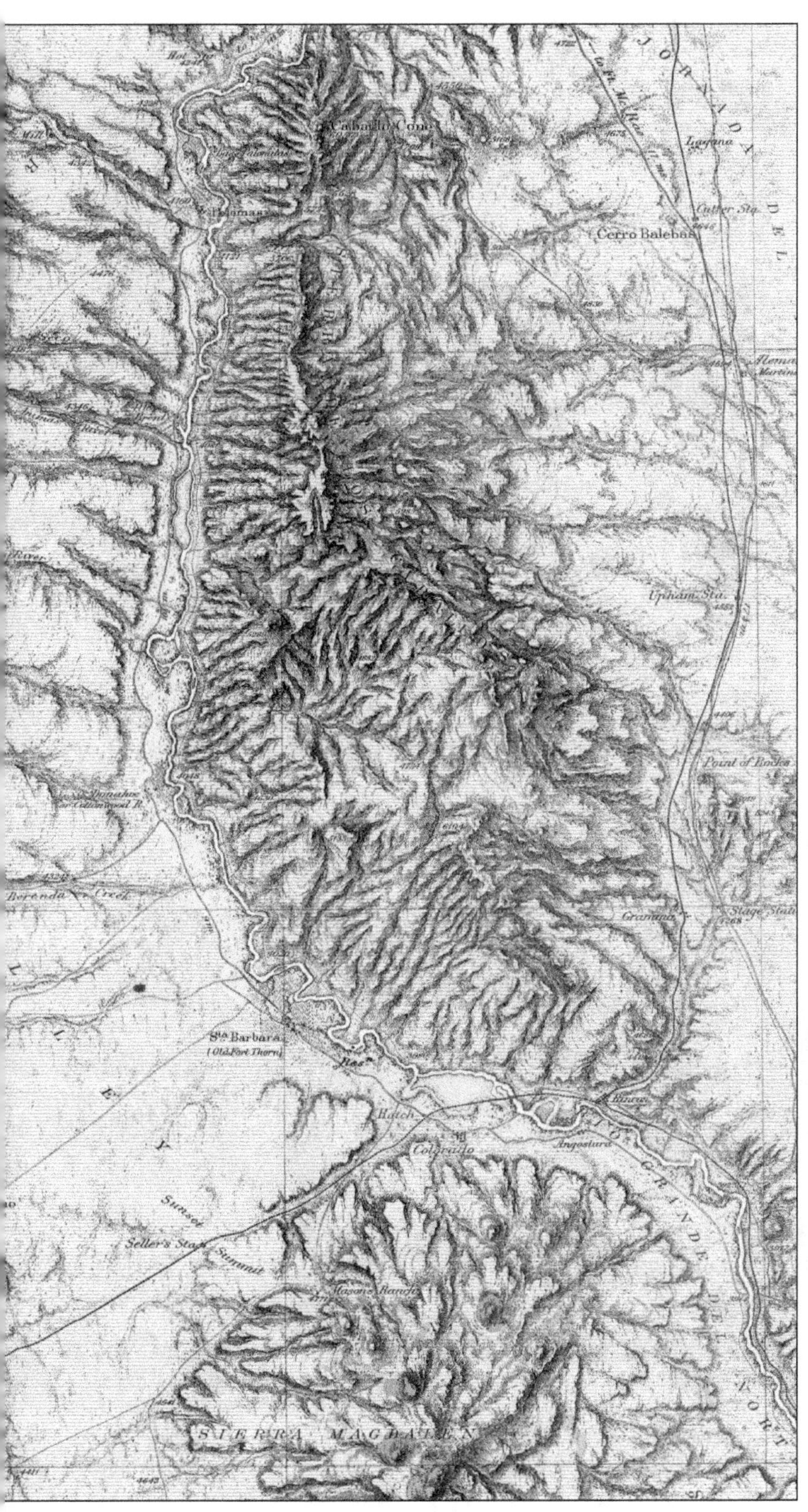

This 1881 George Wheeler map may very well be the first federal map to show Hillsboro as a place name. Kingston was yet to be founded, and Lake Valley and McEver's Ranch were co-located. The Lake Valley townsite would move to two more locations. Pirches Pass would come to be known as Emory Pass to commemorate the topographical engineer of General Kearney's army that moved over the Mimbres Mountains and up Berrenda Creek in 1846, during the Mexican War. The Apache called this place home for centuries, at least on a seasonal basis. (Murray Hudson)

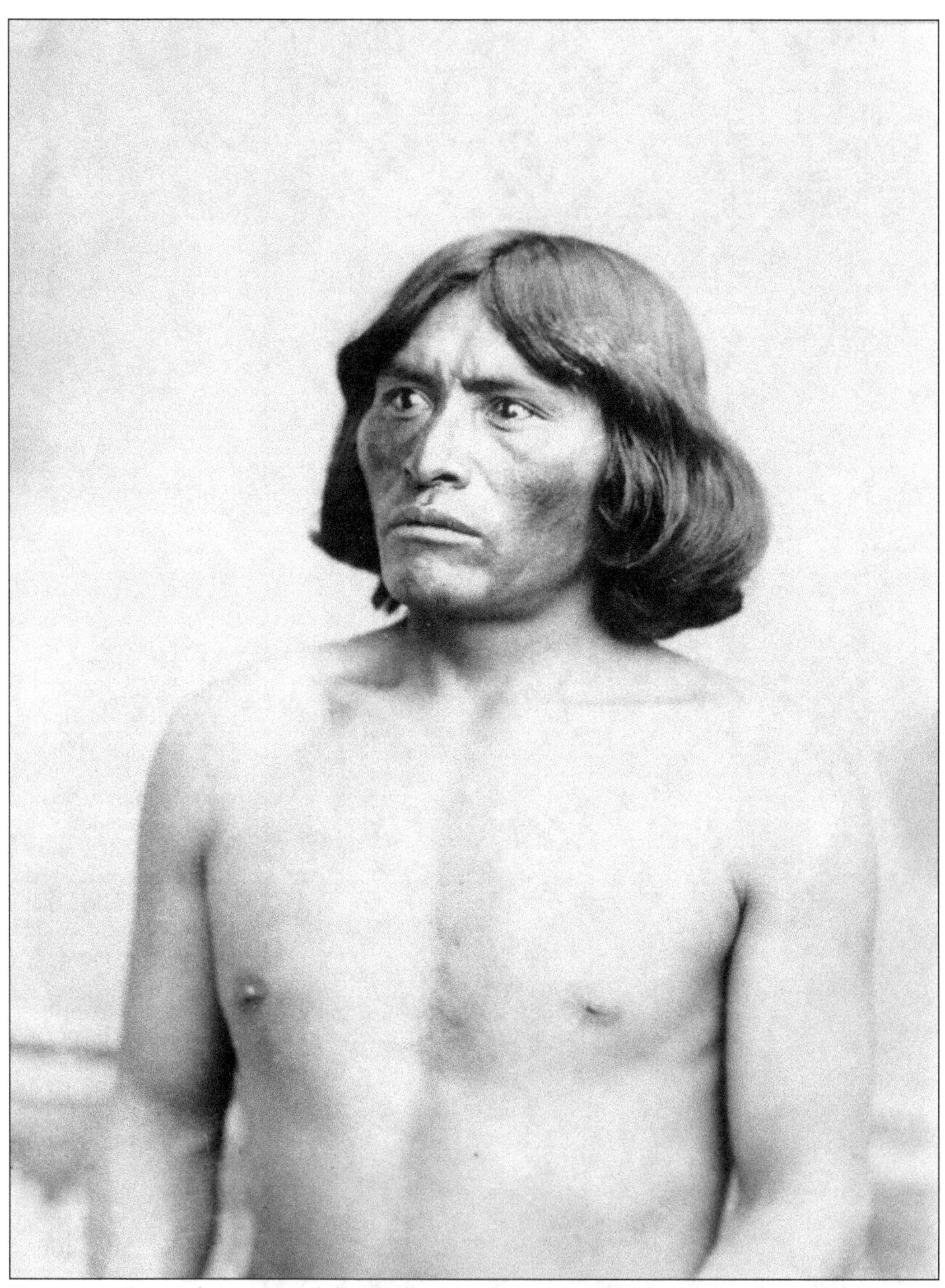

Desiring to live at his ancestral Ojo Caliente northeast of Hillsboro, Apache leader Victorio refused life on the San Carlos Apache Reservation in Arizona. A fickle federal government and an indictment for murder sent Victorio on a rampage in September 1879. The *New York Times* reported a 10-hour fight at McEver's Ranch with 100 Indians. Victorio died in an engagement with the Mexican military in 1880. (Arizona State Library)

Nicholas Galles led a posse of 15 men to McEver's Ranch on September 11, 1879, to fight Victorio. Eight died. Galles, who studied law under Albert Fountain and owned a Hillsboro mercantile, later championed the creation of Sierra County in the territorial legislature. His daughter, Georgia, married attorney Mark Thompson, who prosecuted Sheriff Pat Garrett's accused murderer and defended Albert Fall in the Teapot Dome scandal. (Mark Thompson III)

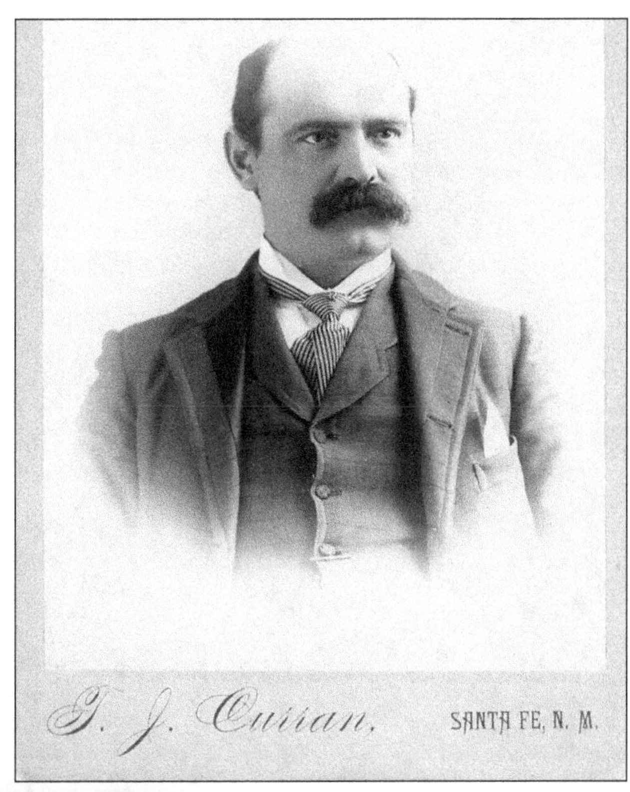

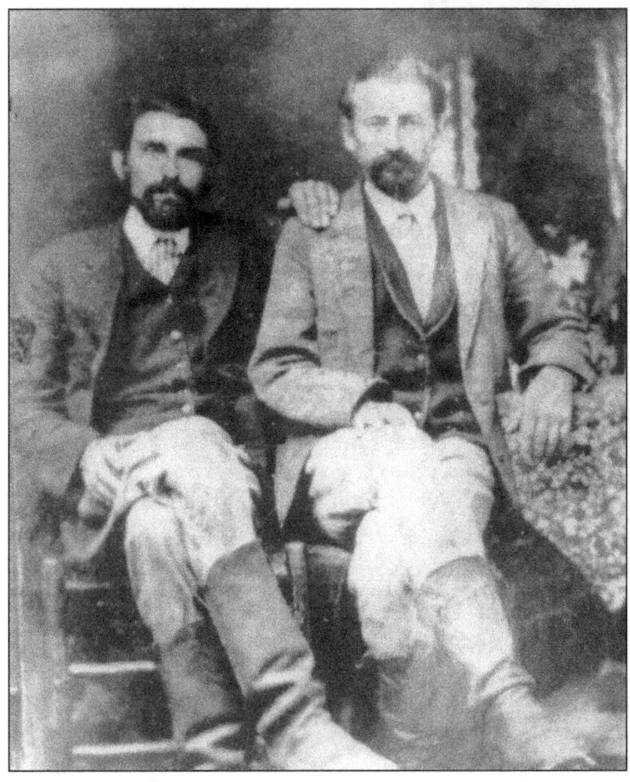

Joseph Yankie (right), with brother James, was at McEver's Ranch on September 11, 1879, to battle Victorio. Yankie was one of seven survivors. Newspapers reported that Yankie's daughter was kidnapped by the Apache. Lore has it that Yankie named Hillsboro after his suggestion was drawn from a hat. He was born near Hillsborough, Ohio. Streets in Hillsboro and Silver City bear the name *Yankie*. (Gerald Yankie)

Hillsboro N Mex
June 27th 1885

E L Bartlett
Adj't General
Santa Fe N Mex

Dear Sir

Signal fires and fresh tracks have been reported by prospectors very near every day the passed three weeks yesterday a signal fire was seen from our streets on the Hillsboro Peak.

A dettachment of troops were out in that direction and last night the Officer in Command sent in for additional men saying he had struck a fresh trail and was within a few miles of the fire seen by us and expected to strike them this morning at daylight.

Truly Yours
Nicholas Galles

Nicholas Galles, by then elected to the territorial legislature and soon to be commissioned a captain in the militia, wrote this urgent 1885 letter telling the government in Santa Fe of Apache activity on Hillsboro Peak. The letter shows that federal troops at Camp Hillsboro/Camp Boyd communicated with local leaders. (CSWR)

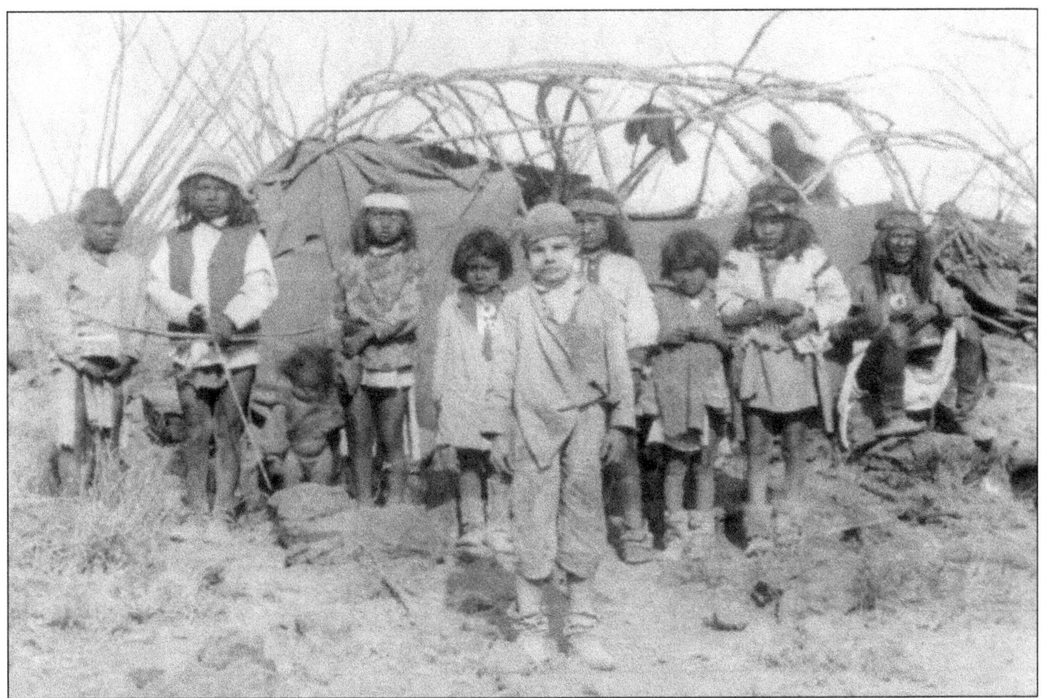

Ten-year-old Jimmy McKinn was kidnapped and his brother murdered by Geronimo at their ranch on September 11, 1885, near the site of Nana's last battle in 1881. The Hillsboro militia, led by Galles and future Supreme Court chief justice Frank W. Parker, chased Geronimo over the Black Range a few days later. McKinn was eventually returned to his parents. (Library of Congress)

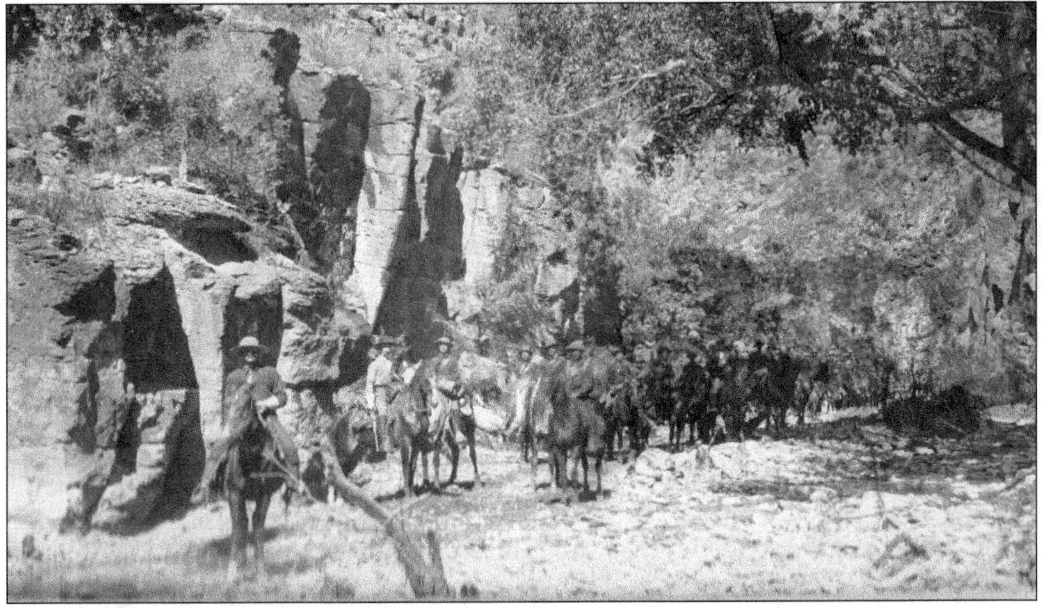

Kingston photographer J.C. Burge captured this c. 1885 image of the 8th Cavalry from Camp Hillsboro/Camp Boyd on patrol. Apache brothers Chihuahua and Ulzana, along with Geronimo, killed civilians at Lake Valley, Hillsboro, and Kingston in the fall of that year, leaving the citizenry on edge and the military on the move. (BRM)

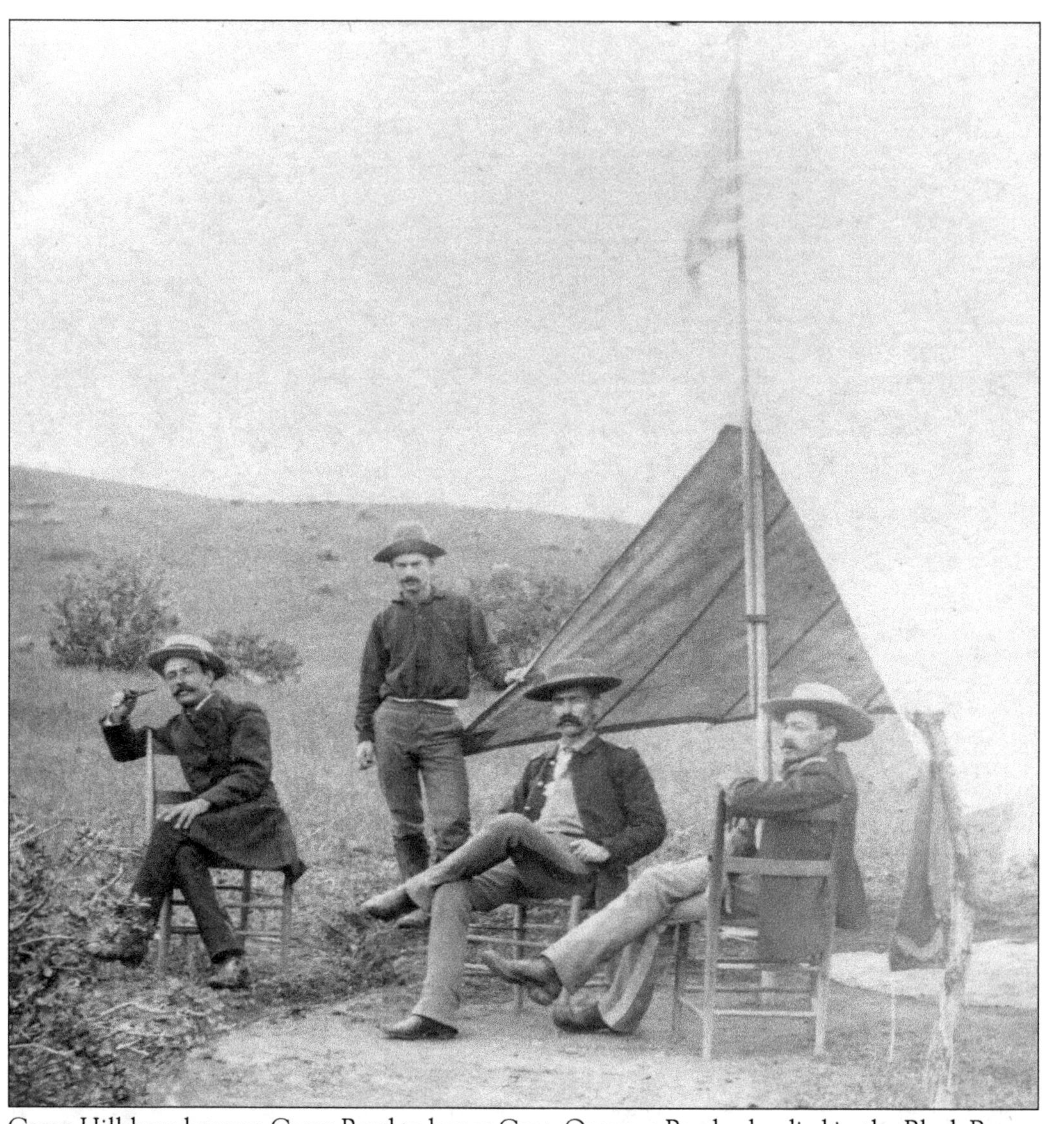

Camp Hillsboro became Camp Boyd to honor Capt. Orsemus Boyd, who died in the Black Range in 1885. Army doctor Emil Muhl (left) was fetched to attend the dying Boyd. Dr. Muhl sits at Hillsboro with an infantry and cavalry officer in a moment of levity. (BRM)

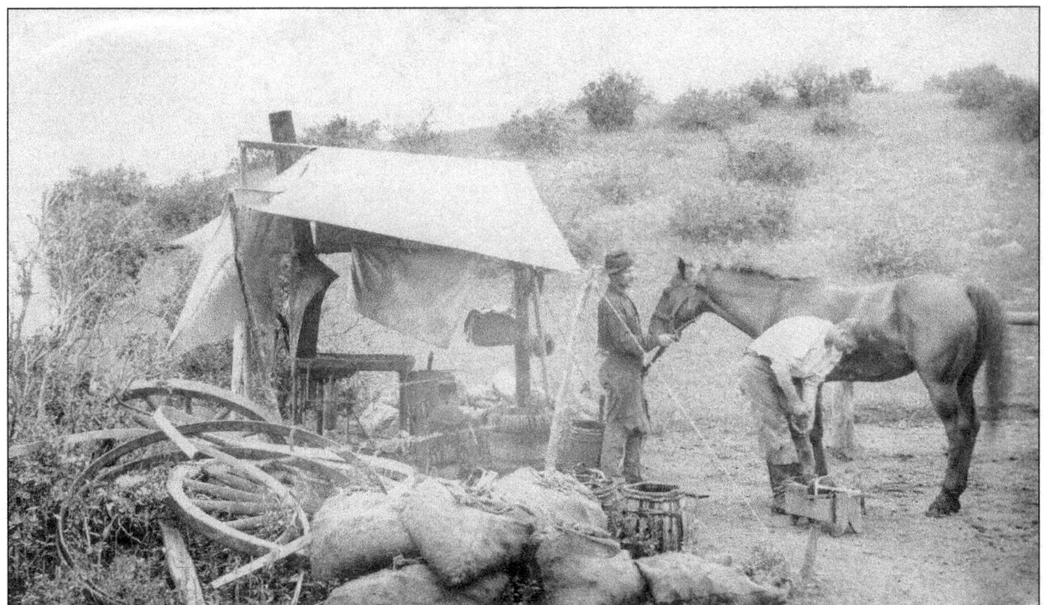

The horse's brand signifies it belonged to Troop G, 8th Cavalry at Camp Boyd. An 1889 court-martial record states that the troop's farrier, Asa Hawkes, deserted. The trial revealed that he "lost" items like his Colt .45 at Hillsboro. Hawkes was sentenced to four years in the infamous Leavenworth prison. This may be Hawkes. (BRM)

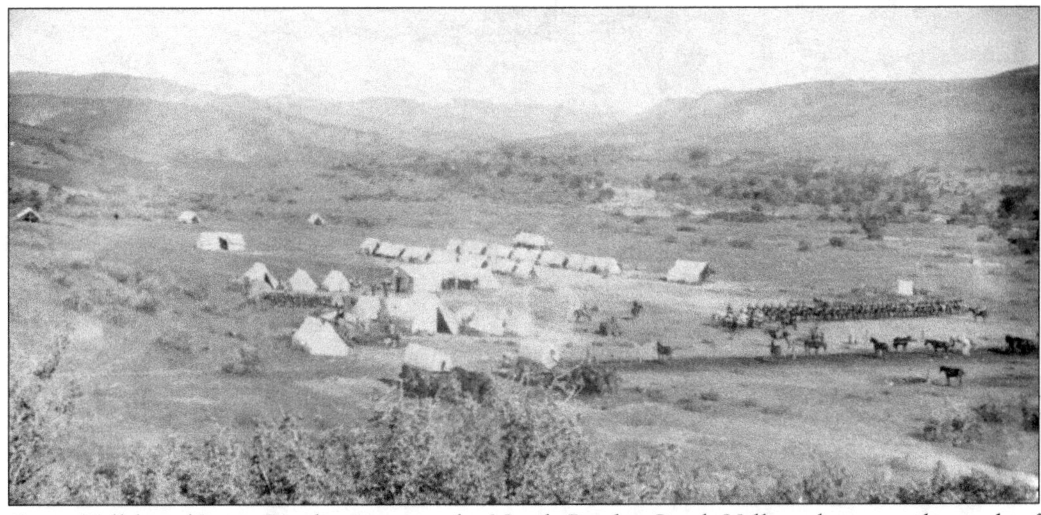

Camp Hillsboro/Camp Boyd was set in the North Percha Creek Valley, about a mile north of the current post office. Troops from the 25th Infantry and the 8th Cavalry occupied Hillsboro for 12 months. Federal troops were there to reign in Apaches who enacted violence in protest of the policy of the US government. (BRM)

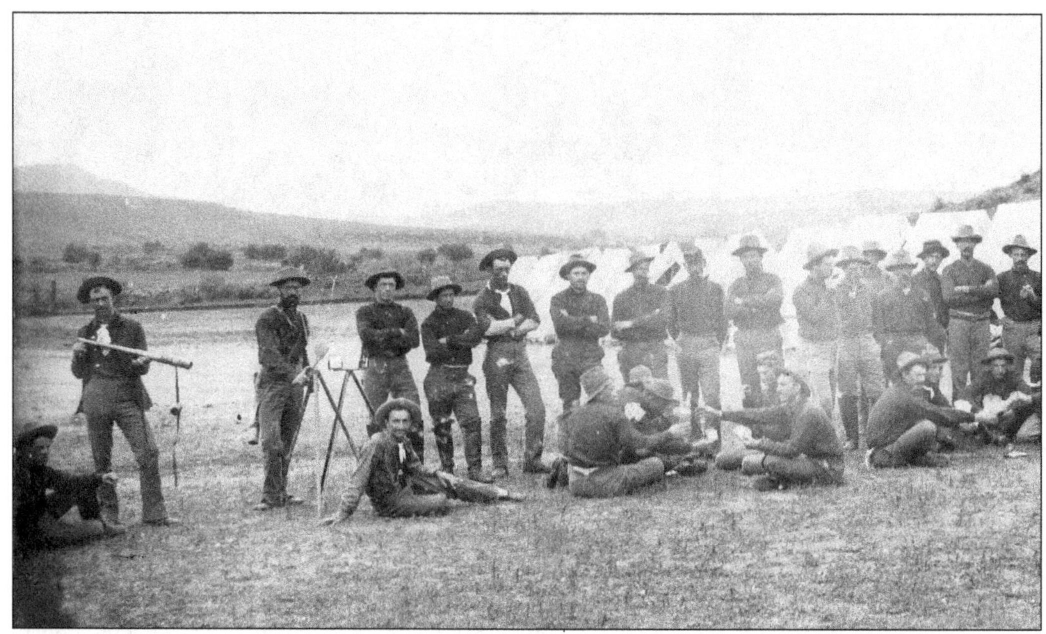

Camp Hillsboro/Camp Boyd was one of many heliograph stations in the Southwest set up by Gen. Nelson Miles in his effort to crush the Apache renegades. The heliograph, seen here at left, was simply a mirror used to flash code. It proved ineffective, given the Apache traveled at night while soldiers slept. The war ended in 1886. (BRM)

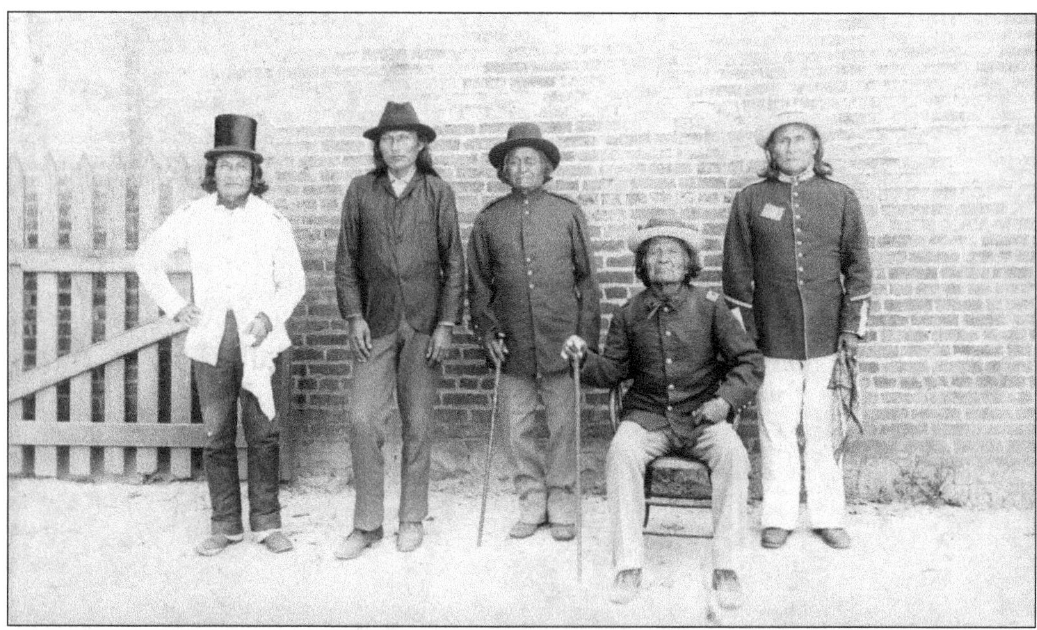

This 1894 images shows Apache paladins imprisoned in Alabama. Chihuahua (left) raided Lake Valley. Naiche (second from left) and Geronimo (far right) were at home in the Black Range crags and were the last to give up. Loco (center), scarred by a grizzly in the Black Range, had sought peace. Nana (seated) remained recalcitrant to his end. He led his infamous 1881 raid as an arthritic old man, yet he still eluded hundreds of soldiers. (Alabama Department of Archives and History)

Two

The Fountain Trial

On the court docket of the Third Judicial District based in Las Cruces, case no. 2618 is the Territory of New Mexico v. Oliver Lee and James Gililland. Lee and Gililland were charged for the murder of an eight-year-old boy, Henry Fountain. Henry and his father, Judge Albert J. Fountain, went missing near the white sands of the Tularosa Basin on February 1, 1896. With signs of a struggle and all the blood, they were presumed dead. Their bodies were never found.

Albert Fountain had a way of bringing out the hate in his enemies, and Lee and Gililland were among them. Fountain, working as a lawyer for a stock association, intended to put Lee behind bars for stealing cattle. Only days before his disappearance, Fountain indicted Lee at the Lincoln County Courthouse. It took three years of investigations, political maneuvering, and chicanery to bring the case to trial. With public sentiment not in its favor in Las Cruces, the defense sought a change of venue to Hillsboro. The trial would be the most sensational event to occur amid the ancient cottonwoods that lined Main Street.

What culminated in a stately Victorian brick courthouse on the rise above Hillsboro in May of 1899 was more than a murder trial. It was a gathering of political factions rooted in the Civil War—Republicans against Democrats. The dead Fountains and the prosecution embodied the "California Column," Union soldiers mustered out in Mesilla at the end of the war. Many of the Union men stayed in southern New Mexico and married Hispanic women. Lee and the defense represented a Texas Confederate heritage. The trial that consumed Hillsboro for three weeks was the epitome of personal and political animus that pervaded the New Mexico Territory. The brutality that the child likely suffered was the collateral damage of taking out a political enemy. It was part and parcel of the lawlessness that delayed statehood for an otherwise deserving people.

At trial, the prosecution faltered. Key witnesses did not show, probably out of fear. The cry of politics worked for the defense, and Lee and Gililland were acquitted of murdering the boy. No one was ever tried for killing the judge. The principal figures in the trial became a who's who of the territory. Some went on to good fortune, others to ruin.

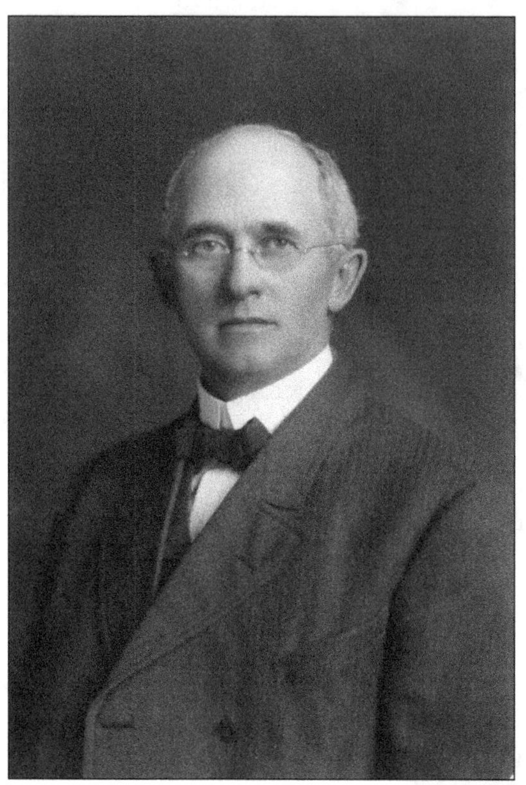

Judge Frank W. Parker presided over the trial of Oliver Lee and Jim Gilliland for the murder of eight-year-old Henry Fountain. A Michigan lawyer, Parker moved to Hillsboro in 1883. President McKinley appointed him to the territorial bench in 1897. Parker also presided over Pat Garrett's murder trial in 1909, and became a justice of the Supreme Court in 1912. He died in 1932. (New Mexico History Museum)

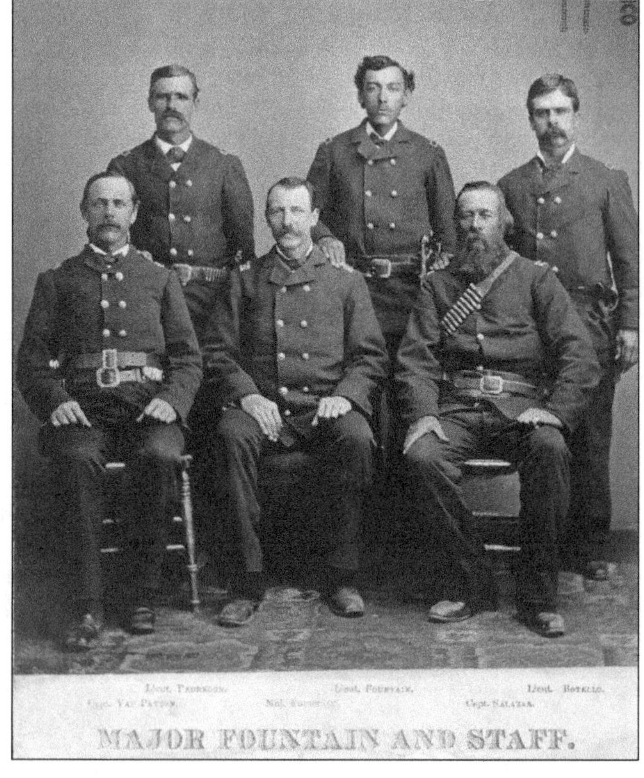

Albert Fountain led a militia that operated around Hillsboro and was noted for effectively rounding up cattle rustlers. His effort to rope in the presumed rustling by Oliver Lee may have been the catalyst that got him and his son Henry killed in 1896. Their bodies were never discovered. Fountain, a former judge and speaker of the house in the New Mexico Territorial Legislature, was a political rival to Albert Fall and associate Oliver Lee. (New Mexico History Museum)

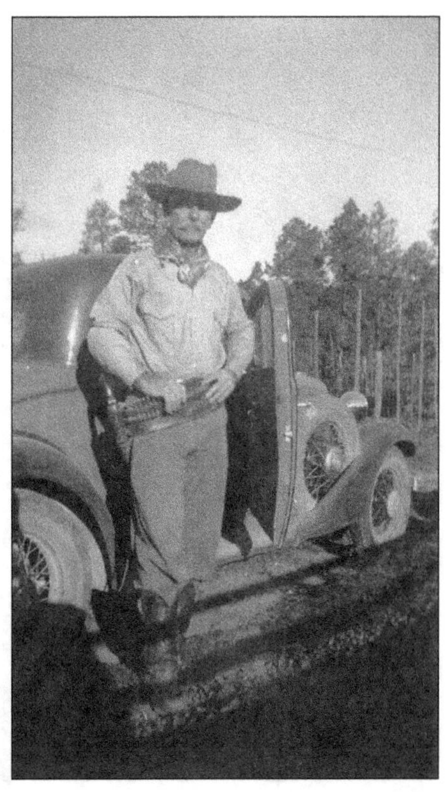

A Hillsboro jury acquitted Oliver Lee (right) and Jim Gililland of murdering the Fountain boy. Freedom was short-lived; they returned to jail for killing Dona Ana County deputy sheriff Kent Kearney but were never tried. Lee went on building a life in politics and a cattle empire that included land belonging to another potential murder victim, Francois Rochas. That land is now part of the Oliver Lee Memorial State Park. Gililland (below) bought a ranch in 1902. He lived less visibly than Lee, but he may have been haunted for having cut the boy's throat, or so said a close friend many years after the fact. Gililland's sister lamented in a 1915 letter to the Fountain family that she shaded the truth to protect her brother and Lee associate Bill McNew. McNew murdered her husband and shot her in the neck. (Both, New Mexico History Museum)

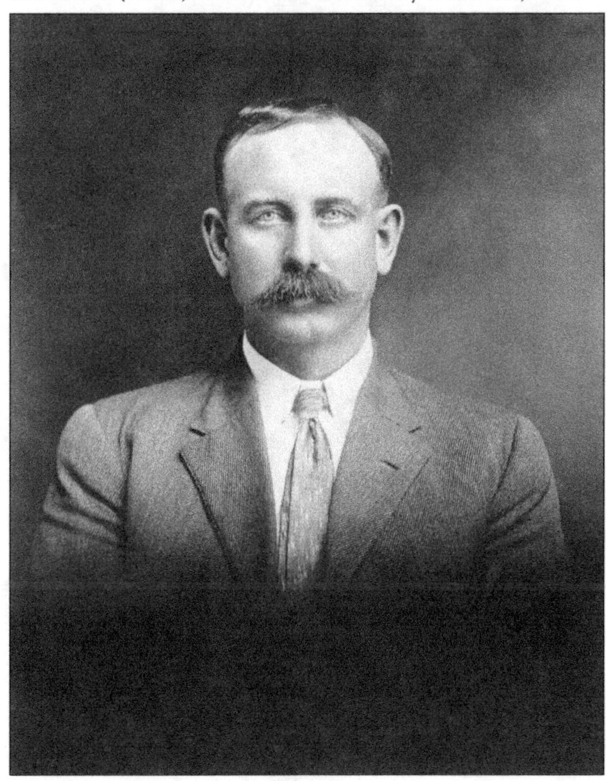

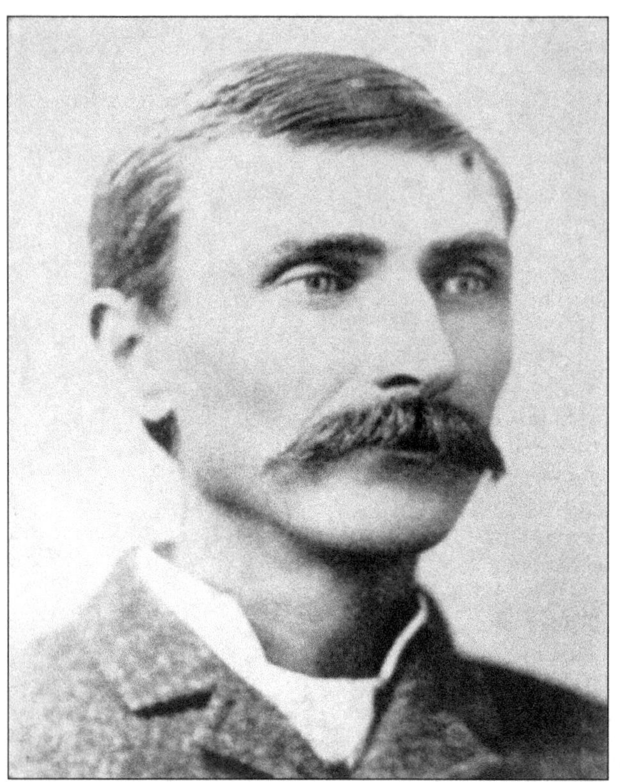

Sheriff Pat Garrett, famous for killing Billy the Kid, pursued Lee and Gililland for months. Citing fear for their lives, the wanted men evaded arrest. The real reason may have been the need for favorable political circumstances to ensure their survival. At the trial, attorneys quizzed Garrett on Lee shooting deputy Kearney and the character of another deputy, Ben Williams. (NMHM)

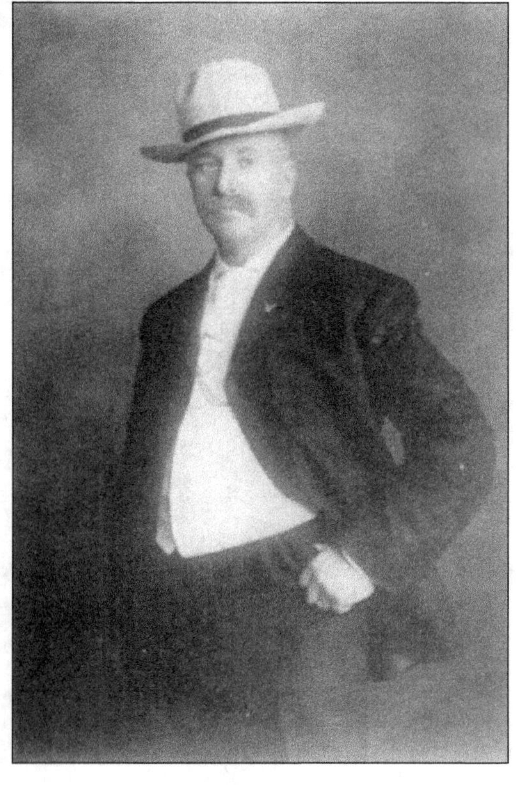

Dep. Ben Williams helped Garrett to ferret out Lee and Gililland. Williams had a history with the accused and their attorney, Albert Fall. When Fall served as a district judge, he had Williams fired as a US marshal and secured badges for Lee, Gililland, and McNew. Fall ambushed and shot Williams on a Las Cruces street in 1895, with Williams taking a bullet in the arm. (NMHM)

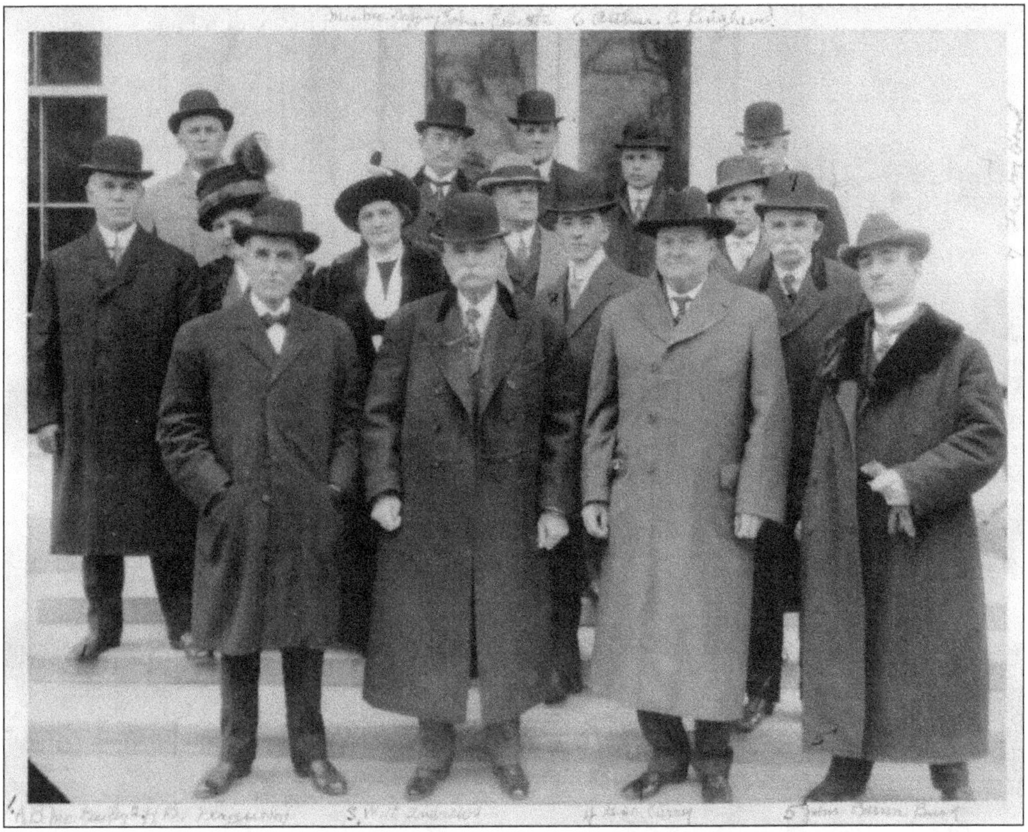

Harvey B. Fergusson (front, far left) and George Curry (front, second from right) were at the trial, and both later served in Congress. Fergusson, formerly partnered with W.B. Childers, defended the accused. Curry was appointed sheriff of Otero County so that Lee and Gililland could surrender to him, thus avoiding Dona Ana County authorities. Late in life, Curry made his home in Kingston, where he penned an autobiography. The man between them, William "Bull" Andrews, lived near Hillsboro and championed New Mexico statehood in Congress. (CWSR)

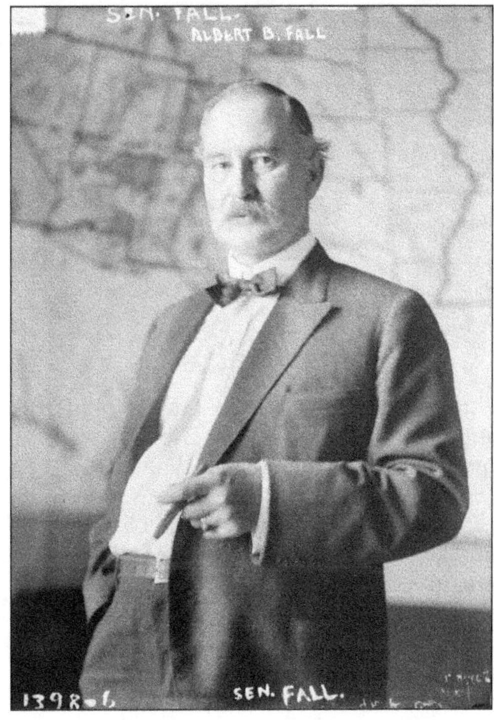

Albert Fall defended Lee and Gililland at trial. His stormy defense even maliciously accused Judge Parker of being part of a political conspiracy. Fall benefited by Fountain's death; his rival was gone. Fall became New Mexico's first US senator and President Harding's secretary of the interior, when his proclivities caught up with him. He went to prison for his part in the Teapot Dome scandal and died broke in 1944. (US Senate)

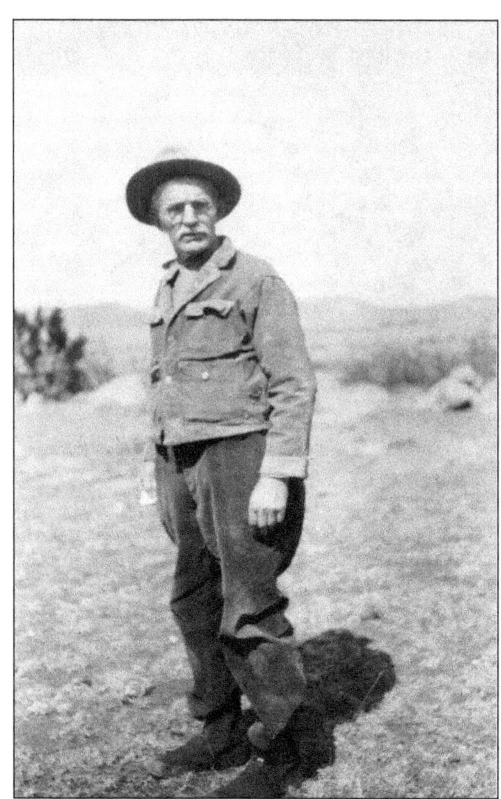

Lee and Gililland hid out on Eugene Manlove Rhodes's ranch, and he escorted them when they surrendered to authorities. Judge Parker deputized Rhodes to protect the accused. Rhodes, a skilled mason, had built a hut on Animas Creek in 1883 with two other young men who were murdered by Apaches shortly after Rhodes had parted. Later a literary icon, Rhodes's novel *The Proud Sheriff* was set in Hillsboro. (NMHM)

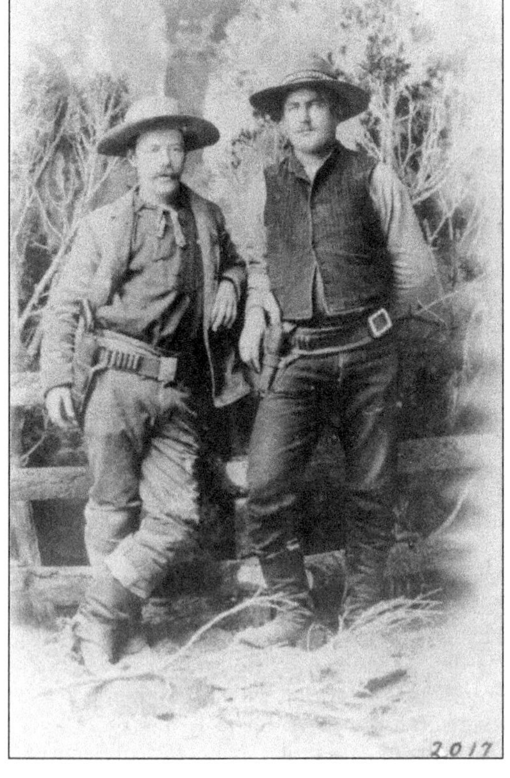

Tom Tucker (right), a bona fide gunfighter and Lee bodyguard, was described as a "professional killer" by Gov. Bradford Prince. Bullets punctured Tucker's lung and earlobe in an 1887 feud. He and Lee were implicated in another killing near Lee's ranch. A Pinkerton detective investigating the Fountain murder reported that Tucker trailed his moves. Tucker was at the trial, not only to testify but to be alert for his boss. (Arizona Historical Society)

District attorney Richmond P. Barnes from Silver City prosecuted the case along with Tom Catron, a future US senator, and William B. Childers. Barnes had troubles at the trial from the start. Witnesses failed to show, and in the closing arguments, Barnes used lofty rhetoric that an interpreter could not capture for three Spanish-speaking jurors. (NMHM)

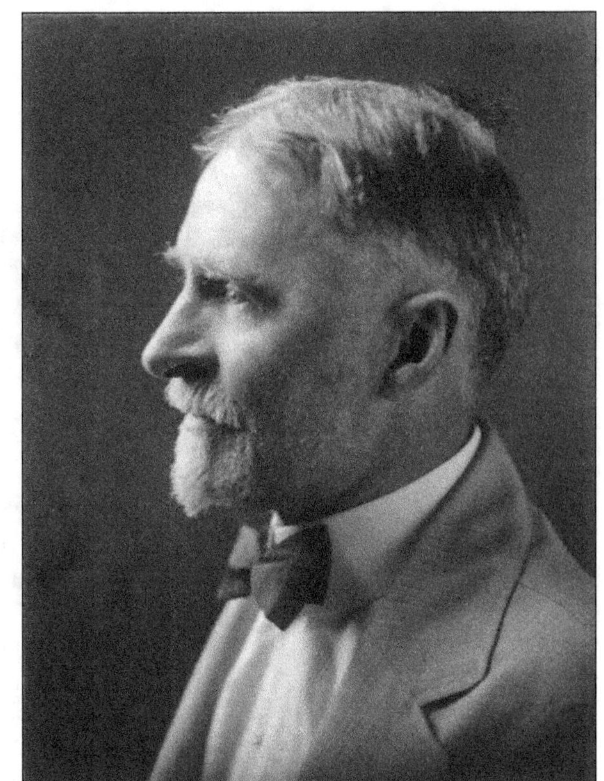

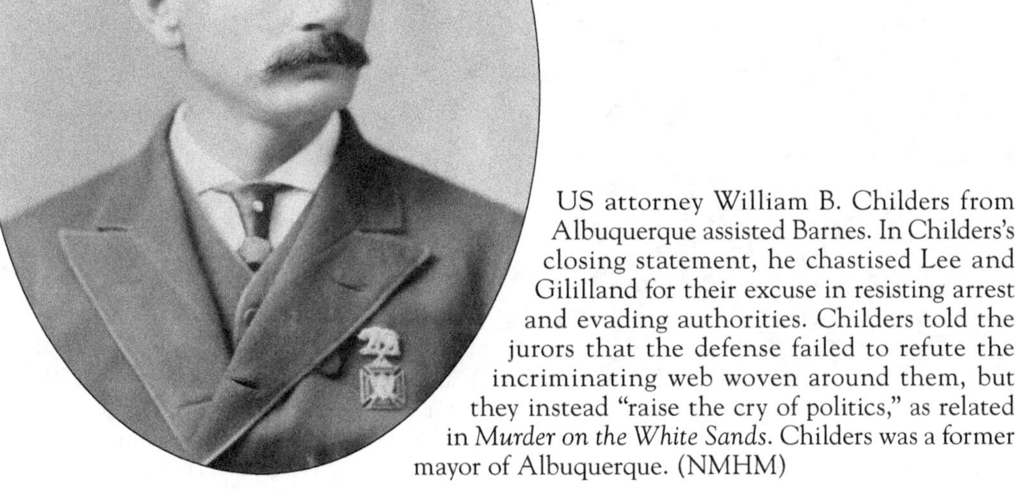

US attorney William B. Childers from Albuquerque assisted Barnes. In Childers's closing statement, he chastised Lee and Gililland for their excuse in resisting arrest and evading authorities. Childers told the jurors that the defense failed to refute the incriminating web woven around them, but they instead "raise the cry of politics," as related in *Murder on the White Sands*. Childers was a former mayor of Albuquerque. (NMHM)

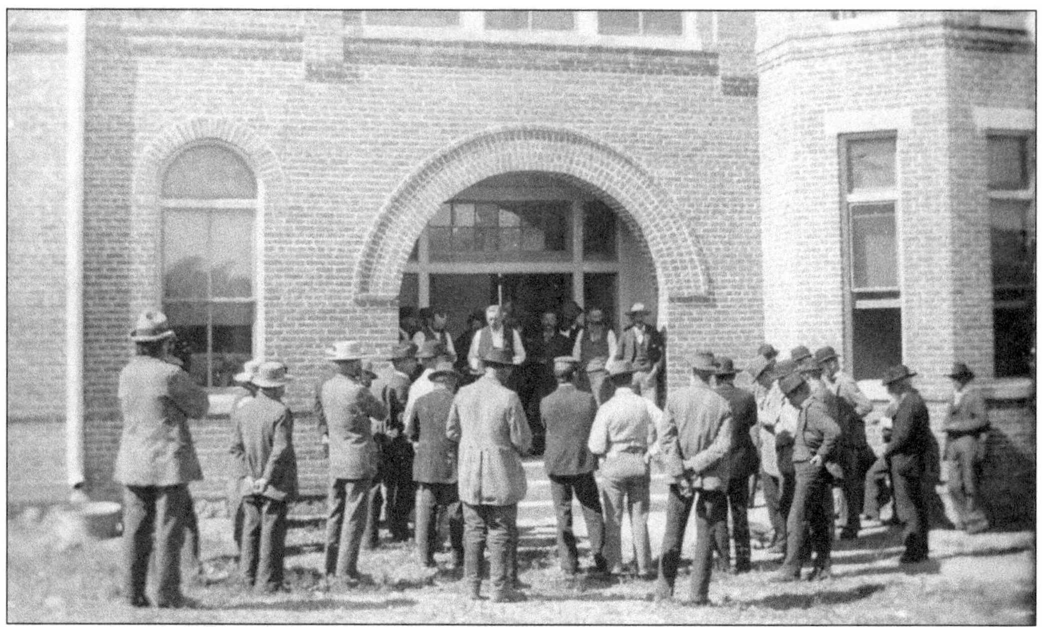

While details of this image are not known, it is plausible that the photograph was taken during the trial by George T. Miller. The trial was a media sensation and brought national attention to Hillsboro and the lawlessness exemplified by the child's murder. (BRM)

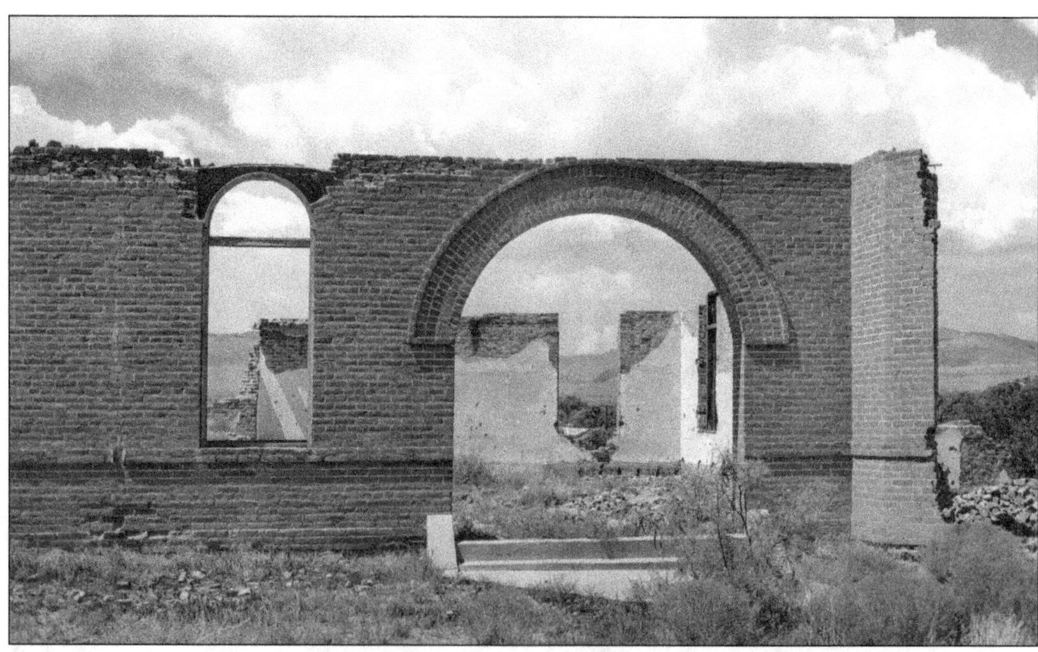

Time has been unkind to the former Sierra County Courthouse, captured in this 1955 photograph. Fighting the pull of gravity, the ruin looks very similar today. The gravity of the Fountain murders still reverberates and continues to be the subject of books and magazine articles. (Patricia Heydt)

Three

Mining

Mining created Hillsboro, Lake Valley, and Kingston. In 1877, placers and gold quartz veins were found in the hills surrounding Percha Creek, and in 1880, gold ore deposits were discovered near Kingston as well as in Tierra Blanca, Gold Dust, Andrews, and Percha City. By 1885, some 150 claims had been registered in the Kingston District alone. Almost simultaneously with the location of gold along the tributaries of the Percha, rich silver deposits were found in Lake Valley. Each of the towns developed its own character, at least partly in keeping with the nature of the respective ore deposits. Hillsboro had rich gold-bearing veins as well as multiple drainages with valuable placer gold deposits. The existence of placer loads allowed less wealthy prospectors to develop claims. As a result, Hillsboro retained the longest and most stable and dispersed economy of the three and, being centrally located, became the Sierra County seat.

The very nature of the hard-rock lodes and the expenses involved in mining ultimately attracted a relatively wealthy and elite set of investors throughout the area. Lake Valley was largely dependent on a few very rich silver deposits that were limited in extent. Fortunes were made quickly from these deposits, and they just as quickly played out. Tierra Blanca, Gold Dust, Andrews, and Percha City disappeared early, and virtually nothing remains of them. Lake Valley is a true ghost town and a historic site maintained by the Bureau of Land Management. A brief resurgence occurred in 1922–1923 and through the Depression years of the 1930s.

With the exception of the opening of the large Copper Flat pit during the 1970s, mining efforts since that time have been insignificant. Only Hillsboro continues to attract hobby prospectors who sift the sands of Percha Creek, Ready Pay Canyon, Wick's Canyon, and Warm and Cold Springs Washes.

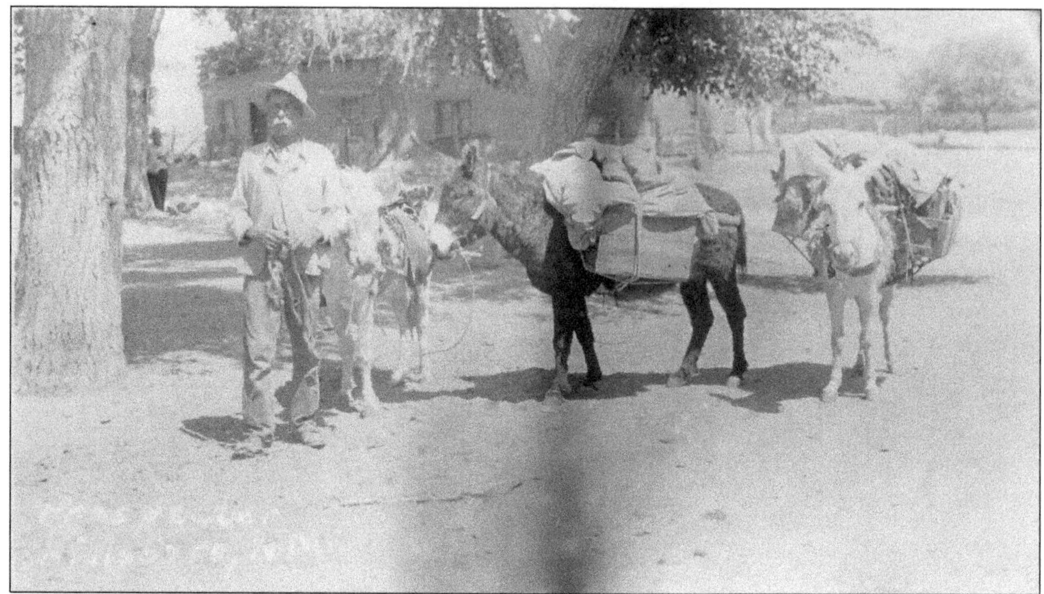

Adventurous prospectors were essential in the early mine discoveries. Manuel Taylor, shown here around 1920 in Hillsboro, was born in 1863. He lived in Silver City from 1880 through 1910 and wandered throughout the Black Range. The crude pack boxes on his burros were used to haul ore to town or to haul supplies to camp. Here, he appears to have come to town for supplies. (BRM)

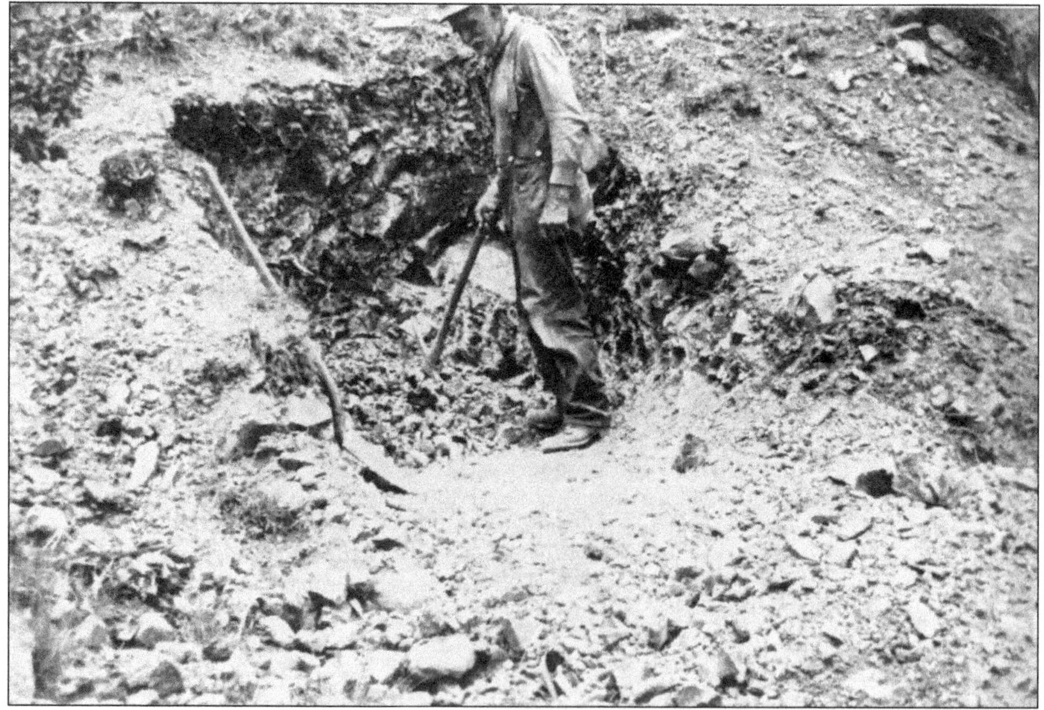

Prospector George Jones is doing typical pick and shovel assay work around 1920. Most individual prospectors like Jones hoped to stake a claim on a vein that they could then sell to a larger mining company. Jones was born in 1853. He lived in Faulkner, New Mexico, by 1910 and was a widower at that time. Faulkner was located northeast of Hillsboro on Animas Creek. (BRM)

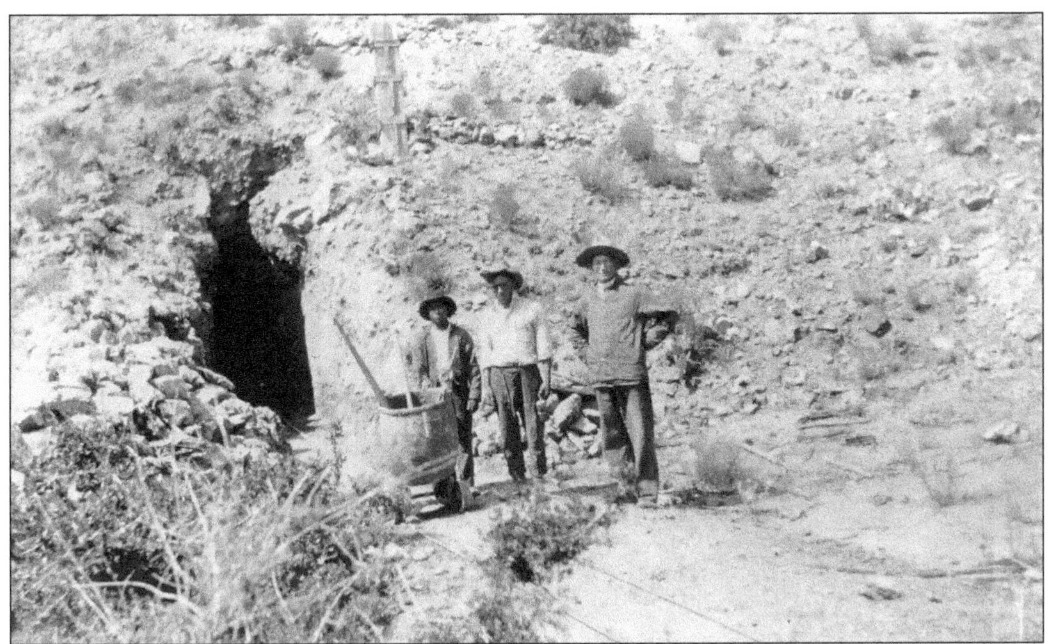

A.L. Bird, on the right, was involved in mining and many other enterprises in Hillsboro. Here, he is working an early claim with an unknown Mr. Duran. When he was married to Ninette Stocker Miller, Bird also ran the Miller Drugstore in Hillsboro. He later married Romelia Luna. (SR, BRM)

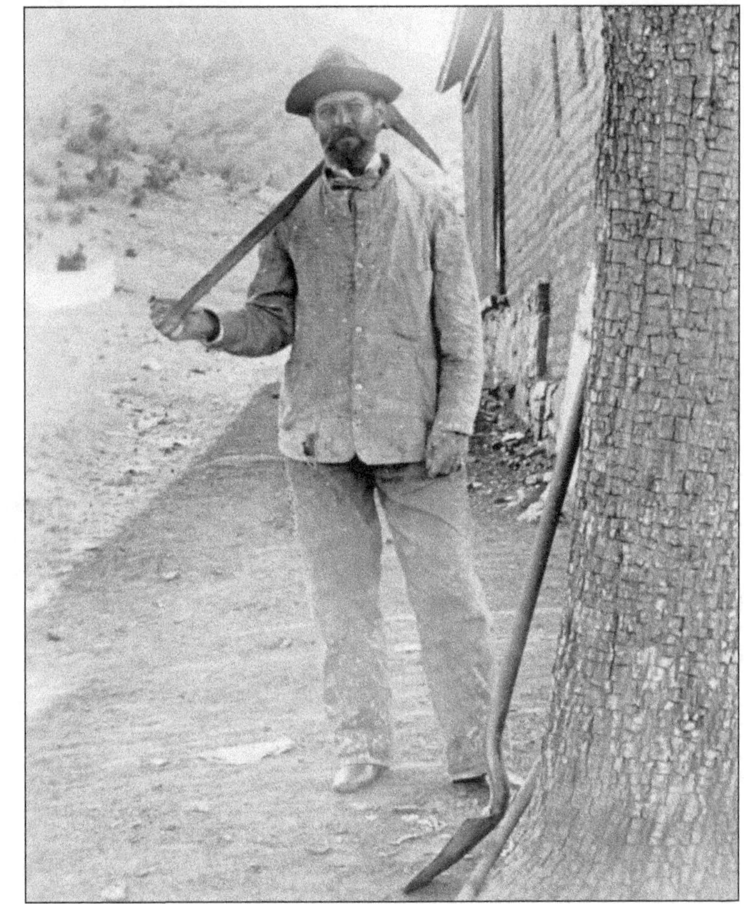

The clothing worn by this miner was standard attire for underground workers around 1890. The tight neckline and untucked shirttail prevented dirt and debris from getting inside the clothing. The conical, small-brimmed hat was also commonly worn by miners of this era. The pick and shovel were the ever-present tools of the trade. (BRM)

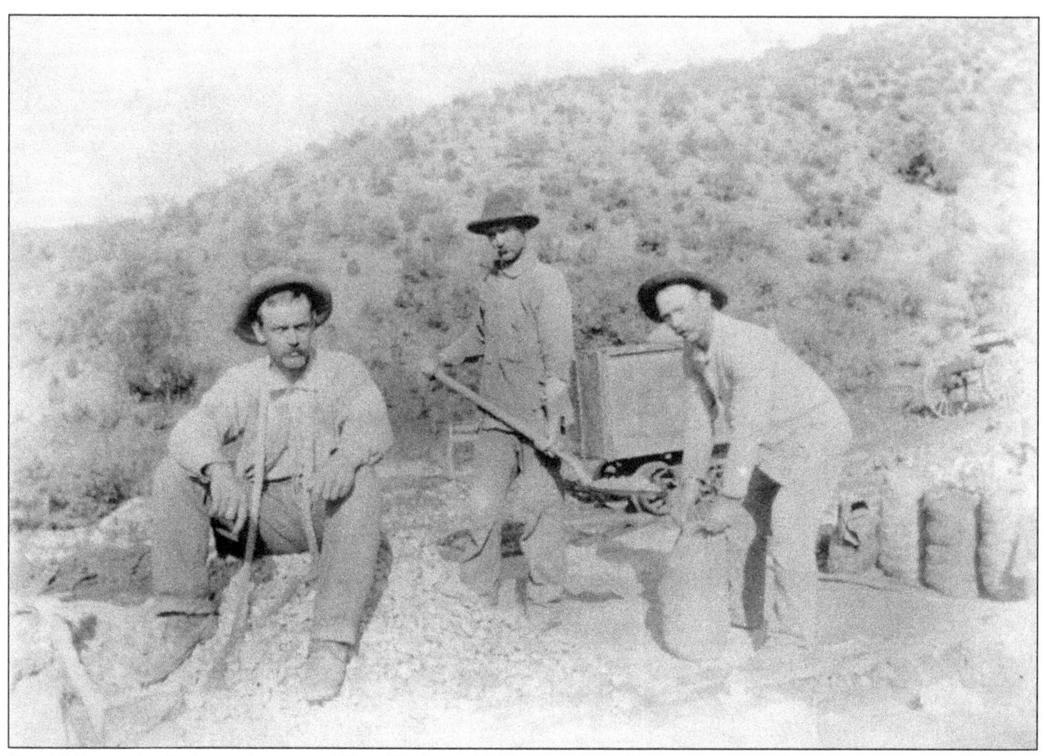

Fred Mister (right) was born in New York in 1860. By 1900, he was married and living in Hillsboro. His occupation was given as butcher. Whatever their main source of income, many businessmen in the area dabbled in mining. Here, Mister and two others are working a placer claim.

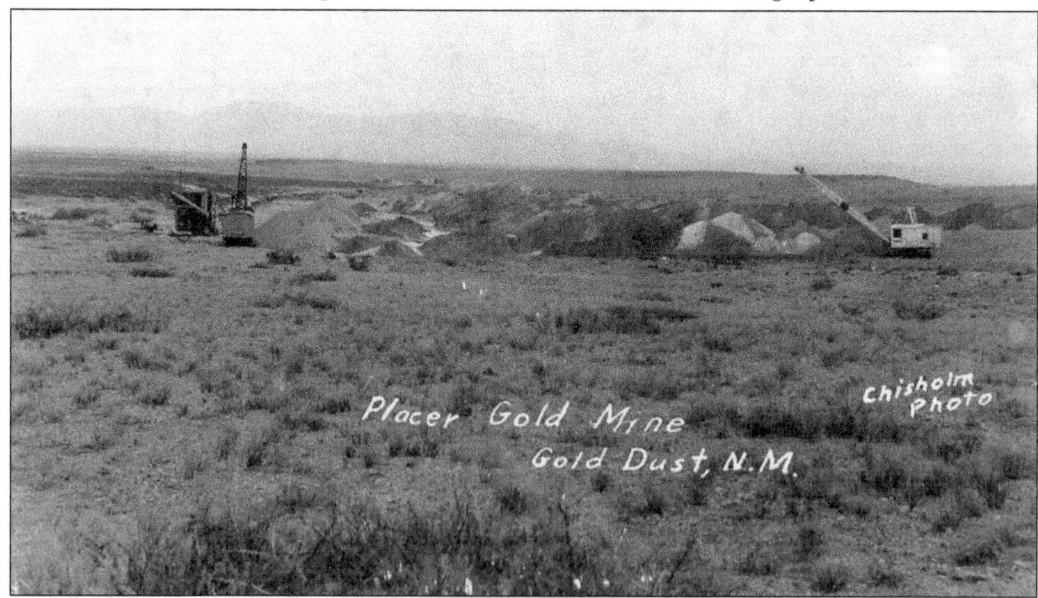

Placer mining was originally done by solitary prospectors panning gold. Discovery of minerals in the alluvial outwash surrounding the mountains near Hillsboro, however, resulted in larger scale placer operations. By the 1930s, heavy equipment was being used to move and screen large amounts of soil for gold and other valuable ore. (GSM)

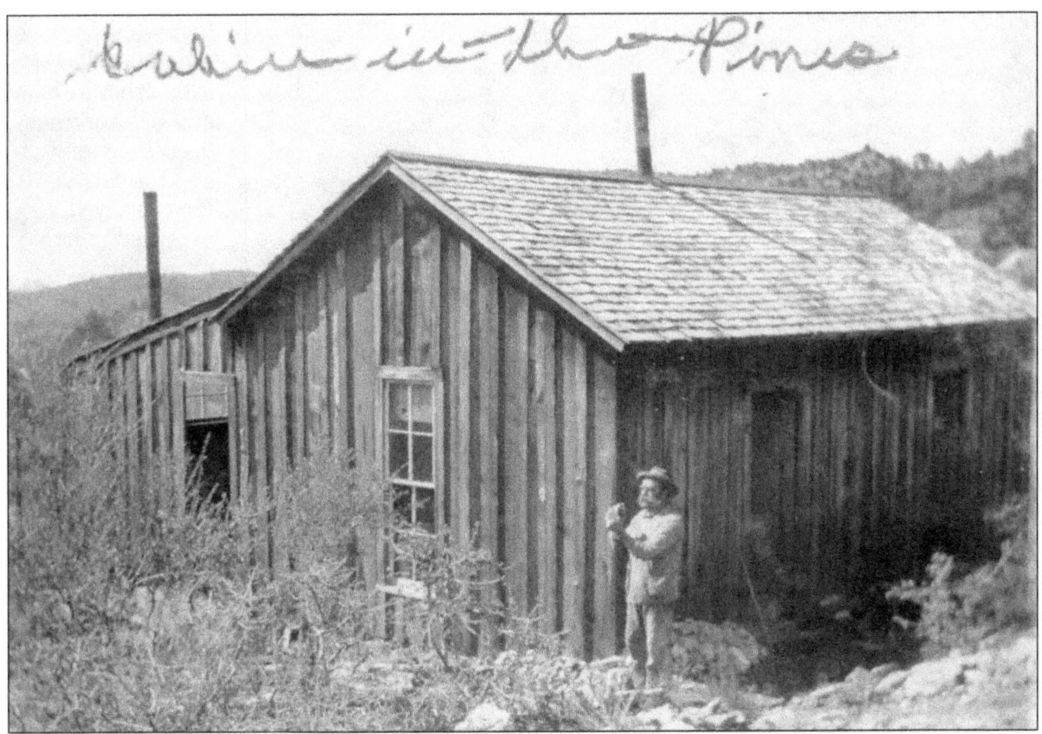

As mining developed, structures near mines were often frame buildings intended to be temporary. Once a mine played out, these were abandoned or, more often, salvaged for use at a new claim. Here, a solitary unidentified miner scrutinizes an ore sample.

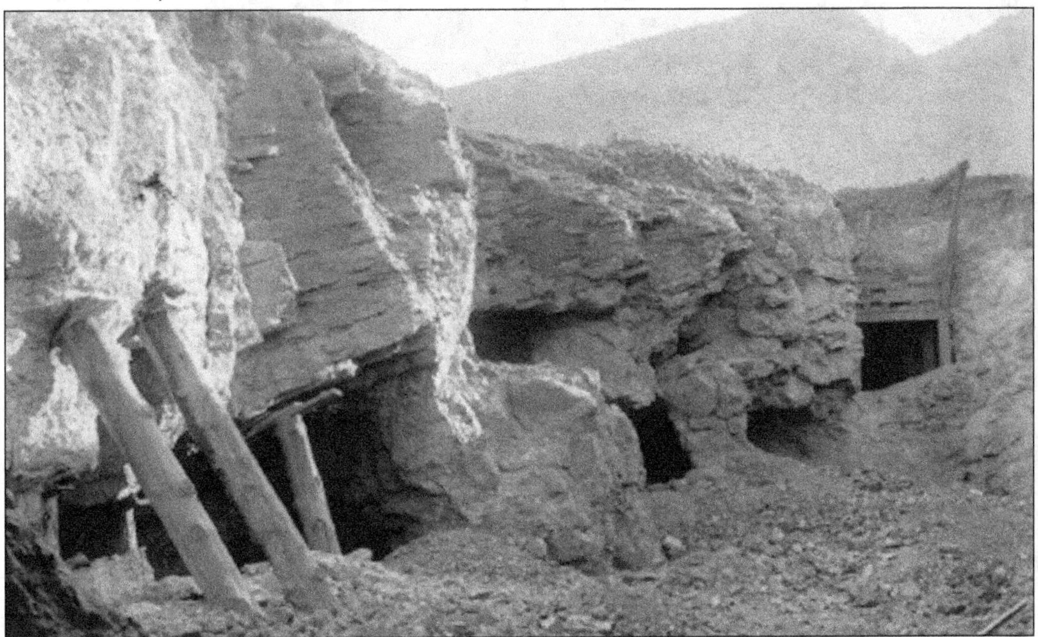

George Lufkin first discovered silver in the Lake Valley area. The famous Bridal Chamber Mine, shown here in 1890, was discovered in 1878. It had walls of pure horn silver and produced almost $3 million in ore before it was exhausted. (GSM)

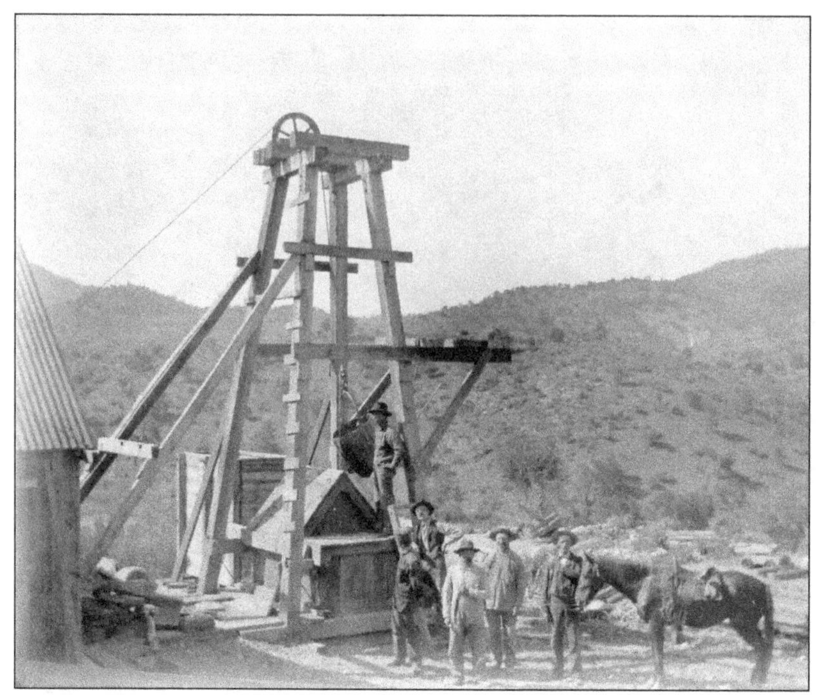

Over time, mines developed infrastructure that allowed working deeper shafts and tunnels. Here is a well-managed mine near Kingston, with ore bucket in place for lowering. The saddle on the horse appears to be a McClellen, the standard saddle for the US Cavalry for many years. Perhaps this one was military surplus of the day or belonged to an ex-soldier. (DW)

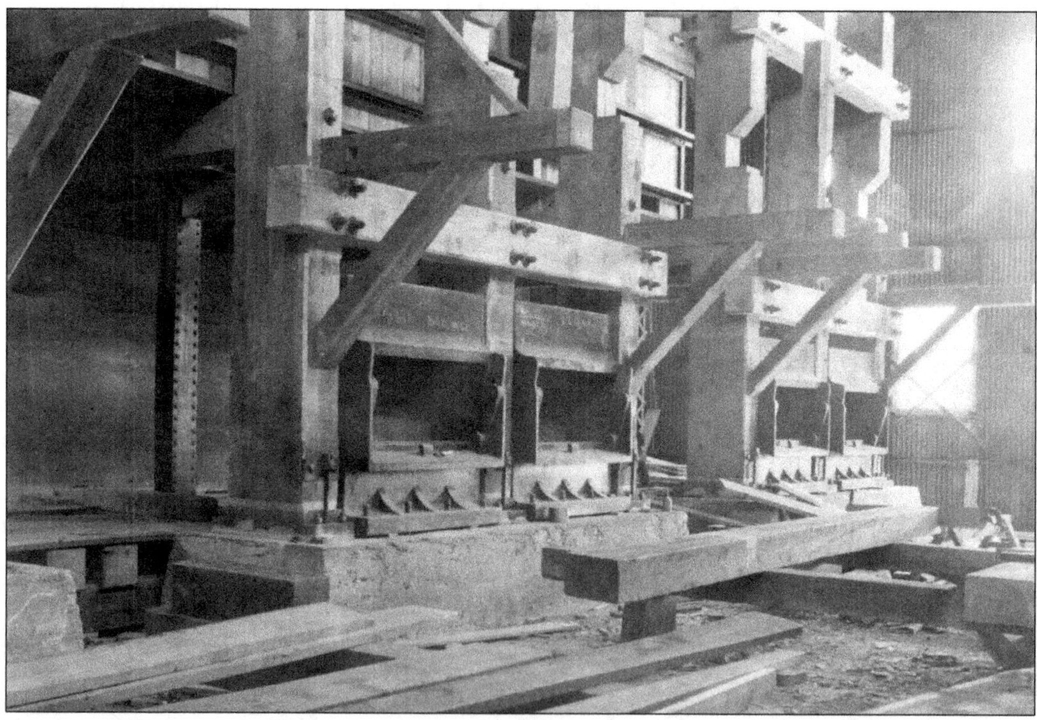

A stamp mill was powered by steam or water. The heavy stamps, rising and falling like pile drivers, pounded ore to a fine powder. This picture from a glass negative depicts the inside of Snake Mine Mill during its construction. (BRM)

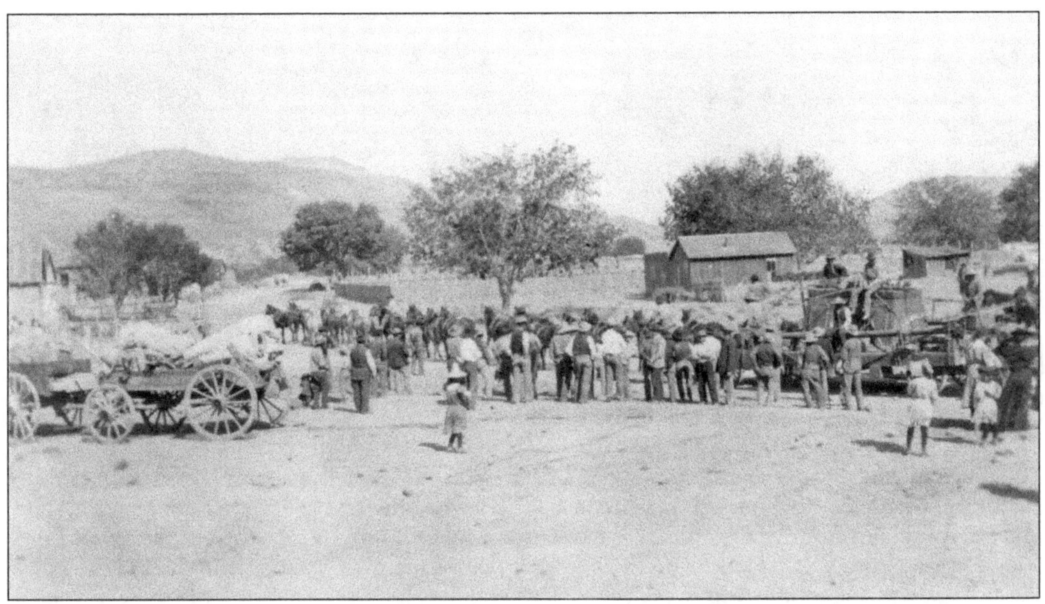

Moving a heavy piece of mining equipment along early-day Mattie Avenue in Hillsboro takes a 20-horse team. The gathered crowd indicates that moving such heavy equipment was not an everyday event. No doubt, the teamsters are receiving a lot of advice. This piece of a boiler is headed for the Snake Mine. (BRM)

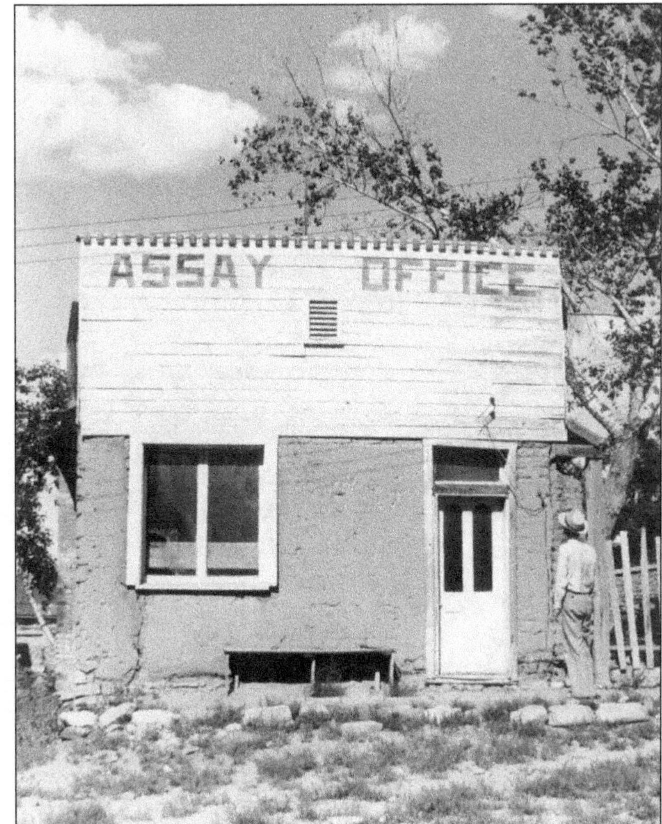

The assay office was an essential part of a mining district. Ore samples could be evaluated before bearing the expense of shipping. This photograph showing a weathered sign and crumbling adobe walls appears to have been taken during the 1930s or 1940s, sometime after the office ceased to operate. (DW)

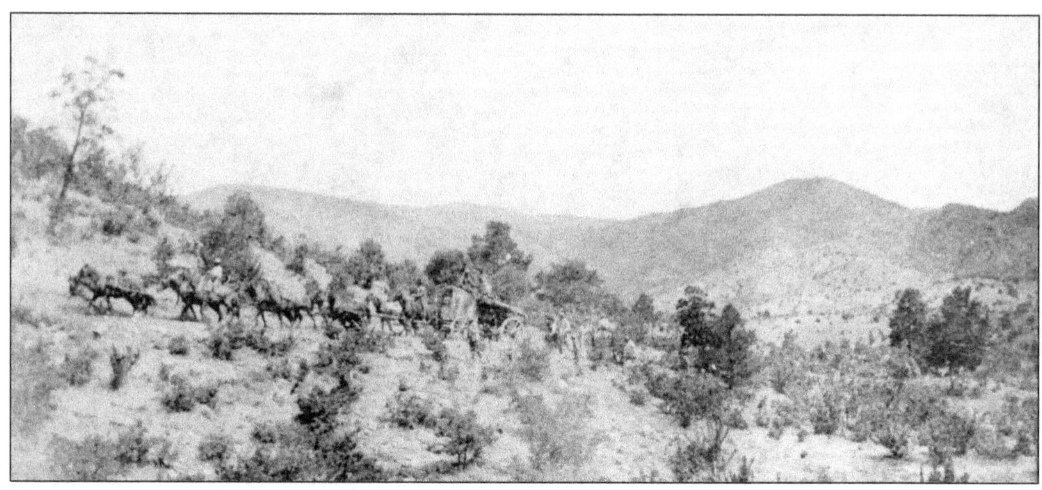

Heavily constructed wagons with large teams of horses or mules were used to haul materials and ore, often over terrain with very rough or nonexistent roads. In this photograph taken about 1890, a load of silver ore is headed for the smelter. A group of men is walking behind, ready to put a shoulder to the wagon on steep slopes where the load may be too great for the horses. (DW)

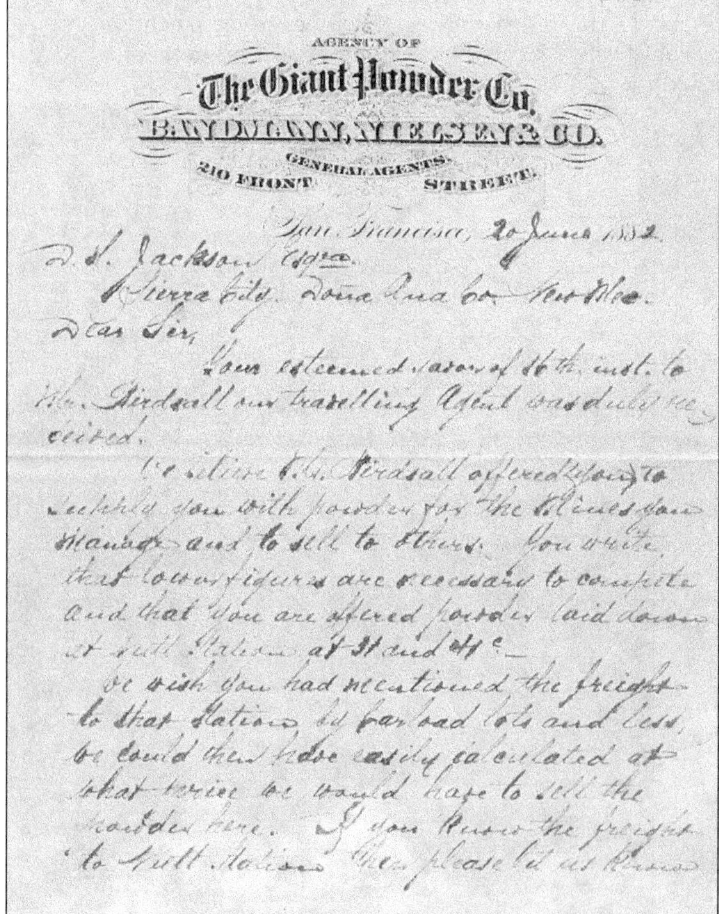

AGENCY OF
The Giant Powder Co.
BANDMANN, NIELSEN & CO.
GENERAL AGENTS.
210 FRONT STREET.

San Francisco, 20 June 1882

D. H. Jackson Esqre.
Sierra City Dona Ana Co. New Mex.

Dear Sir,

Your esteemed favor of 16th inst. to Mr. Birdsall our travelling Agent was duly received.

We believe Mr. Birdsall offered you to supply you with powder for the Mines you manage and to sell to others. You write that lower figures are necessary to compete and that you are offered powder laid down at Nutt Station at 31 and 41 c —

We wish you had mentioned the freight to that Station by carload lots and less, we could then have easily calculated at what price we would have to sell the powder here. If you know the freight to Nutt Station then please let us know

This letter was written in 1882 to D.H. Jackson in Sierra City (later named Lake Valley). Jackson became manager of the Bridal Chamber Mine after George Daly was killed in an ambush by Apaches on August 19, 1881. In this correspondence, the Grant Powder Company of San Francisco is trying to resolve a conflict over the price of powder.

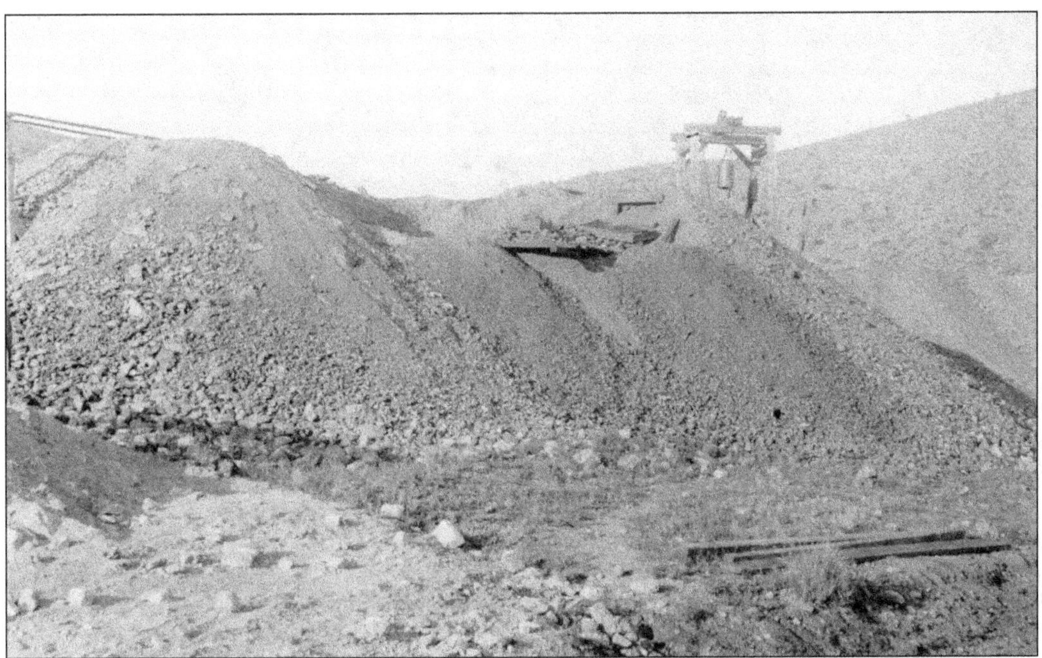

The Caroline Mine (above) was surveyed in 1887 for Walter C. Hadley (below, right) and his father, Hiram (below, left). It was undoubtedly named after Walter's daughter Caroline. A Walter C. Hadley Company is listed in Lake Valley in the 1880 tax rolls. A mine by this name does not show up on later plats for Lake Valley. Its name may have changed to the Carolina Mine, which does show on the mining area maps. Hiram Hadley was the founder of the state college in Las Cruces, now New Mexico State University. (RGHC)

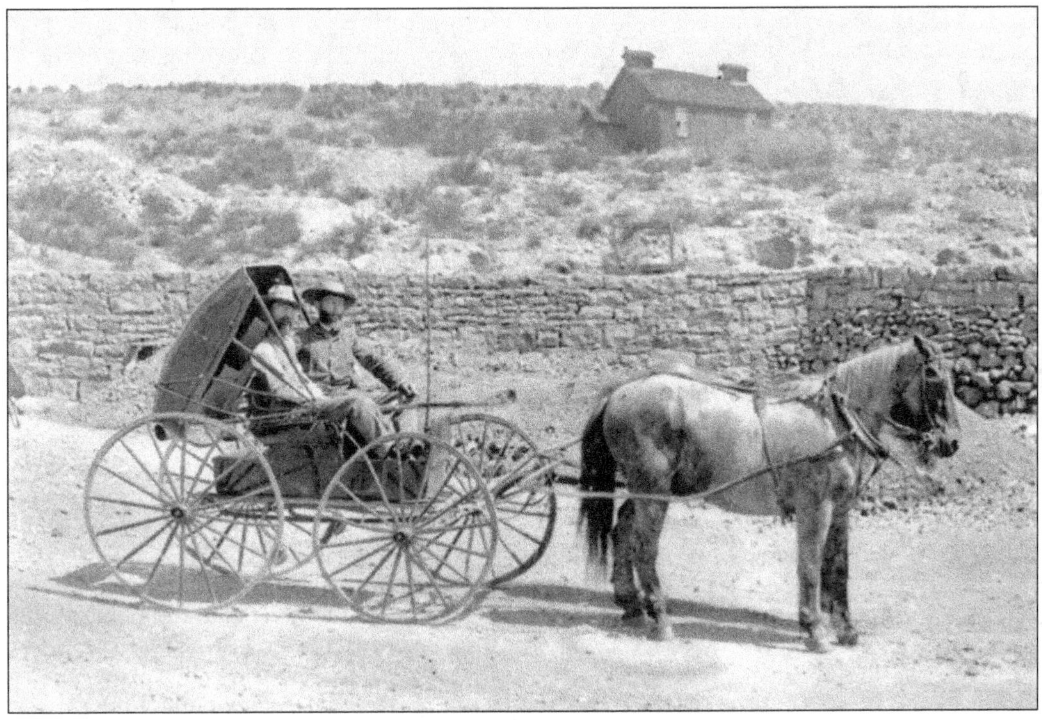

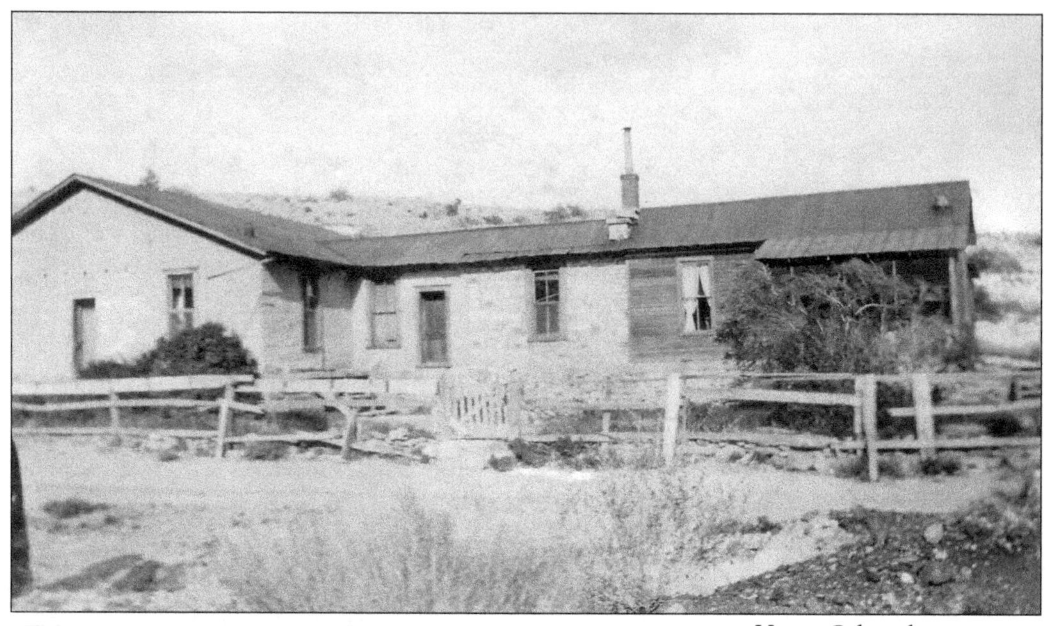

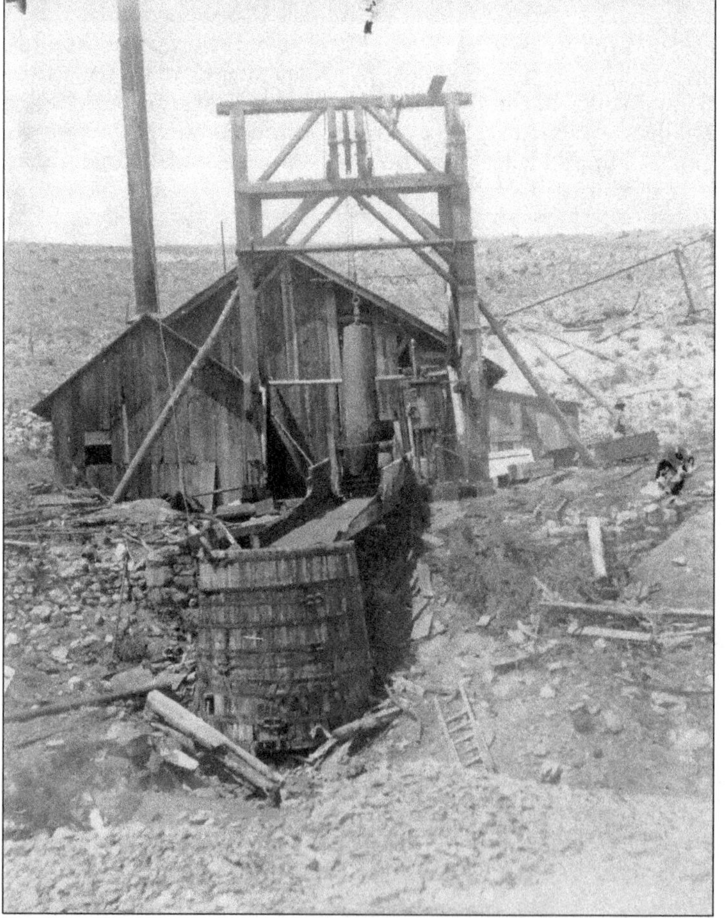

Henry Schmidt was a professional photographer who took many pictures of Lake Valley. He lived for a while in the superintendent's house in "Company Town," where his children were born. At that time, he served as superintendent of the Lake Valley Mill. He later ran a photography studio in Chloride, New Mexico, for many years. (DW)

Unproductive mines quickly fell into disrepair. Underground mining was extremely hazardous. Here, the cylinder attached to the cable had been used to lower miners, one at a time, into the narrow shaft as well as to bring ore to the surface. This was definitely not work for individuals who were claustrophobic, and miners took pride in their ability to work underground. (DW)

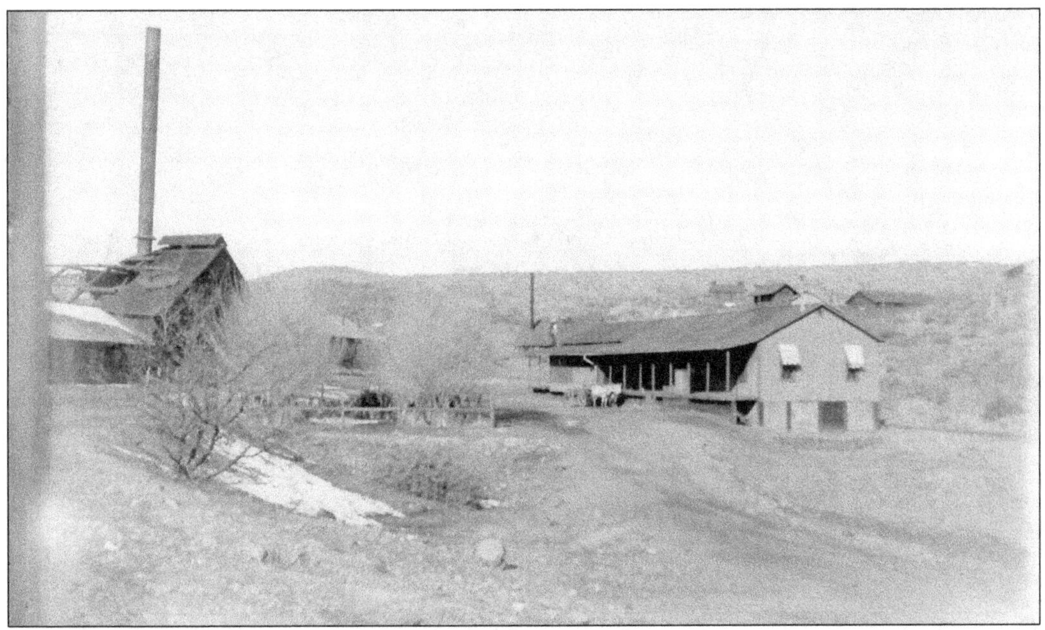

This is the boardinghouse for the miners in Lake Valley. In addition to housing miners, it was used by passengers when they arrived on the trains in Company Town. While this adobe bunkhouse undoubtedly provided comfortable quarters in winter, it appears to be poorly ventilated and was probably uncomfortably warm in summer. Air-conditioning was unheard of, and the tin roof gave little protection from the desert sun. (DW)

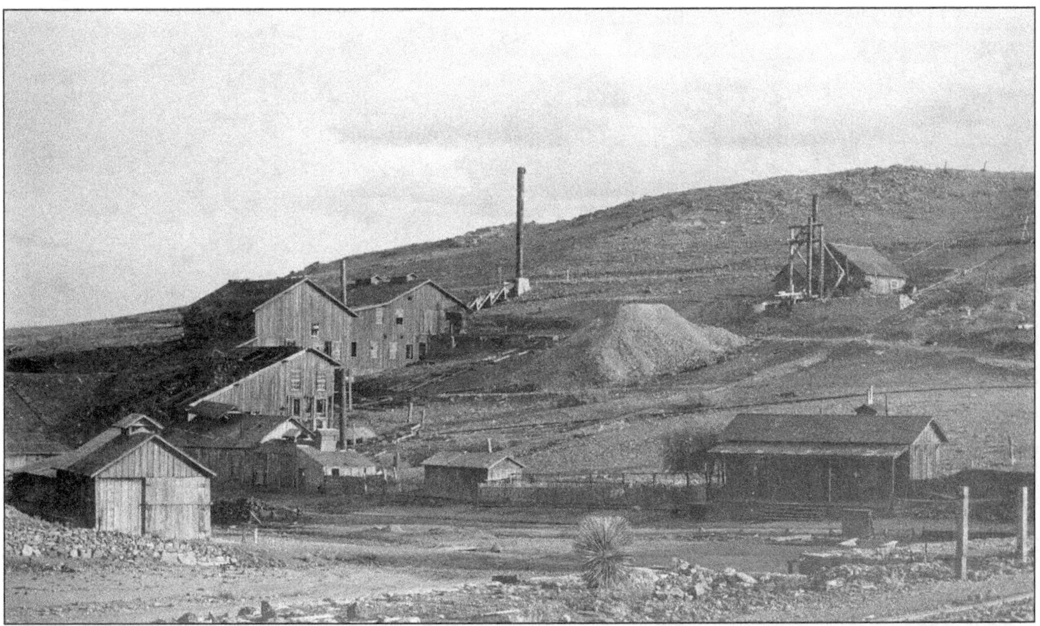

The Lake Valley Mill was developed quickly after discovery of silver, but it was dismantled in the late 1880s. As shown here, the mill contained four offices, two houses, two warehouses, a blacksmith shop, and a boardinghouse. Raw ore was hauled to the chute high on the hill behind the mill and processed downhill through crushers and washers. The crushed ore was then loaded on a train (tracks in foreground) for shipping. (RGHC)

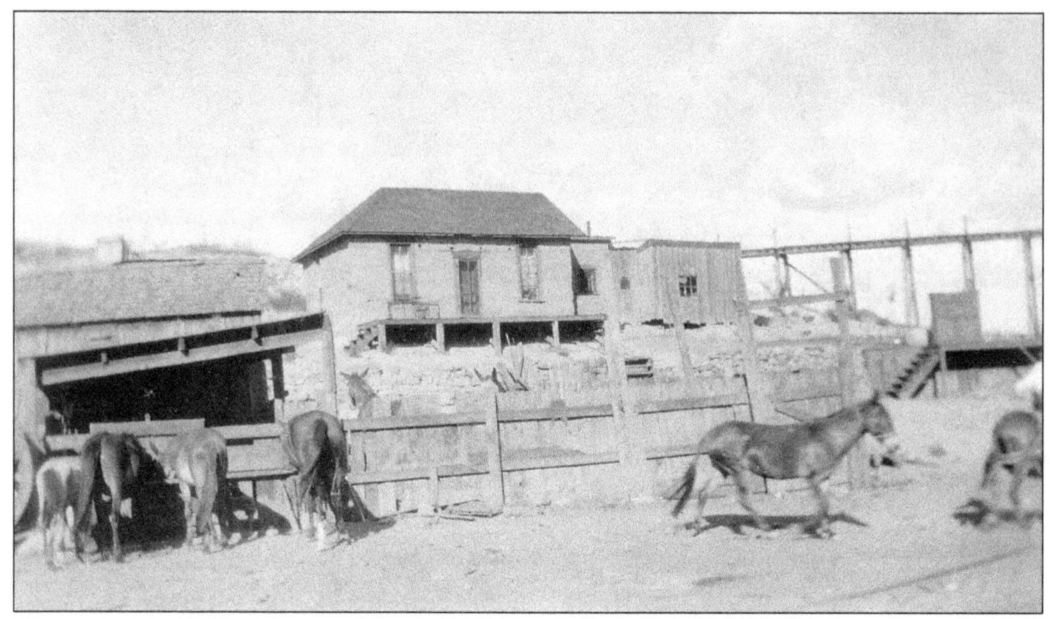

This is the McCardle House in Company Town at Lake Valley. James and Susan McCardle were living in Lake Valley as late as 1920. James's occupation is given as plumber in the mining industry. The trestle behind the house may have come from a mine and carried ore carts to awaiting wagons, or it may have been a trestle on the main railroad track coming to Lake Valley. (DW)

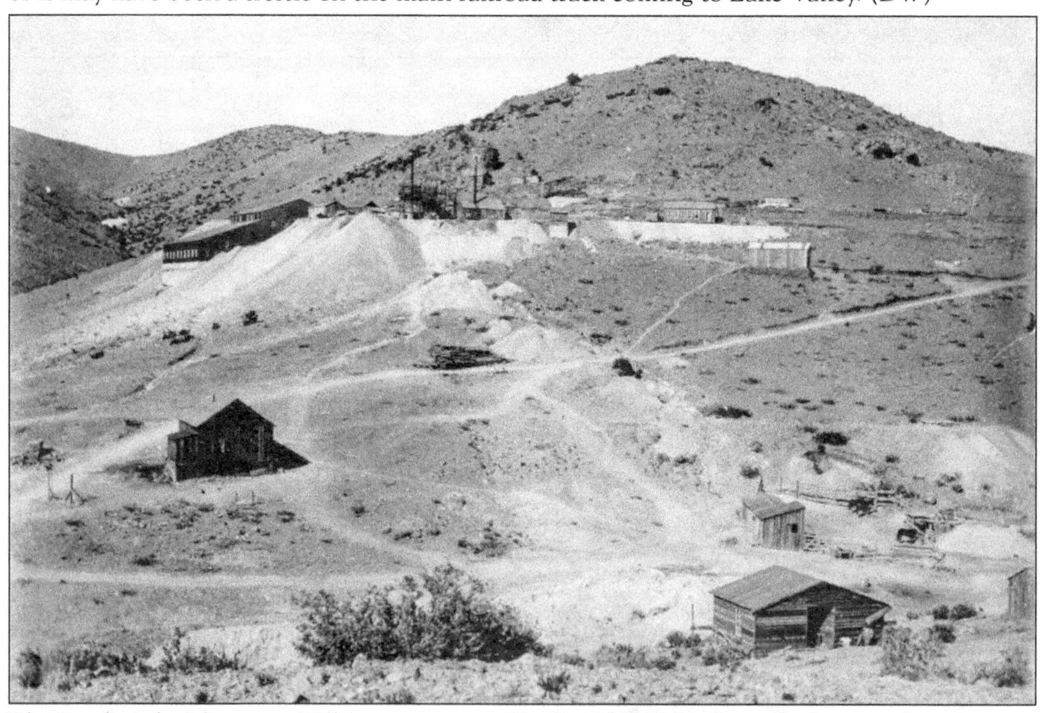

The Rattlesnake Mine near Hillsboro was named by David Stitzel, who picked up a rock to throw at a rattlesnake and discovered that it contained gold. The name was later shortened to Snake Mine. It was the longest-lived mine in the Hillsboro area and is seen here near its peak of operation. It was close enough for miners to live in Hillsboro and walk or ride daily to the mine. (BRM)

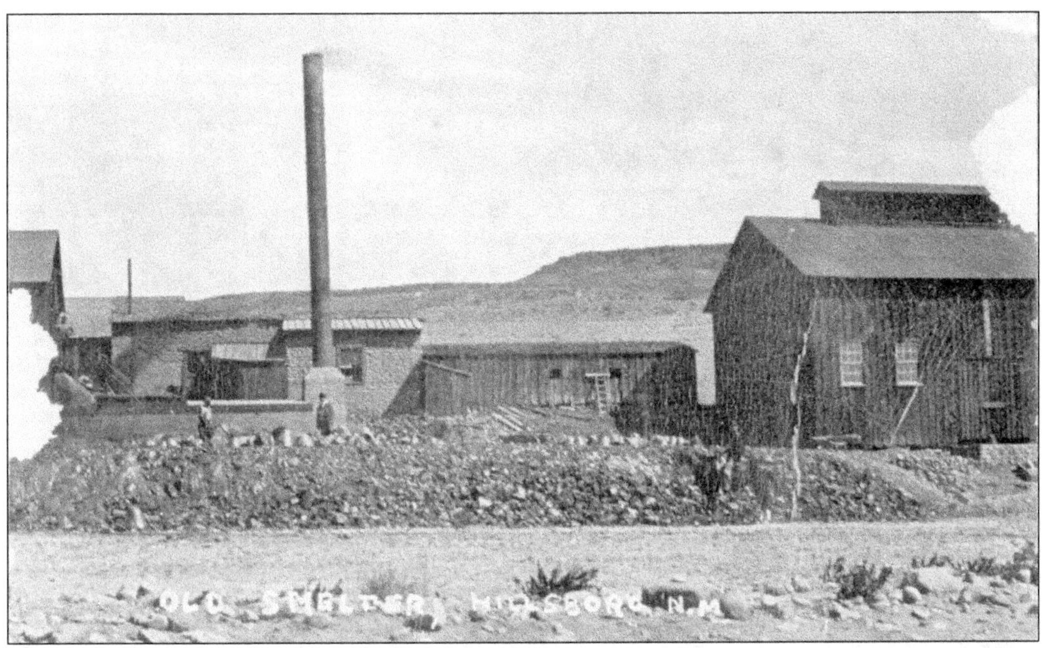

The Hillsboro smelter was on the north side of Percha Creek. It no longer exists, although some of its slag deposits lie alongside State Highway 152 just east of the lower bridge in town. Several buildings in Hillsboro were constructed using foot-long slag blocks that weighed near 110 pounds each. These structures still stand, and one is a fine historic home. (BRM)

Another mine associated with Hillsboro was the Mamie Richmond Mine, shown here about 1890. Located northeast of Hillsboro, it was one of the more remote mines, and miners stayed in the bunkhouse shown here. The wagons had to haul ore several miles over rough and steep terrain to the Hillsboro mill. (BRM)

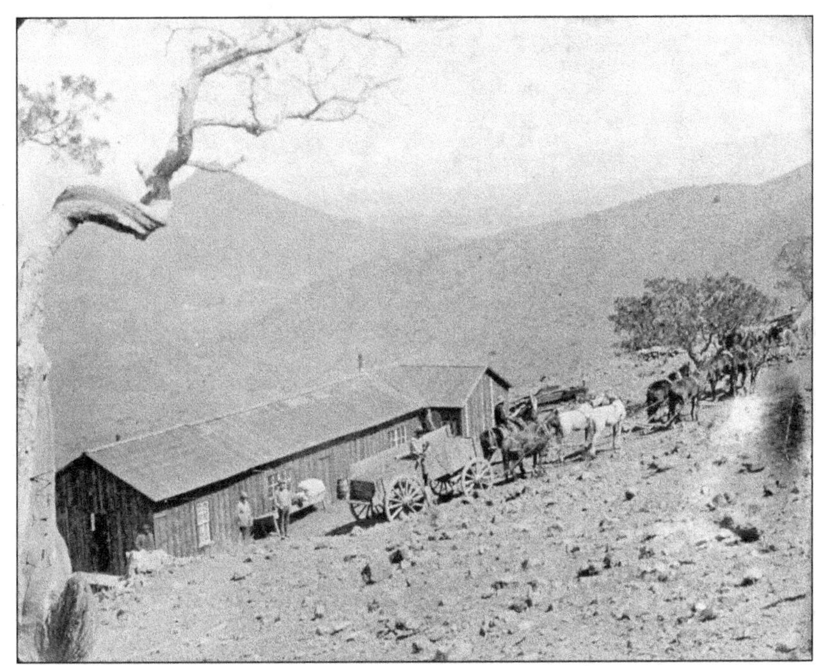

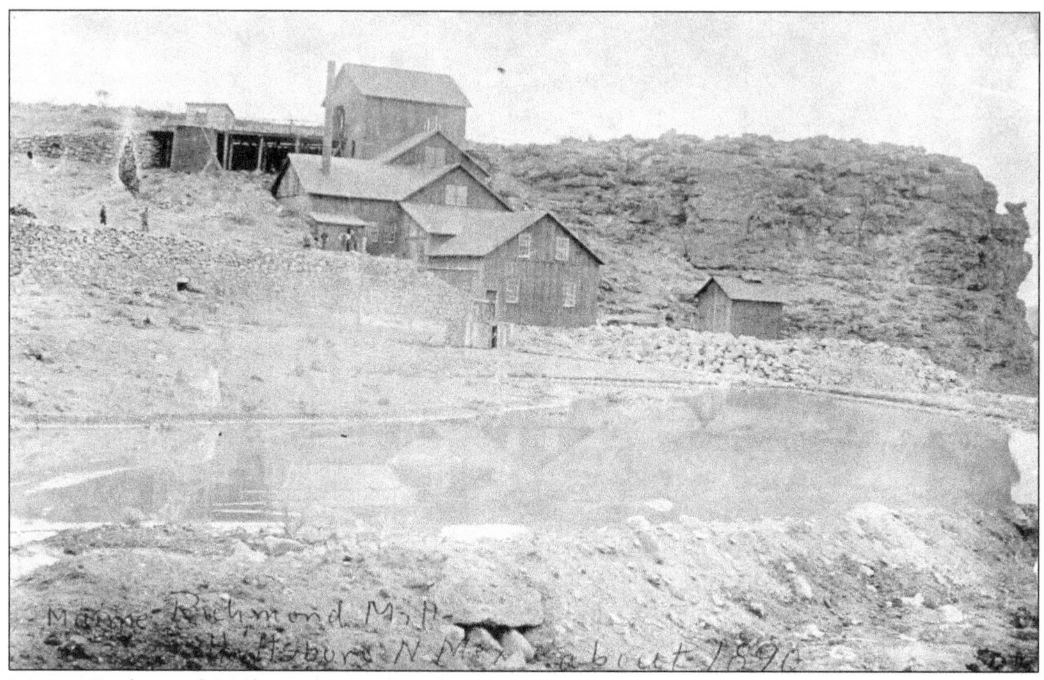

Mamie Richmond Mill was located at the junction of Warm Springs Wash and Percha Creek, east of Hillsboro. Its foundations are still visible. Water was piped from a nearby well for washing crushed ore. Ore processed here was probably hauled to the Hillsboro Smelter. The person for whom the mine and mill were named remains a mystery. (BRM)

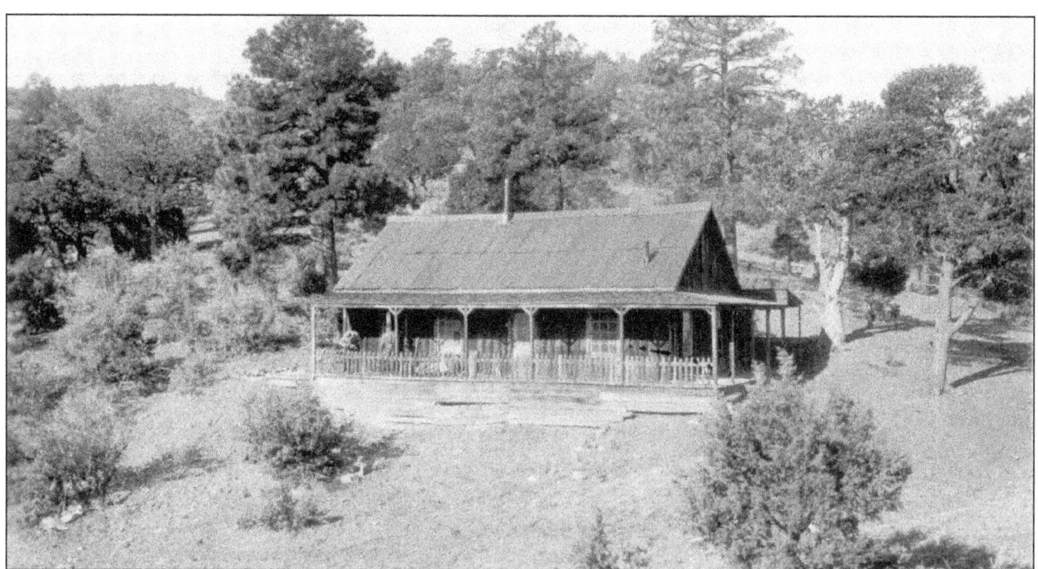

The Lady Franklin was one of several successful mines clustered at the head of Picket Springs Canyon, about two miles north of Kingston. The mine was located in 1881 by Dan Dugan, John Donahoe, and John McNally. The building shown here was probably the bunkhouse for miners. Located near 7,000 feet in elevation, it was undoubtedly one of the more pleasant places to work during summer months. (BRM)

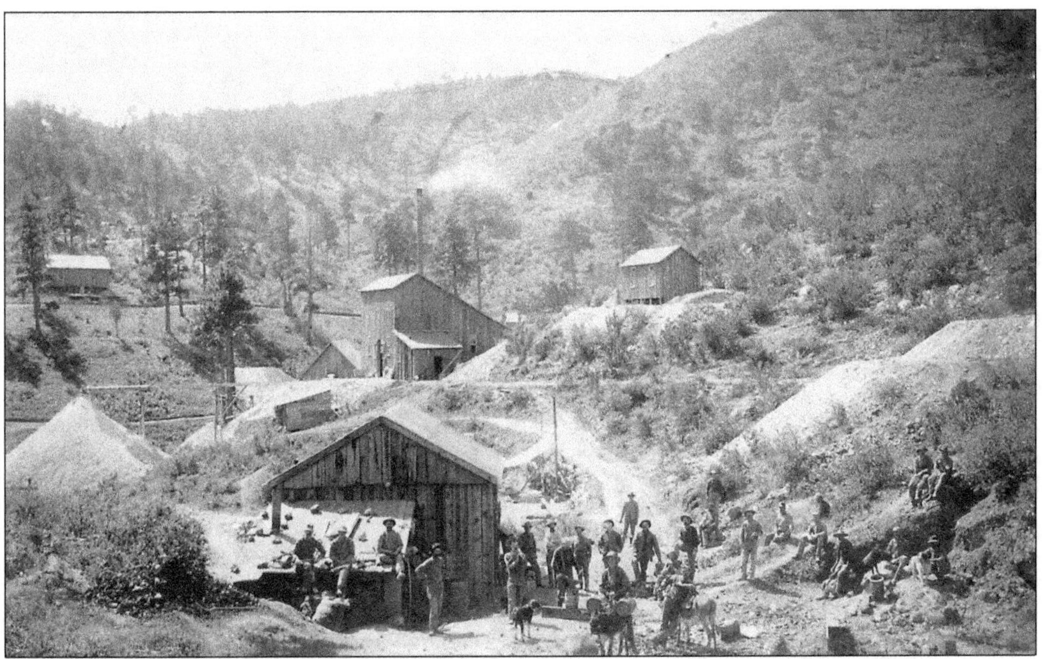

The Lady Franklin Mine was one of the main producers near Kingston by the time this photo was taken in 1892. The mine, located in 1881, belonged to Dan Dugan and John Donahue. Here, what appears to be the entire crew at the mine is assembled. Names of these miners are unknown. The photographer was J.C. Burge of Kingston. (PBM)

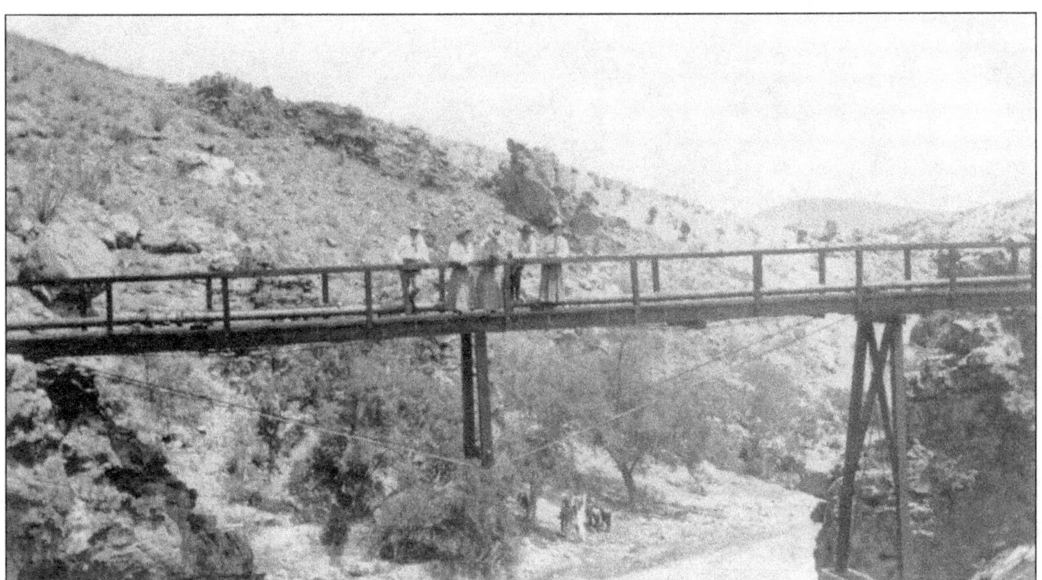

The mining boom at times led to unrealistic schemes. This bridge was built at the lower end of the narrow and rough Percha Creek Box, east of Hillsboro. It carried a large pipeline across the canyon. Clothing in the image suggests that the bridge was built around 1900 or earlier. Its concrete abutments are all that remain. (IHSF)

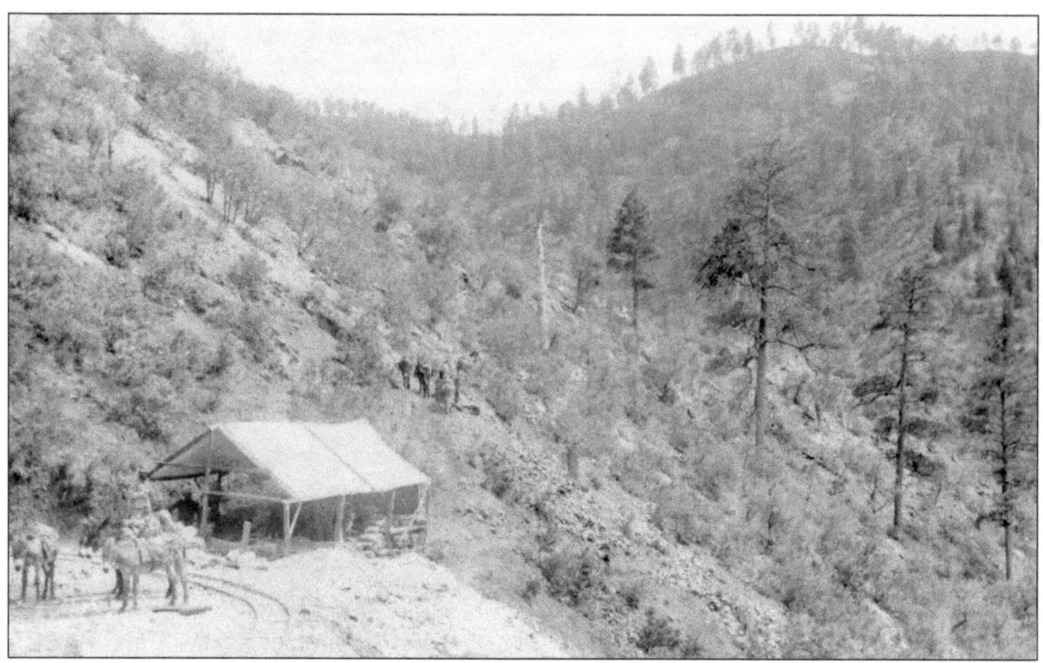

This is a primitive camp at a mine near Kingston. On such rough terrain, wagons could not be used, and ore and supplies were hauled with burros. Here, four burros are waiting for a load of ore to be taken to the mill at Kingston, while others are being driven up the trail with a load of supplies. Unlike horses and mules, pack burros were often driven ahead of the miner. (PBM)

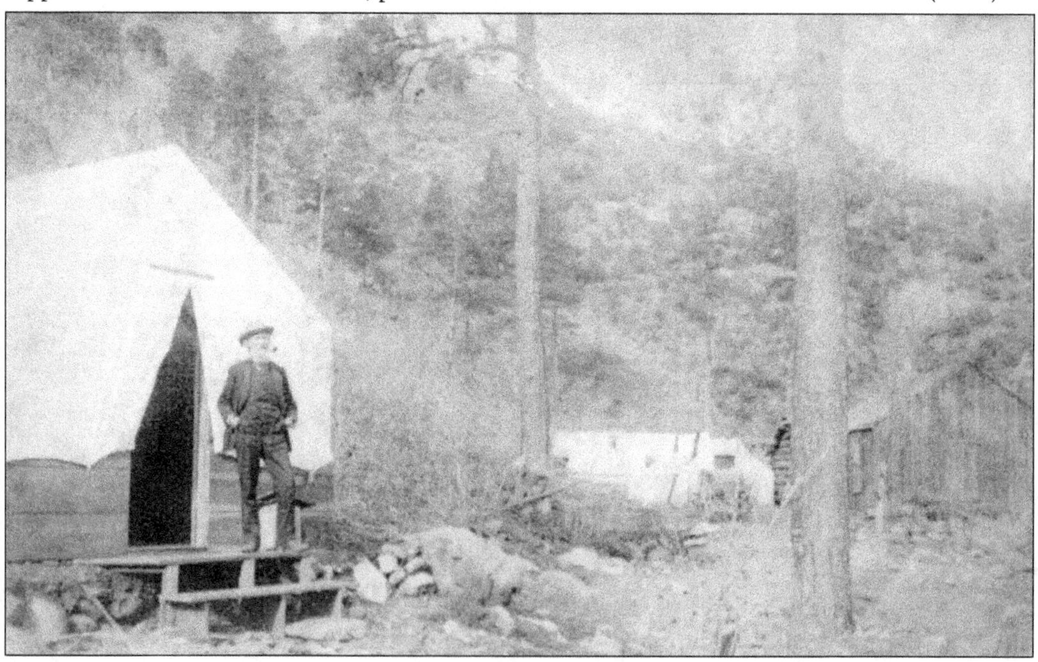

Even when living in primitive conditions, such as the wall tent shown here, miners would turn out in finery for a photograph or when an occasion demanded an appearance of success. This successful-looking gentleman is unidentified, but it may be that he was one of the few who truly struck it rich. (PBM)

Four

RANCHING

Ranching developed concurrently with mining. Early efforts likely involved small herds kept in communal pastures around the settlements to provide meat and dairy products for miners and businessmen. The lush grasslands, however, quickly attracted more ambitious cattle- and sheep men, and, as the danger from marauding Apaches declined through the 1880s, remote ranches developed near reliable springs and waters. Improved well-drilling equipment and windmills allowed even further expansion of ranches, and the range was fully occupied by 1890. Excessive stocking of the range through the 1880s and 1890s, combined with severe droughts in the 1890s and 1920s, resulted in heavy losses.

Until the public lands were allocated and administered by the US Forest Service and the Bureau of Land Management and private lands fenced, range ownership conflicts resulted in occasional outbreaks of violence. Opportunistic cowboys "mavericked," or rustled (depending upon point of view), thereby starting their own herds, and a few went so far as to round up legally branded cattle and market them to less-than-respectable slaughterhouses. Posses and local militia formed to capture or kill rustlers or to convince them that Sierra County was not a safe place for their enterprises. Sheep played a small role in Sierra County ranching, and the wars between sheep ranchers and cattlemen apparently never developed as they did in other parts of the West.

Between 1890 and the 1940s, raising Angora goats became especially profitable. In many ways, goats were better adapted to browse on the steep, brushy slopes of the Black Range, and their multiple products—mohair, meat, dairy—created healthy profits for dedicated operators. Near Kingston, Margaret Armer-Reid began raising goats in 1893 and became known throughout the world as the Angora Queen; her heirs remained in the goat business until 1961.

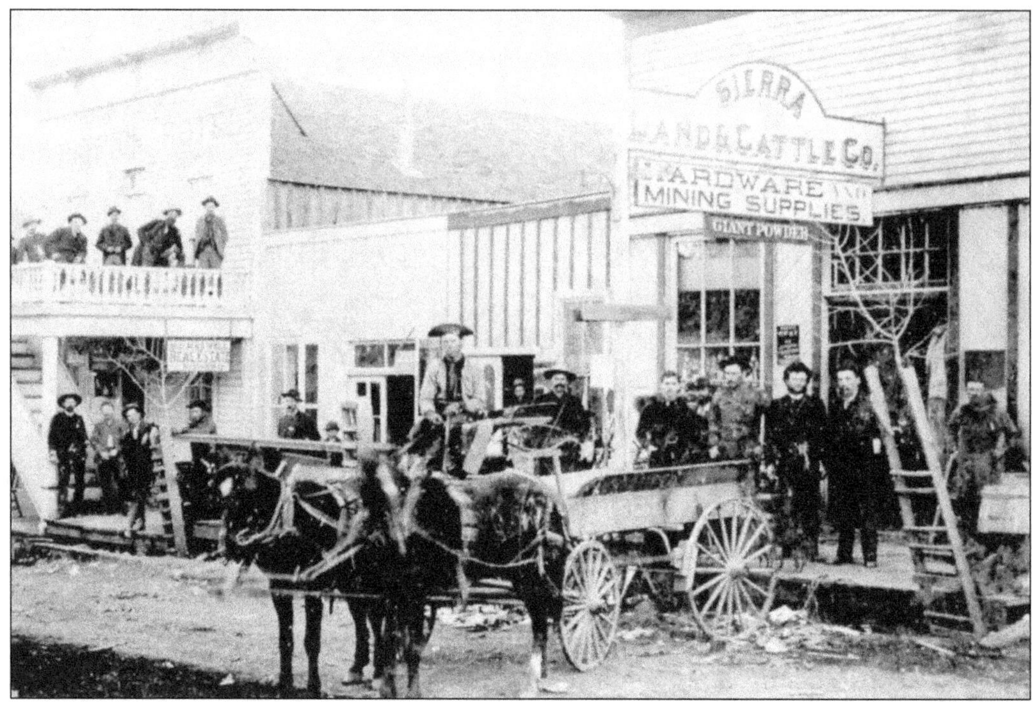

The Sierra Land and Cattle Co. ran a large number of cattle in Sierra County when it was still open range. The SLC brand was owned by Ridenour and Baker Grocery Co. from Missouri. Harvey A. Ringer and Israel King bought all of the SLC cattle and horses sight unseen, and uncounted, in August 1895. In December 1909, Greely Nunn and sons Pryor and Emmett, along with brothers Arch and Jim Latham, bought the SLC Brand. They ran approximately 10,000 head of cattle and 18,000 sheep. Because of a severe drought in the early 1920s lasting several years, hundreds of cattle died, forcing the SLC and other ranchers to move their livestock to pasture in Mexico. Pryor Nunn wrote from Palomas, Mexico, to his wife, "We crossed yesterday about dark and held up here for a day as there were so many cattle we couldn't get by." (PBM)

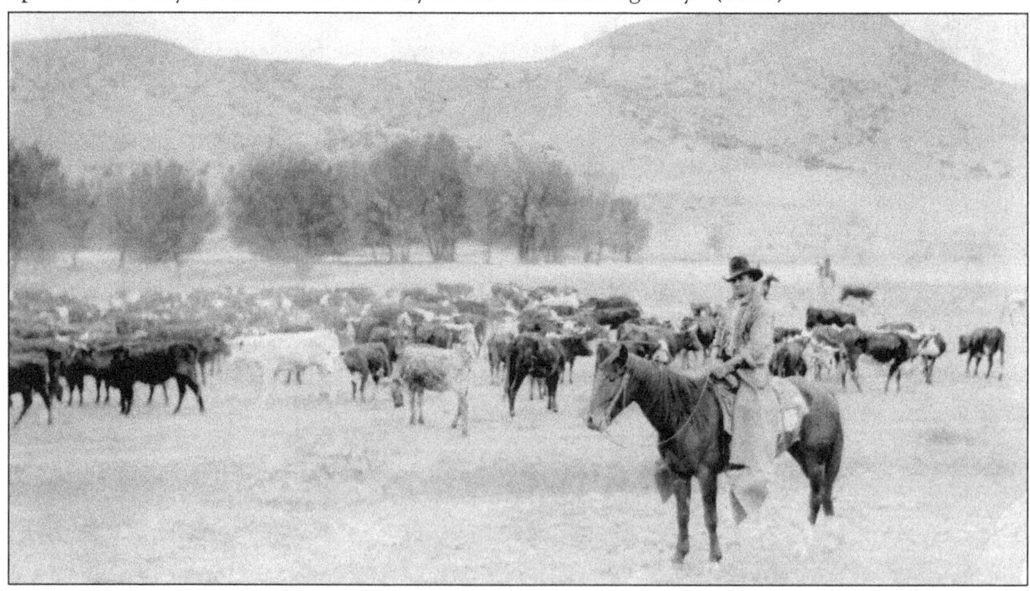

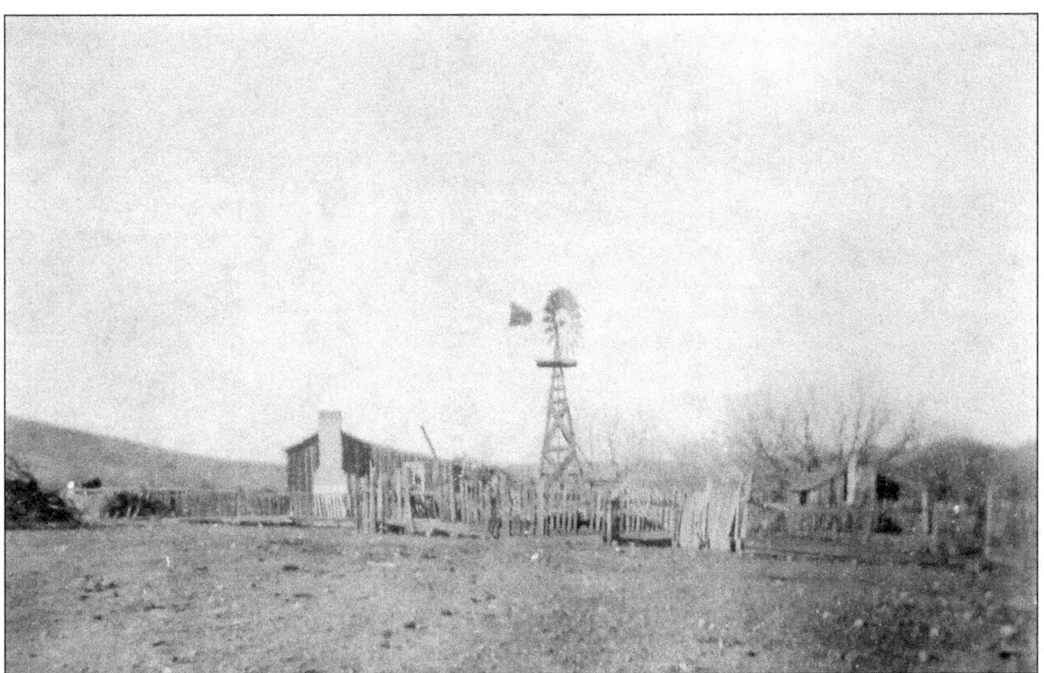

The Stock Raising Homestead Act of 1916 permitted people to obtain a section (640 acres) of free land in exchange for developing a homestead within a certain time. In the arid Southwest, one section was not enough land for a ranch, so many small homesteads were sold to larger ranches. This photograph shows the Ed Latham homestead on Berrenda Creek. (DW)

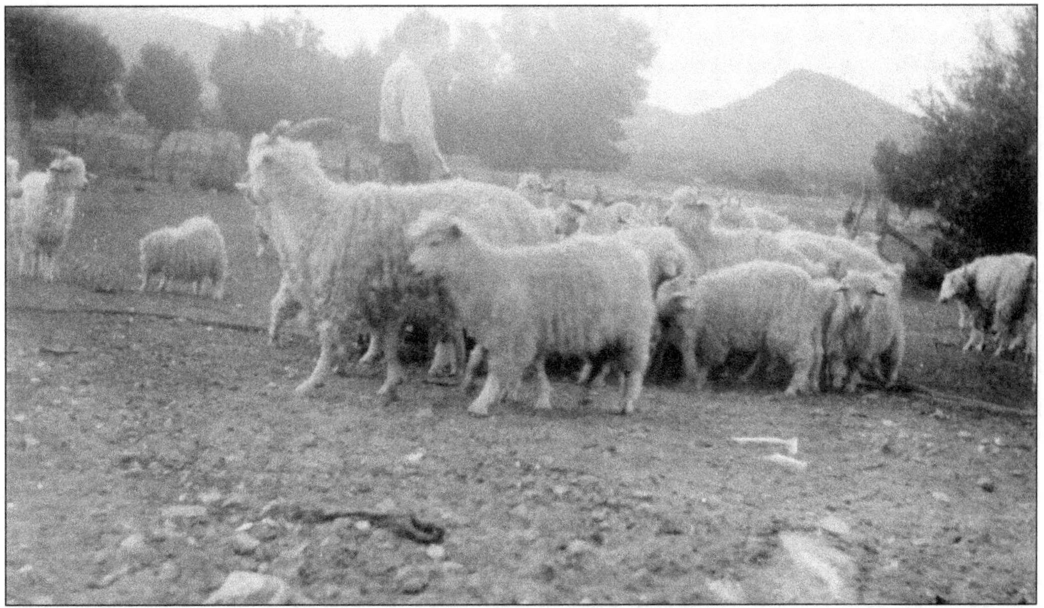

Louis Faulkner came to Sierra County from Texas with members of the Latham family who were driving a large herd of cattle. Faulkner, a great nephew of Daniel Boone, homesteaded on Berrenda Creek and raised Angora goats. Today, a windmill and water tank are still called "Uncle Louis." (DW)

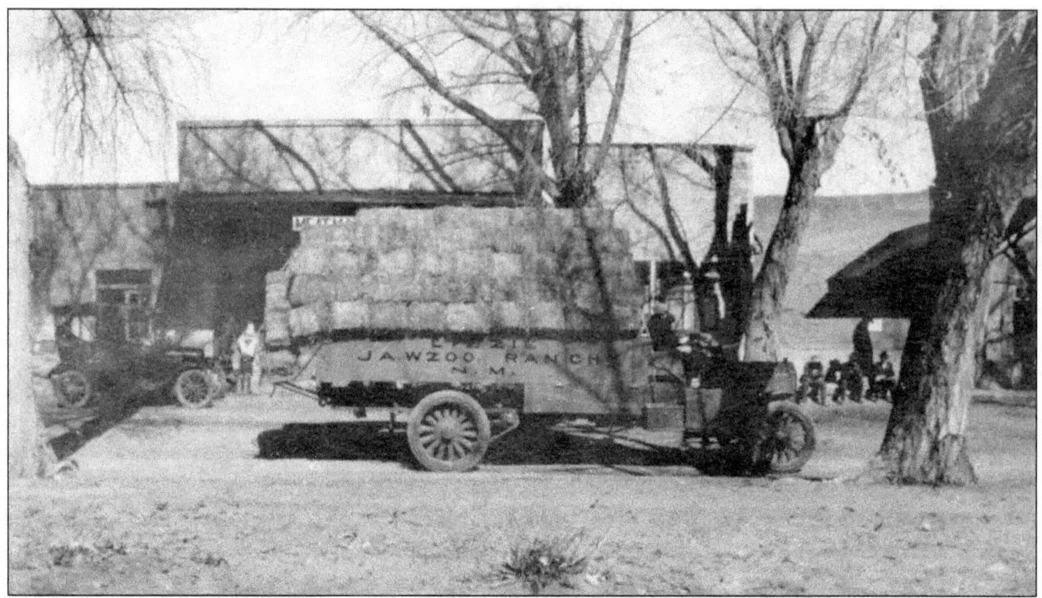

J.A. Wigmore, founder of the Dr. Pepper Co., once owned what is now the Ladder Ranch. JAW was his brand. A woman commented that his ranch was a zoo, so the name was changed to the Jawzoo. Other wealthy owners of the ranch have included Willard H. Hopewell, Sam S. Lard, Robert O. Anderson, and, presently, Ted Turner. (GSM)

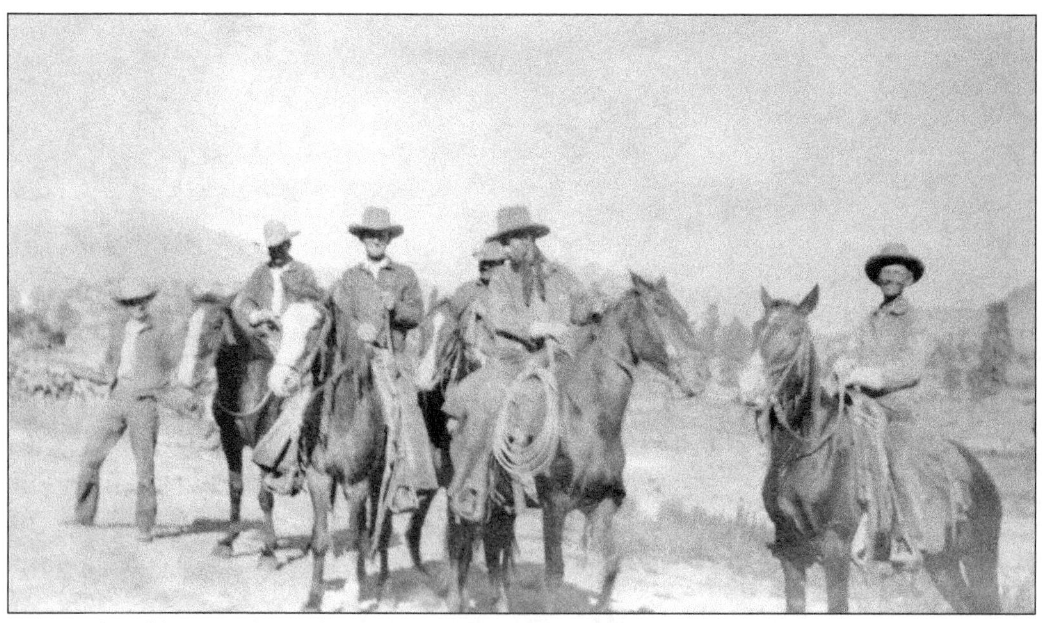

Mounted Ladder Ranch cowboys (from left to right) Willard Hopewell, Ed Baca, Cliff Crews, unknown, Henry Moore, and Sully Farnsworth are ready for a day's work. One of them was up before daylight to wrangle the horses. Each had to rope and saddle his own horse out of the remuda. The town of Willard, New Mexico, was named for Willard Hopewell. (IHSF)

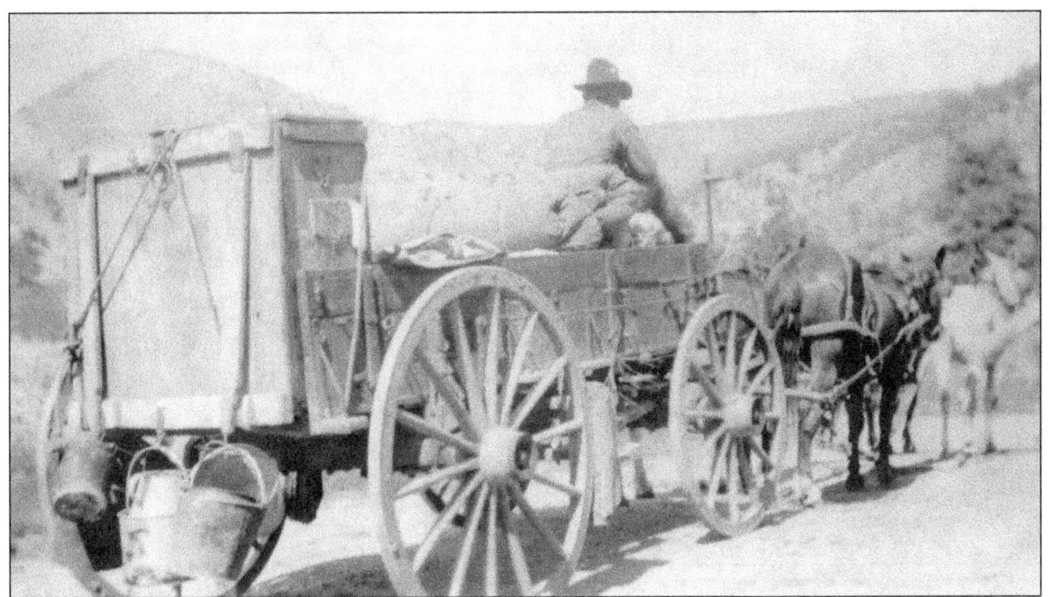

The large Ladder Ranch required a chuckwagon to follow the cowboys from camp to camp as they gathered cattle for branding or shipping. Its main feature was a sloping box with a hinged lid that lowered to become a table. It contained shelves and drawers for holding food and utensils and also held the bedrolls. (IHSF)

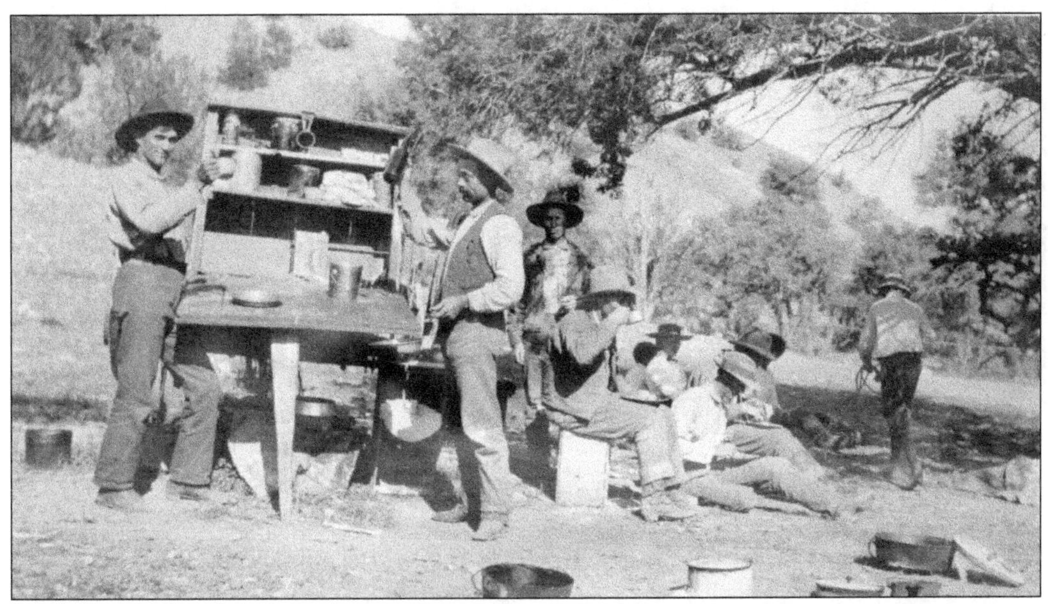

The chuck wagon was the cowboys' headquarters on the range. They did not just eat their meals there; it was their social center and recreation spot. Most meals included beans and meat along with sourdough biscuits and coffee. (IHSF)

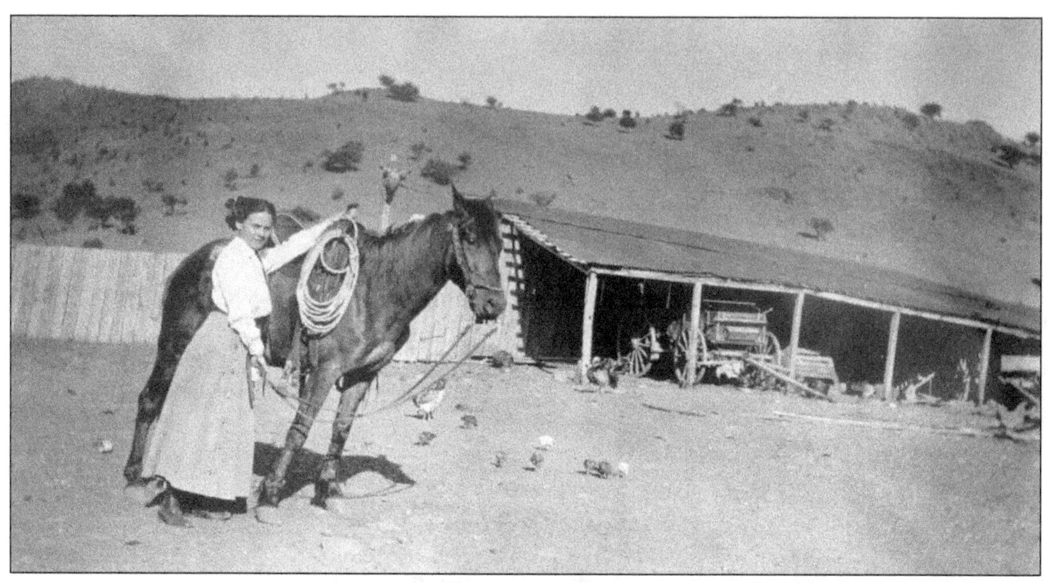

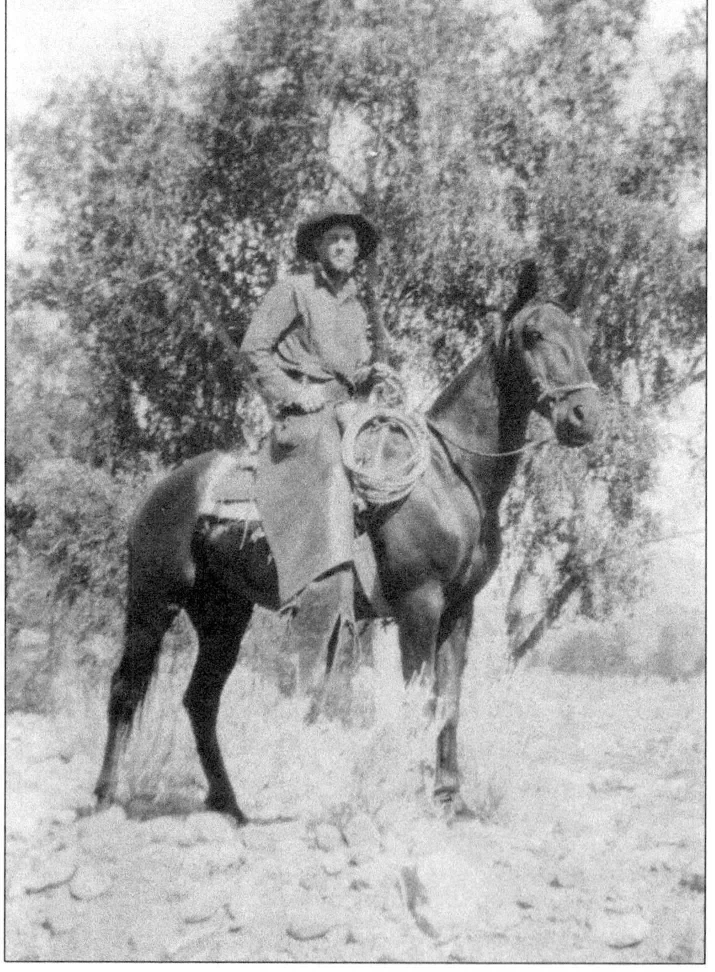

Ann Bucher's father was a successful banker in Kingston and was part owner of the large Ladder Ranch, where Ann spent much of her life. Here, the split riding skirt and roping saddle indicate that Ann abandoned the side-saddle when she helped on the ranch. (IHSF)

Dudley Messer, a grandson of Dudley Richardson, an early rancher on Tierra Blanca Creek, was a lifelong cowboy. To provide protection from the brush in this mountainous country, ranch hands wore chaps and had taps on their stirrups. (BRM)

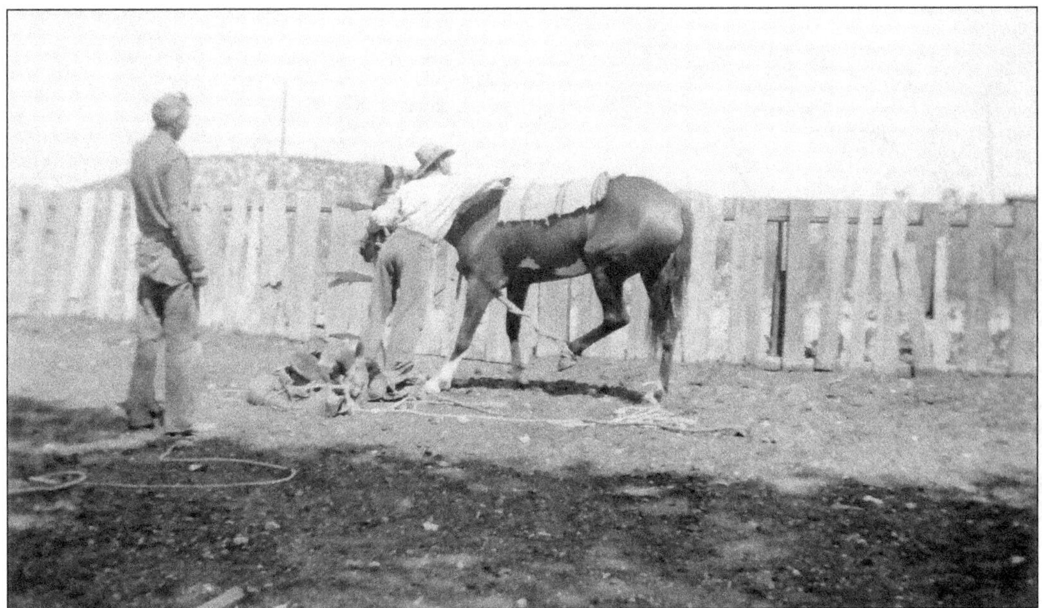

Breaking horses was part of a cowboy's job. Ground breaking horses was done after the horse was grown (about three years old). Tying a hind leg up was one way to control an unbroken horse while saddling it. The rope was usually tied with a bowknot that allowed the rider to release the rope once he was in the saddle. (DW)

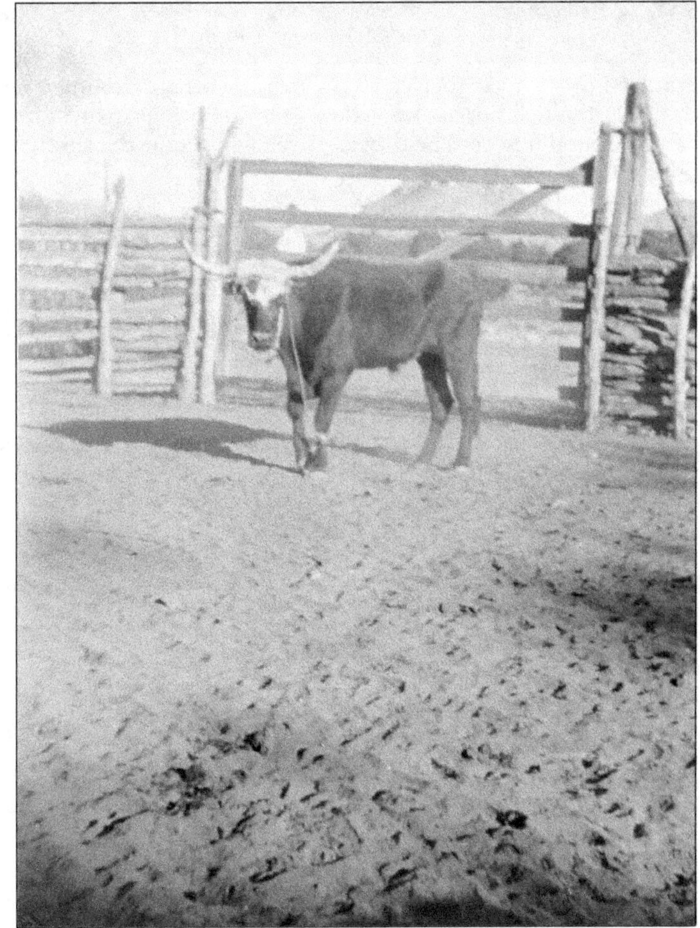

Wild mavericks (unbranded cattle) were sometimes caught in cattle traps in the Black Range. At other times, they were roped. Getting a rope on a wild cow took exceptional skill and no little courage in the rugged Black Range. A front foot was tied to the horns to slow the animal and keep it from running off during the long drive down rugged brushy canyons to the ranch headquarters.

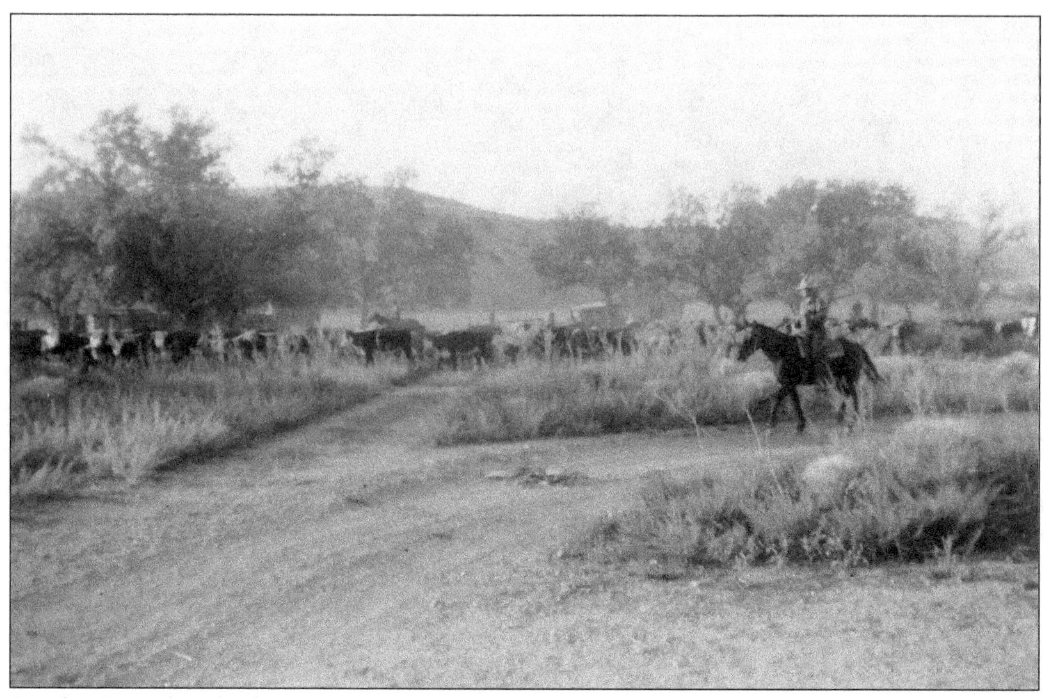

Stanley Dysard and other cowboys are shown here driving a herd of gentle Hereford cattle on the Wilson ranch near Lake Valley. They are bringing them to the corral in order to brand the calves. Round-ups were held twice a year—once in the spring to brand and once in the fall to ship. (DW)

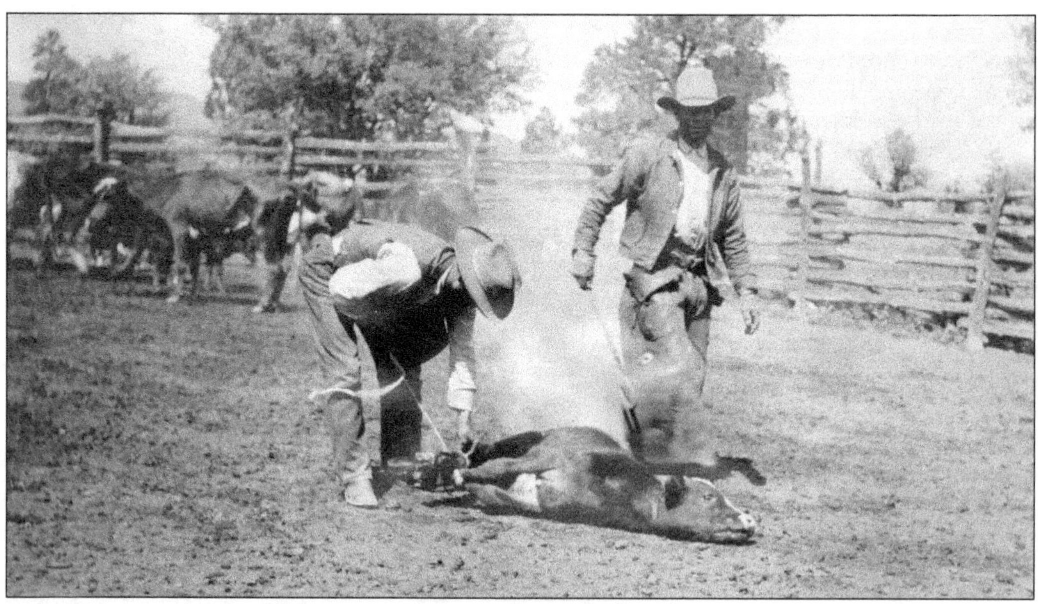

Branding calves was part of the real work of the ranch. Here, two unidentified Ladder Ranch hands are involved in the annual chore. This calf has been roped, flanked, tied down, and branded. One cowboy is carrying a hot running iron back to the fire, and the other is turning the calf loose. (IHSF)

The cowboys here have roped and flanked a calf. Two unidentified cowboys are holding the calf while another is branding as Lucas Apodaca waits to vaccinate. Modern cowboys often use an alley and a branding table instead of roping a calf and dragging it to the flankers.

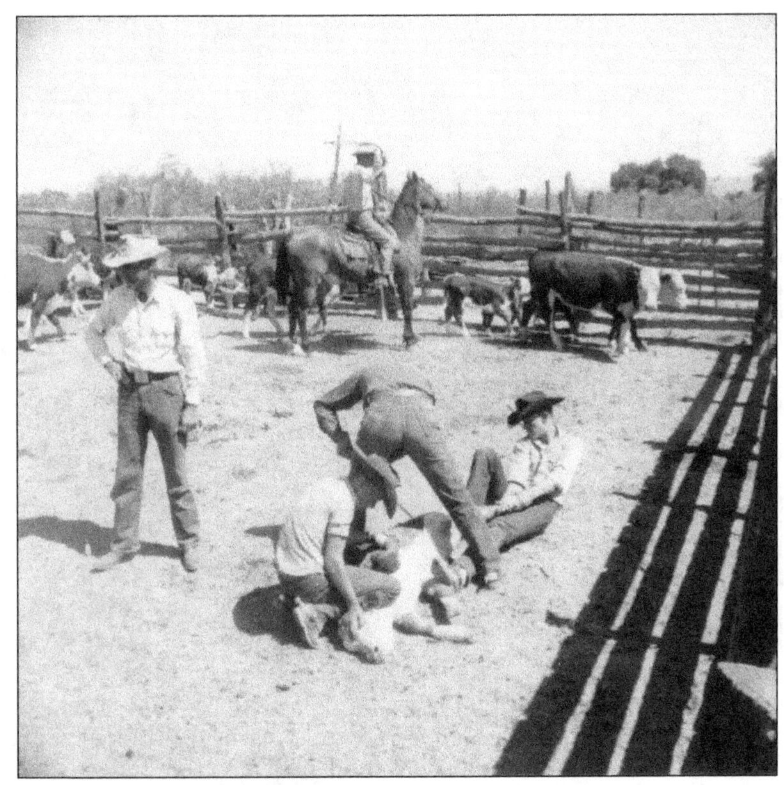

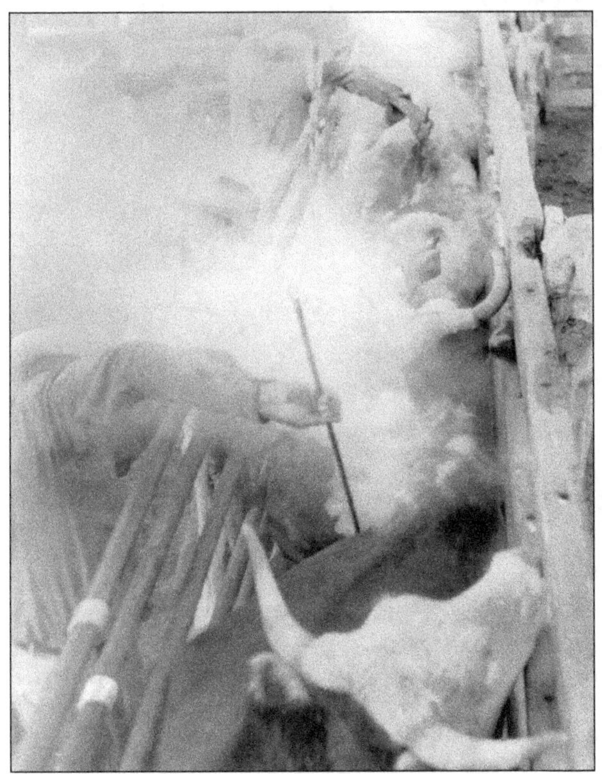

Today's cowboys use a chute so narrow that cattle cannot turn around or move when crowded into it. Without chutes or when on the open range, grown cattle were headed and heeled by cowboys on horseback.

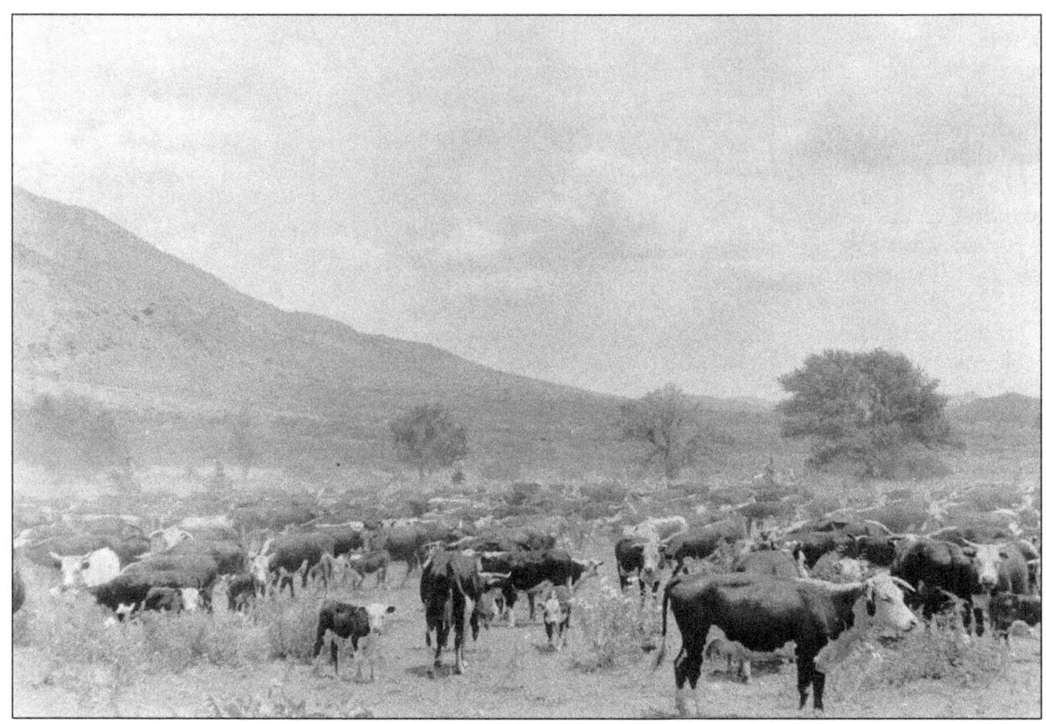

It has taken at least two weeks to gather this large herd of cattle out of the mountains. They are being sorted in preparation for the two-day drive to the shipping pens. Neighboring ranchers always helped each other at round-up time, making it unnecessary to hire extra labor. Women and children often rode and helped work cattle.

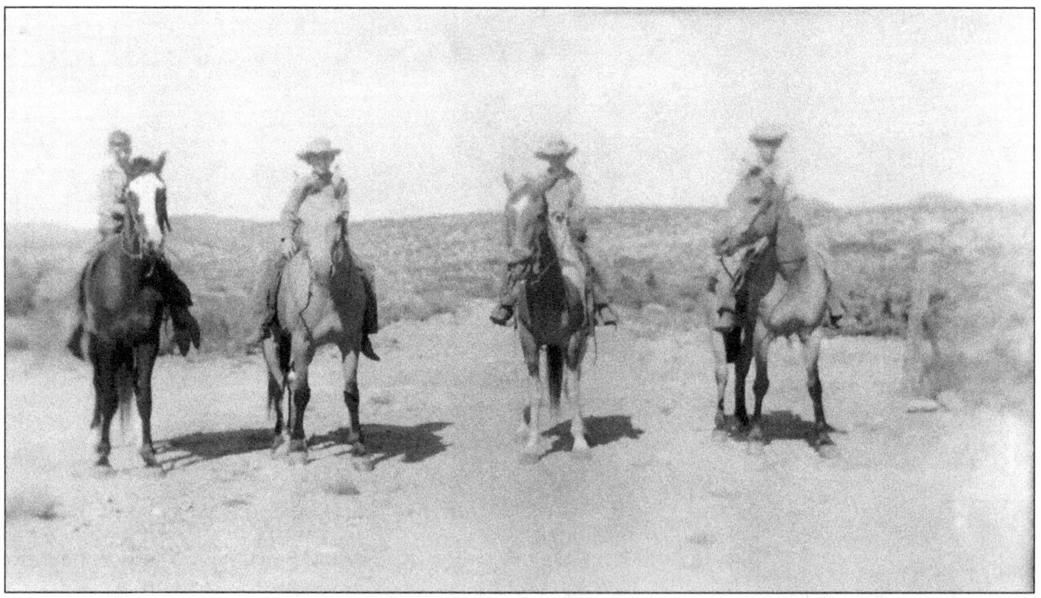

Young cowboys played especially important roles during the two world wars, when many of the experienced hands were serving their country. Shown here, from left to right, are Emory Faulkner, Doyle Nunn, Emmett Faulkner, and Joliver Wilson. Emmett and Emory Faulkner worked all of their lives as cowboys. (DW)

All cattle leaving the ranch had to be inspected to make sure they had the correct brand. This was done to prevent stolen cattle from being sold. Weaned calves were sold by weight and had to be weighed. The cowboys are using long prods to urge the cattle up the chute. This is how they earned the name "cowpokes." (IHSF)

After the railroad track was taken out at Osceola in the early 1930s, shipping pens were built at Nutt. This meant it took the cowboys another day to make the drive. A triangular holding trap, called the Jog, was built to hold the herd overnight between Lake Valley and Nutt. The shape of the trap made it possible to gather cattle before daylight without missing any.

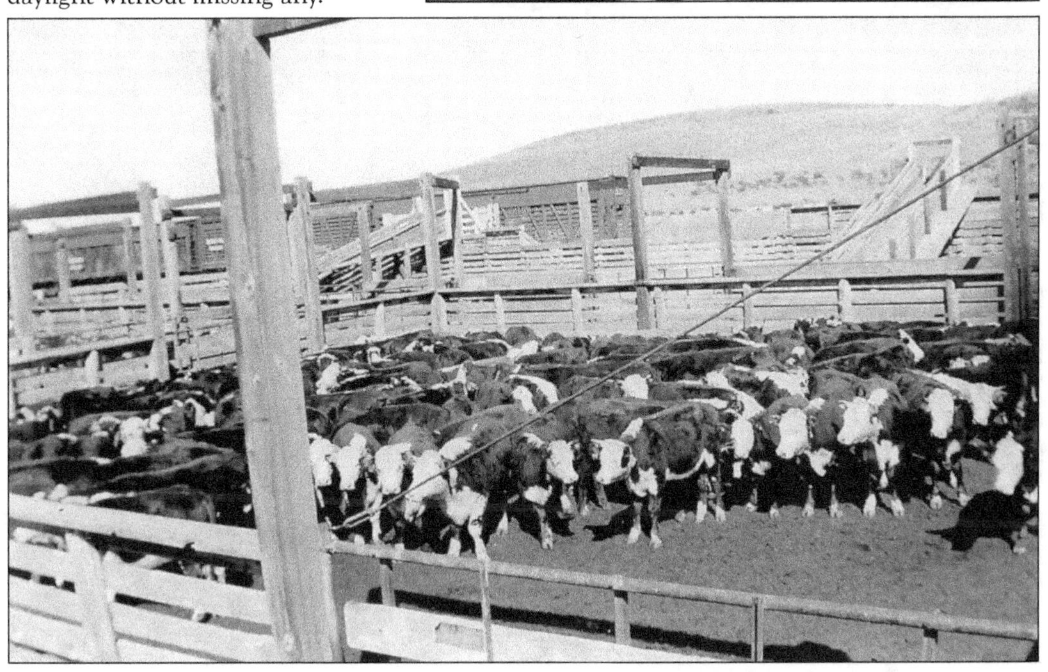

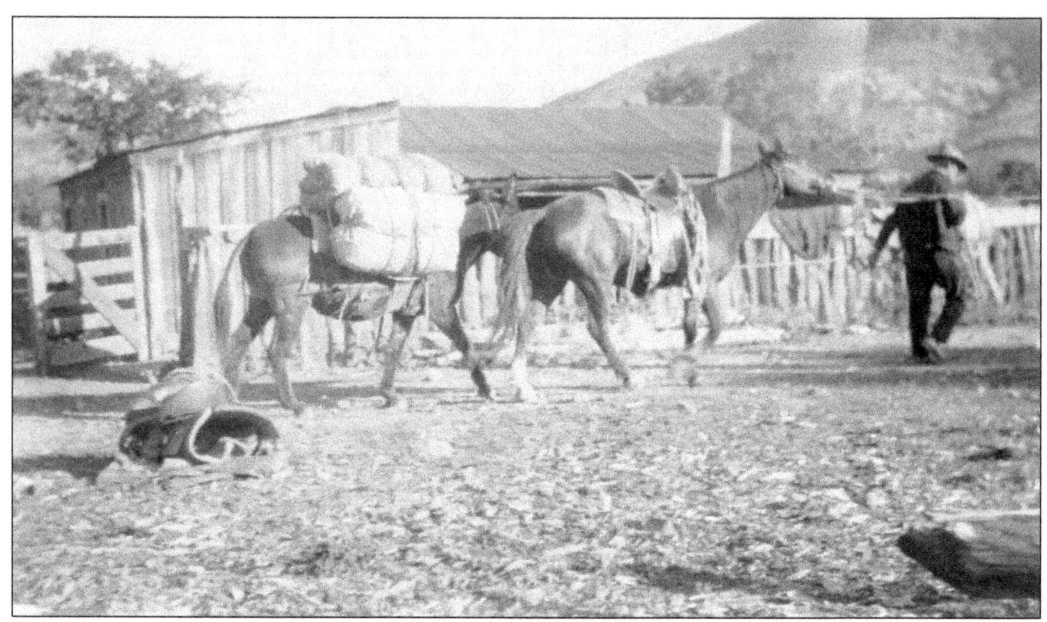

Until the invention of the automobile and the horse trailer, cowboys would ride from one ranch to another seeking work. Most of them brought their own horse and bedroll. One old cowboy was heard to say that if he rode up to a barn that had outside lights, he kept right on going. Ranchers often worked long hours, starting before daylight and ending after dark. (BRM)

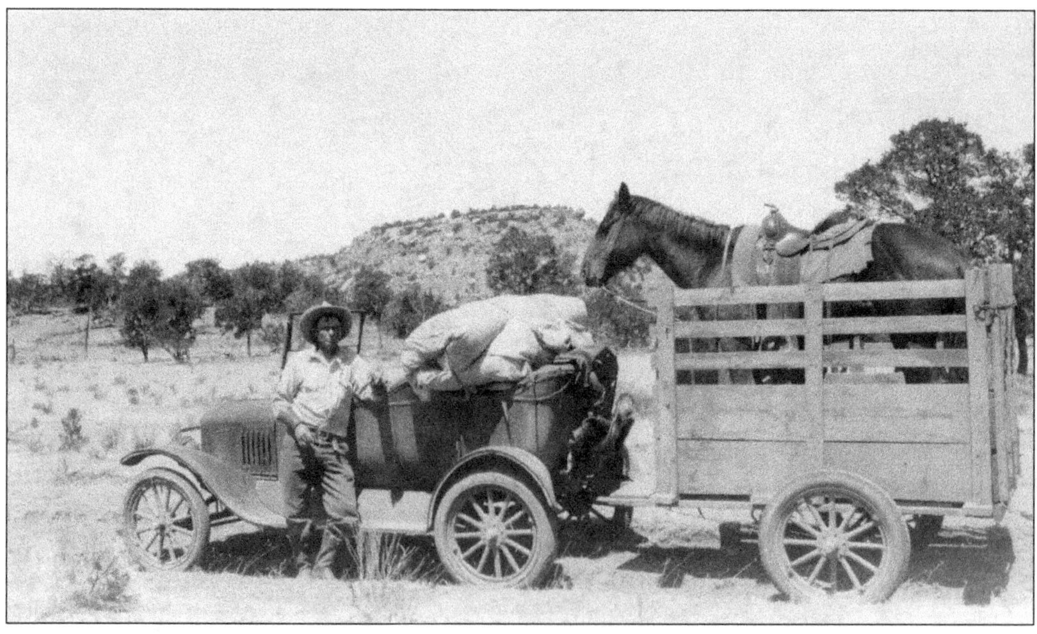

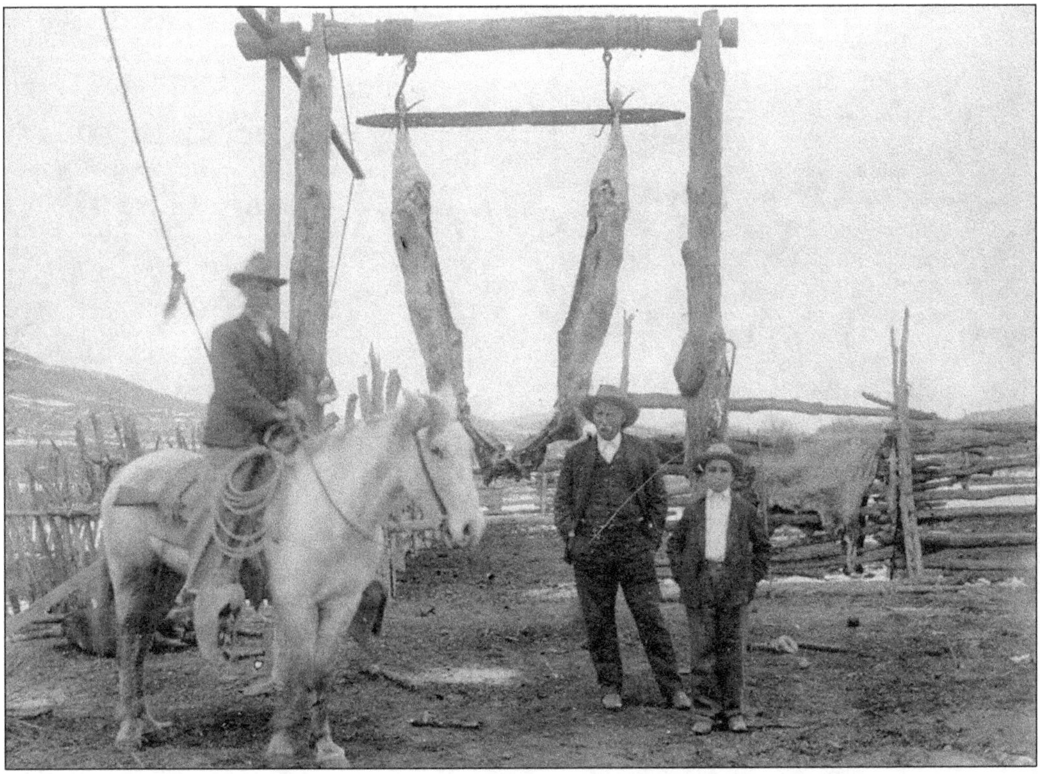

Meat preparation was often done at home. Ranchers butchered their own hogs, chickens, and beef. Here, a steer has been skinned, gutted, and cut in half in the corral.

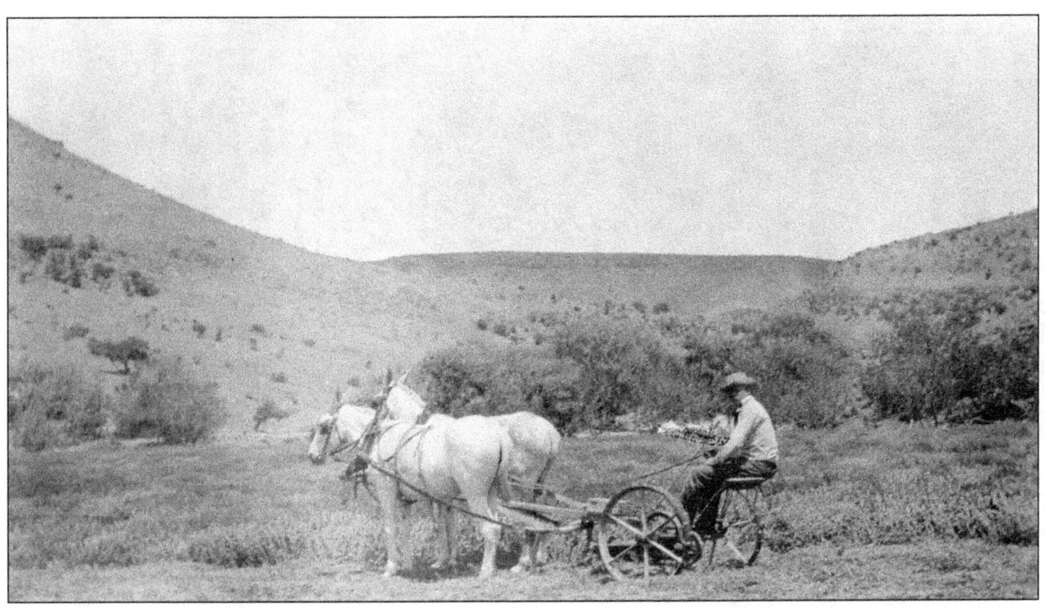

A ranch hand is cutting hay on Ladder Ranch about 1907. Irrigation by way of acequias developed early near the Ladder Ranch headquarters. In a good year with lots of rain, some ranchers even cut grass or prairie hay. (IHSF)

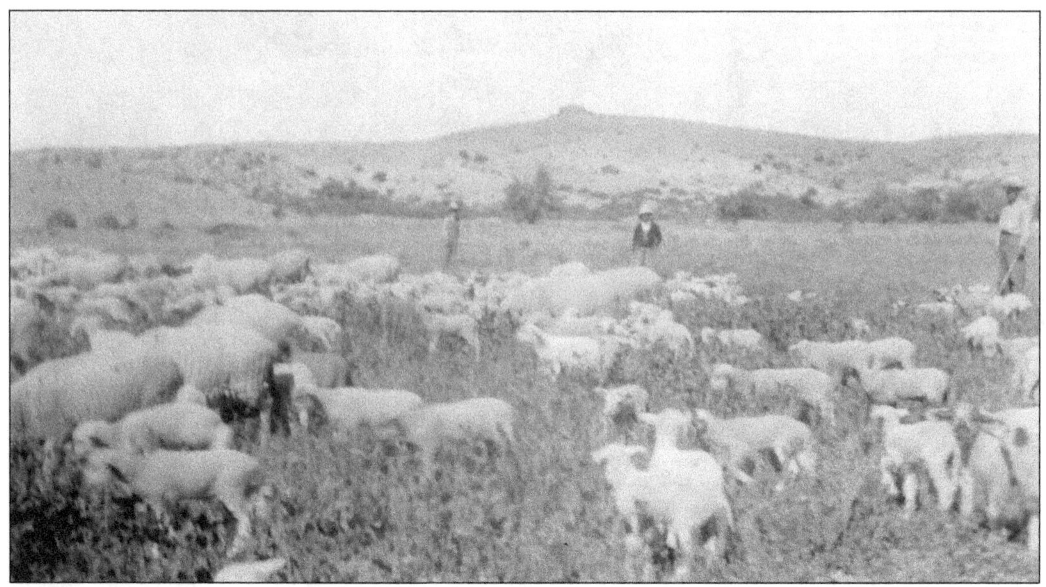

Many ranches ran both sheep and cattle. While conflicts over land ownership erupted at times, Sierra County never experienced the violent sheep/cattle conflicts that occurred in other areas. These sheep are on the ranch belonging to Clarence Wilson, son of early Kingston pioneer Oliver Wilson. (DW)

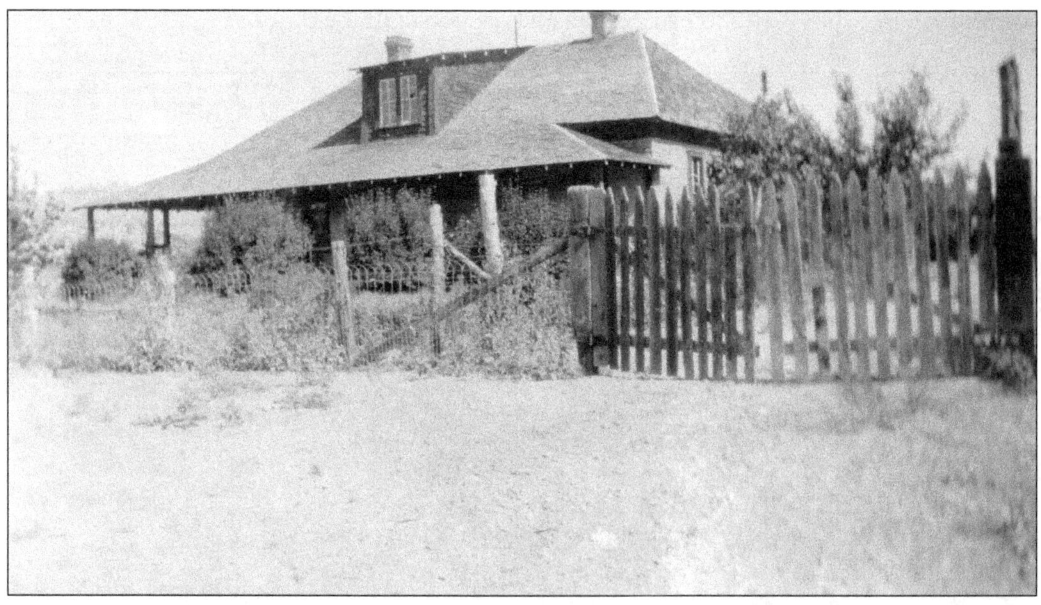

This is the house near the original site of the first Lake Valley settlement. It still stands and is part of the Lake Valley Ranch Properties. An adobe room that is part of the house was at one time a stage stop. Dan Dugan once owned the ranch and left it to his son Tom Inglis, who branded TI. Harve Ringer was the next owner. After his death, his wife, Mabel Bright Ringer, sold to the Wilson family, who increased the size of the ranch and ran it for years. (DW)

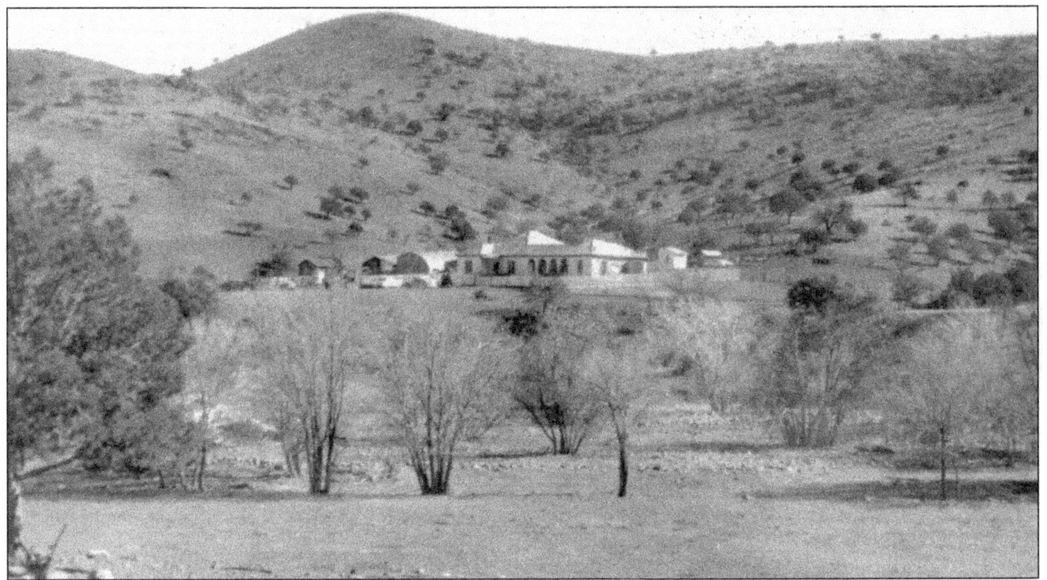

Called the Pitchfork Ranch, this fine old adobe became the headquarters for the Reids' ranch. The house was originally built by Liggett and Meyers Tobacco Company. The owner came to the area for his health. When he died, he left the ranch to his ranch hand. It became part of Bason's F+ ranch and later burned. (SB)

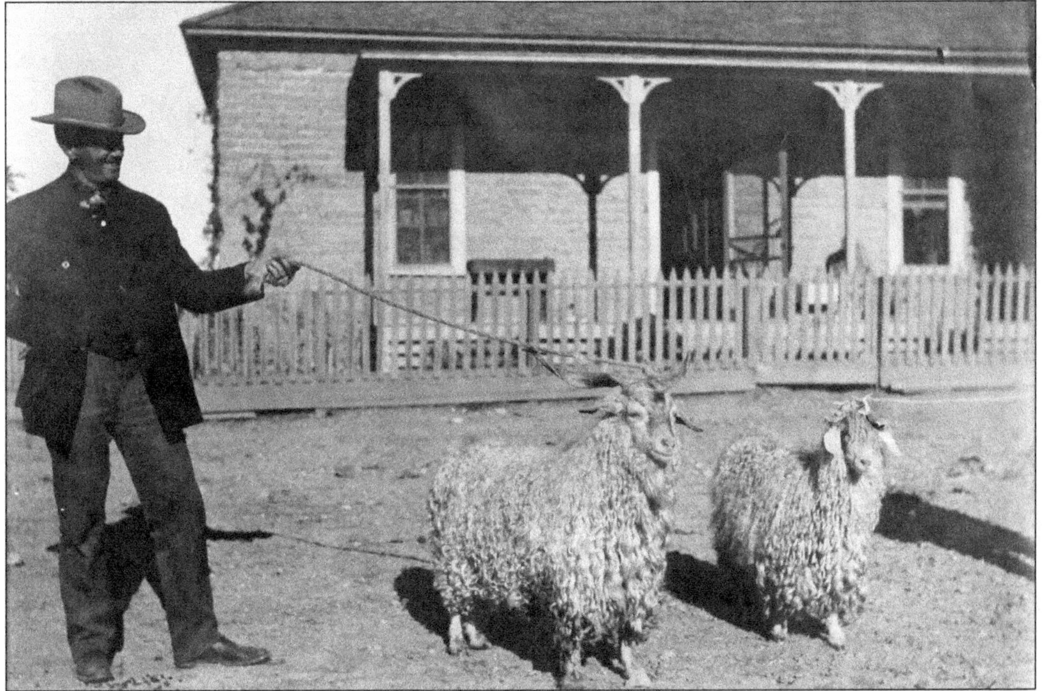

Robert was a son of Margaret Armer Reid, who founded the goat operation in 1893. Raising angora goats was a major enterprise in southwestern New Mexico. Margaret Armer Reid settled just west of Kingston. Descendants of the Angora Queen kept the Pitchfork Ranch until 1961. Robert was an early forest ranger and game warden at Alma, New Mexico. He took over the goat ranch when Margaret's health failed. (DW)

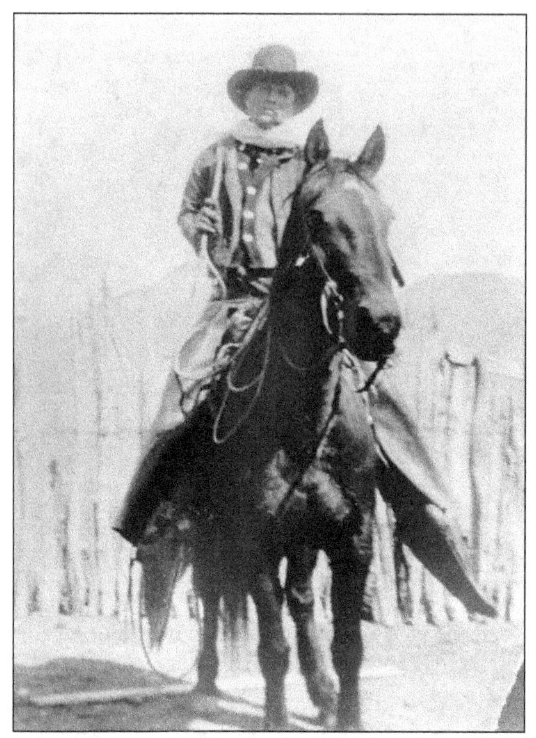

In early 1921, Nunn brothers Pryor (left) and Emmett were involved in what became known as the "Last Range War" in New Mexico. It was a land dispute between the Sierra Land and Cattle Company and the Charlie Sikes family (below). In the first gun battle at the North Well near Lake Valley, John Sikes was shot and killed by Luther Wright, a hand hired by the SLCs to guard the well. Later, another gunfight broke out when Charlie, Hood, Roger, and Lane Sikes, guns across their saddles, rode up to the North Well where Pryor and Emmett, Luther, Jay Barnett, and John Thomas were working. Hood was killed and Charlie was wounded. The SLC men were arrested for murder by Sheriff Neal Sullivan; only Pryor Nunn, Luther Wright, and Jay Barnett were indicted. When Pryor assumed responsibility for the killing at the trial held at the Sierra County Courthouse, the defense was left up in the air, and all were acquitted. The verdict was self-defense.

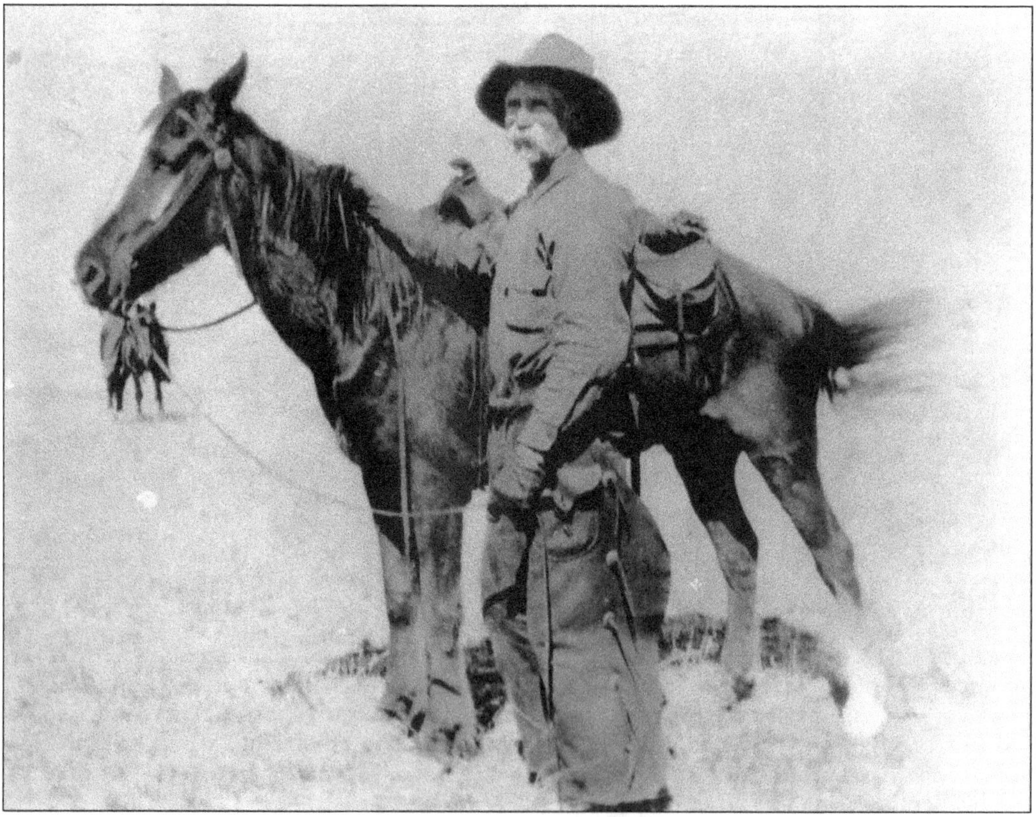

Five

PUBLIC LANDS

Prior to creation of the Forest Reserves in 1891, use of all of the public lands was unregulated. Federal policies encouraged privatization of western lands via mining and homestead laws. With the advent of the US Forest Service, federal ownership of the public domain was proclaimed, and dispersal of lands to private owners deemphasized. Forest rangers, game wardens, and government hunters played an increasing role throughout Sierra County. Regulation of grazing, logging, and hunting gradually emerged, and early forest rangers usually functioned as volunteer state game wardens. Respected citizens within the communities also carried deputy game warden badges, even while New Mexico was still a territory.

By 1900, federal land surveys and timber surveys were underway throughout the Black Range. The US Bureau of Fisheries stocked 1,000 rainbow trout into North Percha Creek in 1904. The Forest Service and, later, the Bureau of Biological Survey, carried out efforts to eliminate large carnivores, including wolves, mountain lions, coyotes, and both bear species. By the 1930s, they had removed the wolf and grizzly, but mountain lions and coyotes survived the early blitz and are now managed for sustained populations. Another species that was targeted by the government was prairie dogs, which were virtually eliminated by the 1920s through use of poison.

In 1934, public domain outside of the forest reserves fell under administration of the US Grazing Service, which became the Bureau of Land Management (BLM). This agency still manages most of the grasslands and desert habitats in Sierra County, although State Trust Lands are also dispersed through the county in one-square-mile blocks. To date, most of these are leased to ranchers and regulated similarly to the federal BLM lands.

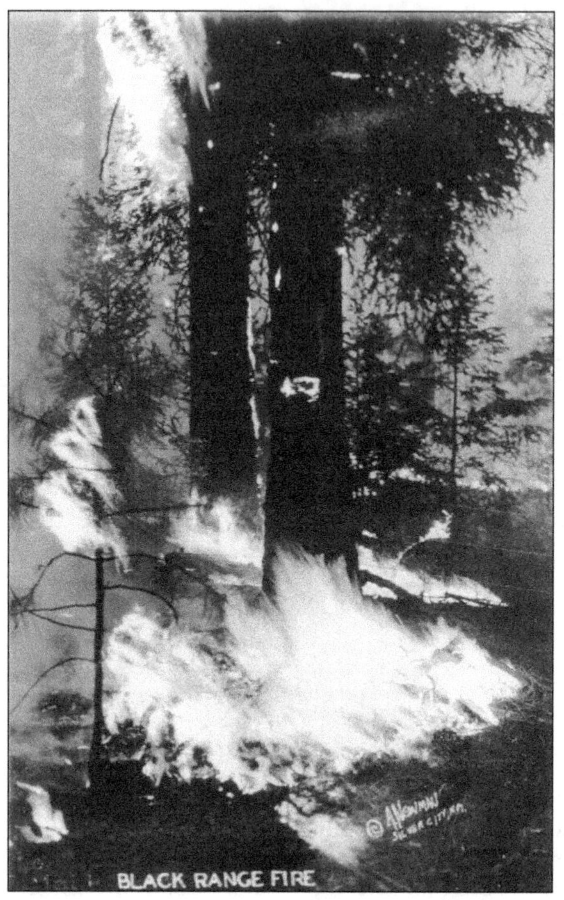

The unclaimed lands in the Black Range surrounding Kingston became part of the Gila National Forest Reserve in 1899. It became the Gila National Forest in 1905. One of the main duties of newly arrived forest rangers was fighting wildfire. In many cases, a single ranger would rush on horseback or on foot to a newly started fire and try to contain it single-handedly until help arrived, if it did. (GNF)

Rangers recognized early the need for fire towers and forest fire guards to spot forest blazes. Getting supplies into a remote lookout sometimes tested the skills of even the best packers. Here, packers are leaving Kingston with a load of unwieldy construction materials to build a new fire tower on Hillsboro Peak. (DG)

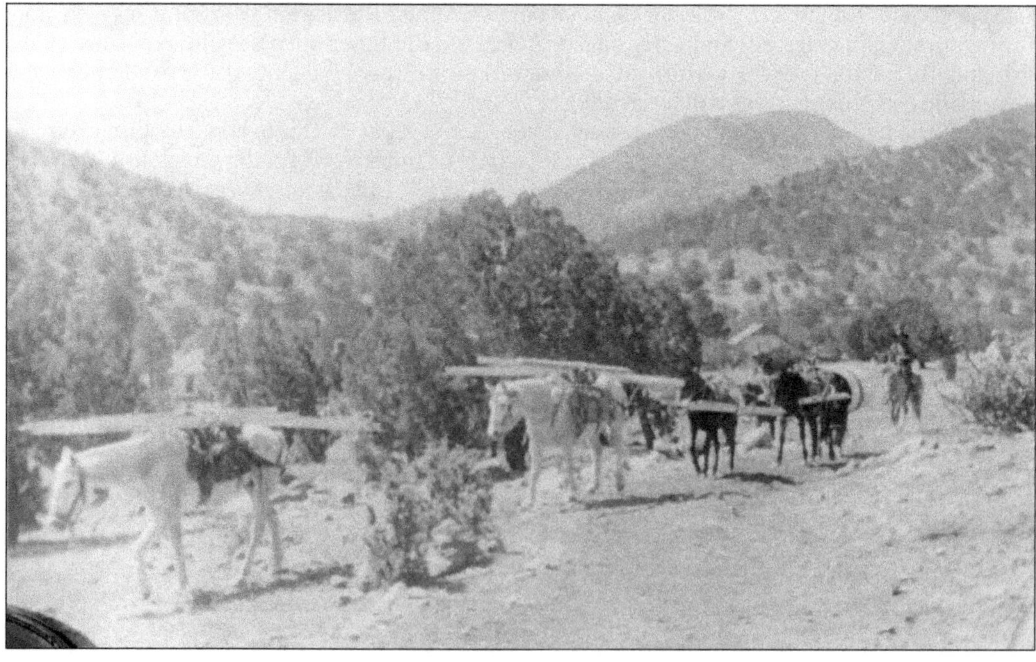

Braving wind and lightning in exposed towers in order to report forest fires before they could get out of hand, fire guards had to spend long hours during the dry months living in remote places. Here, workmen are putting the finishing touches on a newly built tower on Hillsboro Peak. (GNF)

Women began to work as fire guards early in the history of the Forest Service. Cecelia Anderson was the daughter of George and Cecelia Anderson. She lived with them in Kingston in 1930, but she disappears from the record after that. Hillsboro Peak, where this photograph was taken, was about nine miles from Kingston and accessible only on foot or by horseback. (GNF)

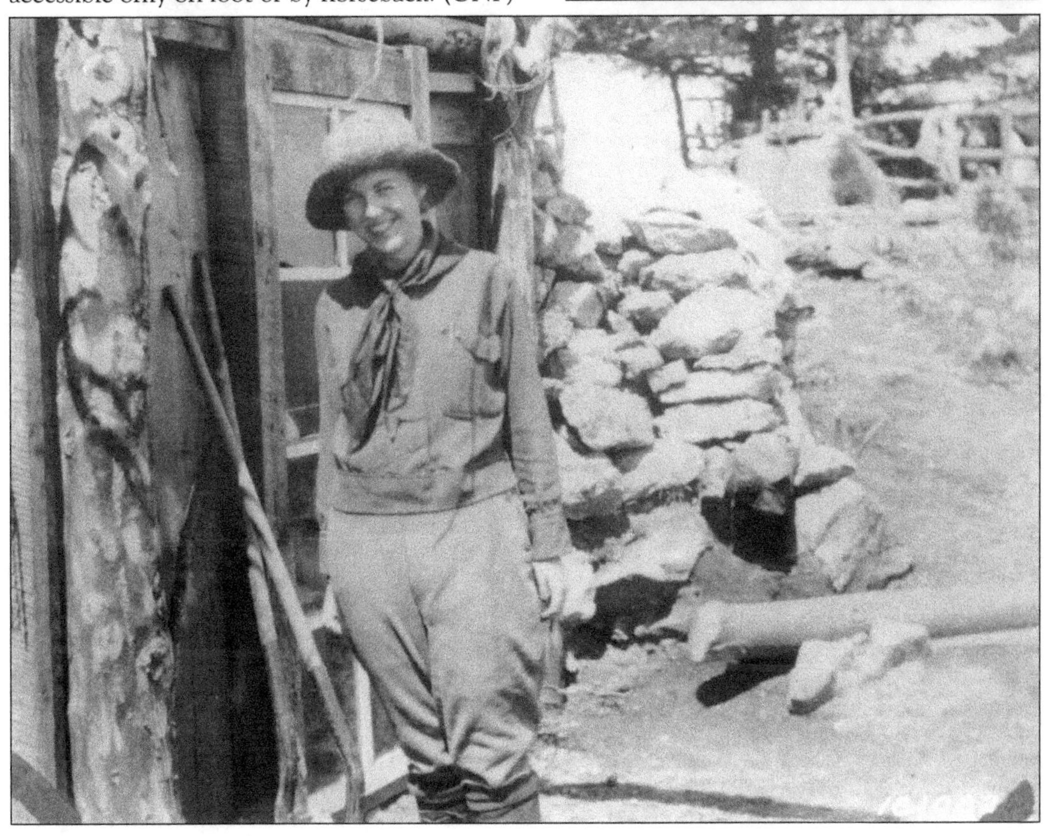

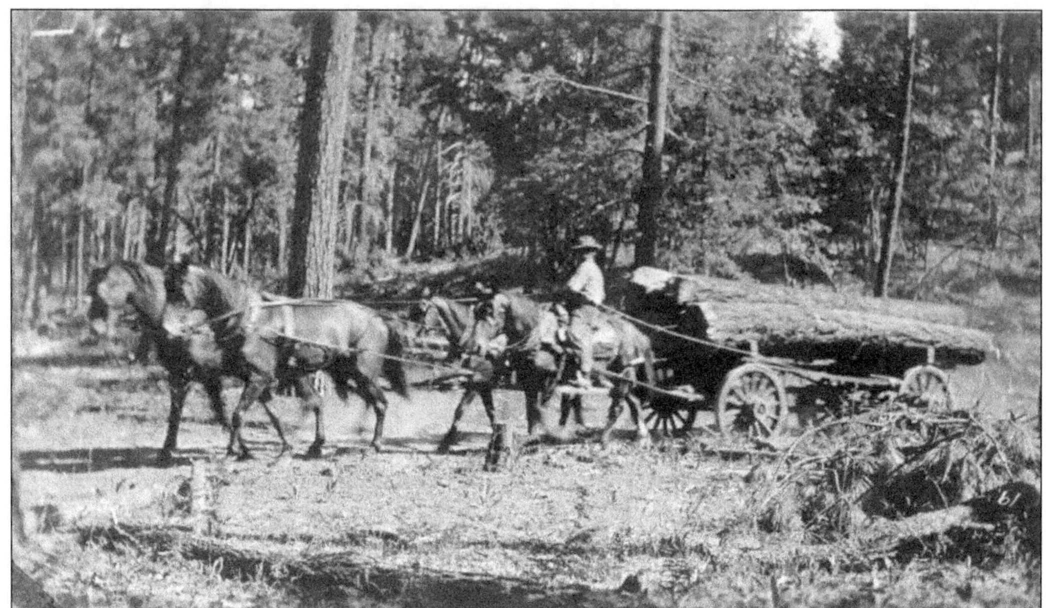

Demand for lumber created a logging industry on the national forest soon after Kingston and Hillsboro were settled. Several small sawmills developed within a few miles of Kingston. Loggers cut trees by hand crosscut saws and hauled timber by wagon. Mills were usually mobile, allowing loggers to cut a site, then move the mill close to an uncut area. Even so, hauling heavy logs by wagon was part of the process. (GNF)

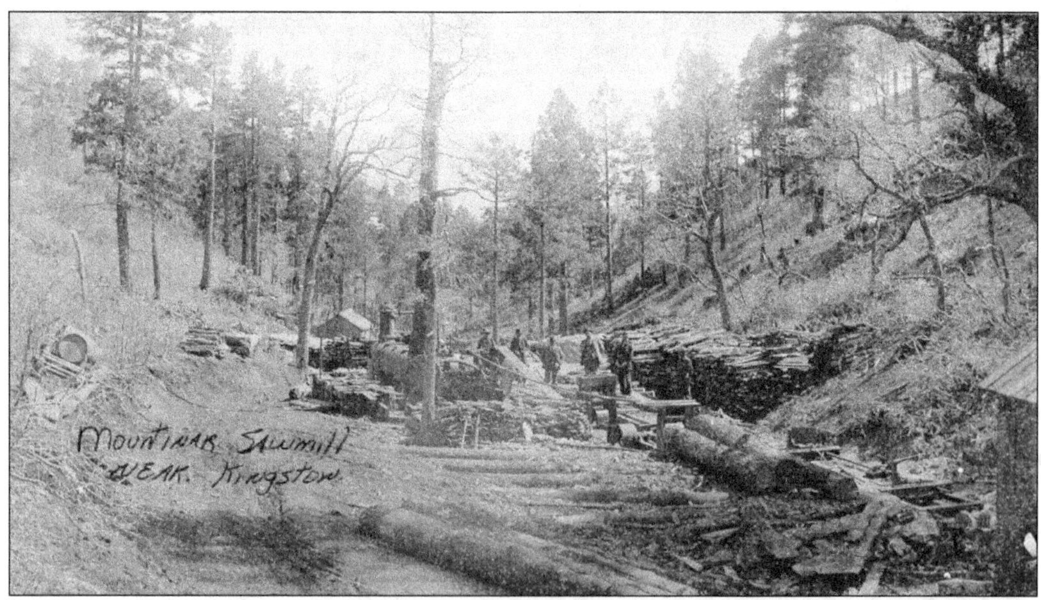

Here is a typical small sawmill in a remote forest site. The large boiler indicates that the mill's saw was driven by a steam engine. Even heavy boilers such as this one were periodically moved to new mill sites. Some of these old boilers remain in the last locations they were used. Today, it taxes the imagination to understand how they were hauled to some of these places. (PBM)

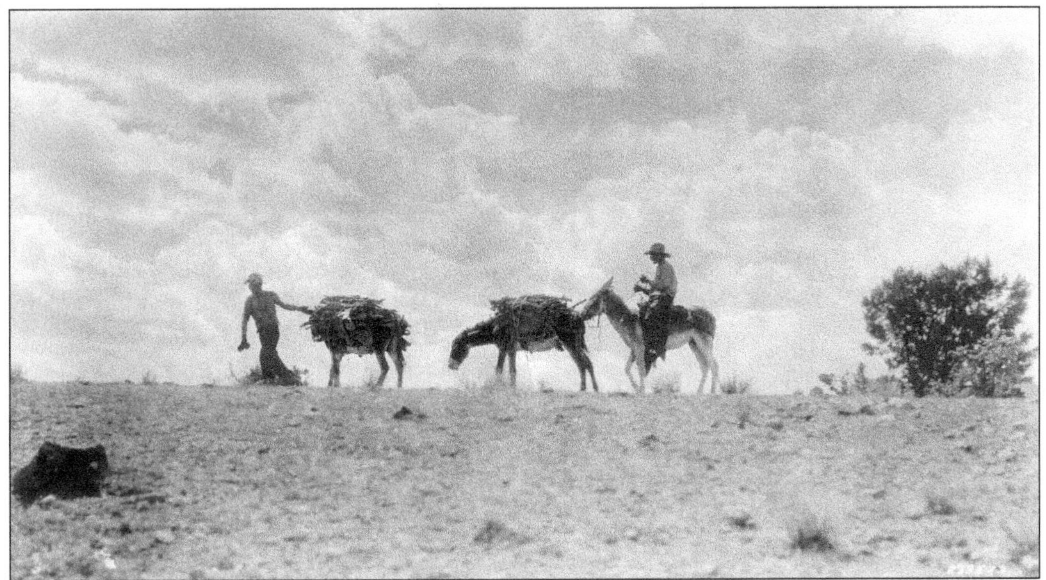

While perhaps less glamorous than logging, cutting firewood was an important occupation in the national forest. Wood was the only easily available fuel, and it was used to heat homes and businesses and run boilers for the steam-driven engines that powered everything from sawmills to stamp mills for mines. The ever-present burro was the main method for bringing wood to town from increasingly distant sites. (GNF)

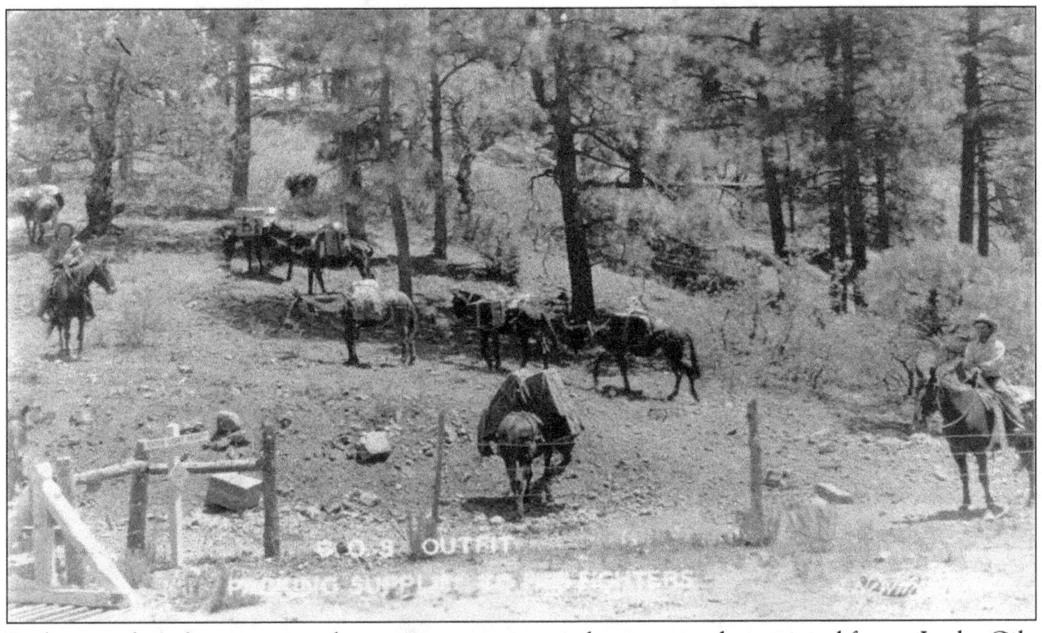

Packing and outfitting was and remains an important business in the national forest. In the Gila Wilderness Area, roads were nonexistent, so quality pack strings were needed to get supplies to isolated ranches, ranger stations, and firebases. In addition, packing and guiding hunters and wilderness campers became a source of income for capable packers. (GNF)

HUNTER'S LICENSE.

No. 5510 — TERRITORY OF NEW MEXICO, — $ 5.00

DEPARTMENT OF GAME AND FISH.

THIS CERTIFIES THAT Ralph E. Werley, a resident of El Paso, Tex., has paid the sum of Five and no/100 Dollars for a Non-Resident Bird HUNTING LICENSE, and is entitled to hunt Birds in the Territory of New Mexico, in conformity with law, during the season of 1910.

DESCRIPTION OF LICENSEE—Age 18 years, height 5 feet and 9½ inches, weight 127 color of hair Light, color of eyes Brown

Dated Las Cruces, New Mex. July 19 1910.

Thomas P. Gable Warden.

Holder's Signature. By Deputy.

This license is not transferable, does not authorize transportation or sale, and must be in the possession of the licensee while hunting. Opportunity to inspect and copy must be afforded to any officer authorized to inspect the same.

Then as now, bird hunting near Lake Valley and Hillsboro was popular among sportsmen. Gambels, Mearns, and scaled quail live in the area. Where this young El Paso man hunted is unknown, but his 1910 Territorial Hunter's License is a work of art. (Craig Springer)

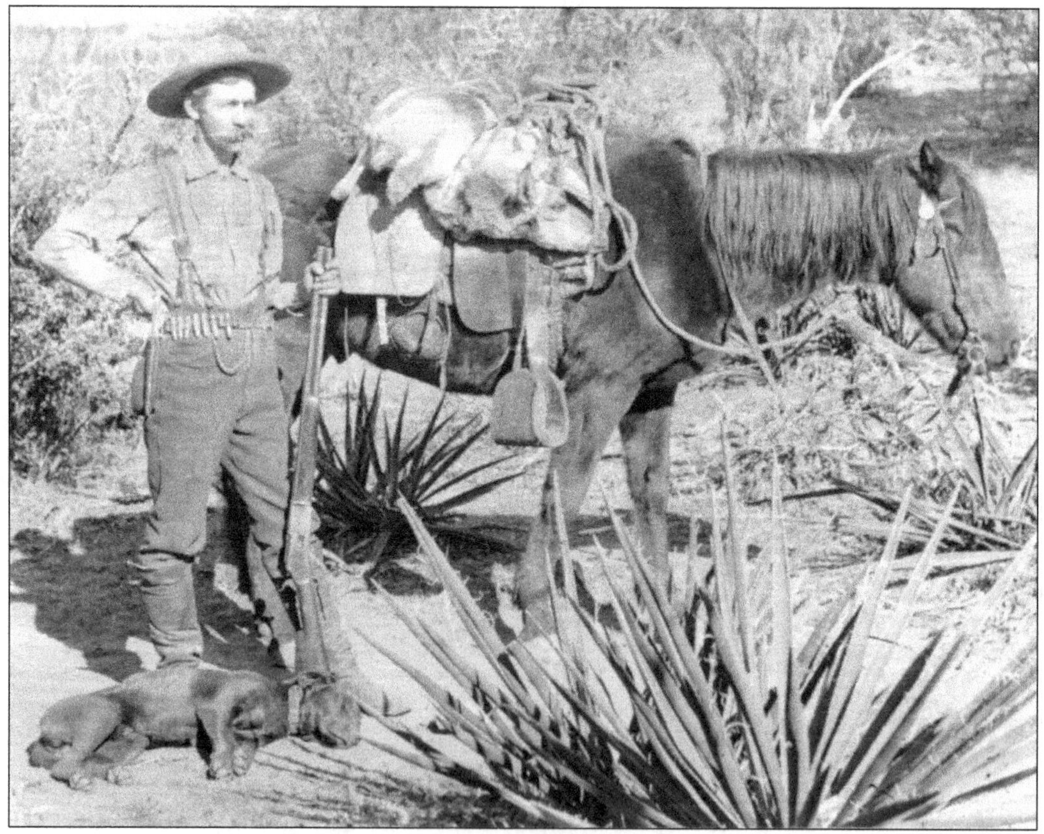

Hunting was a major use of the national forest. Although the grizzly and wolf were extirpated early, the Black Range was a place where hunters pursued all other big game. Here, a successful hunter is packing a pronghorn that he killed. (BRM)

Six

EDUCATION

While most of the stories about Hillsboro and its surroundings emphasize Apache wars, mining, and ranching, photographs tell us that the education of children was important from the beginning. In part, this was because mining and its related businesses attracted young workers who quickly developed families, as well as professionals in the form of engineers and doctors, who placed a high value on education. Whatever the case, schools were obviously important; from the very beginning, all children were invited to attend. Initially, the scattered communities built one-room frame buildings and hired one teacher to teach all grades.

With the demise of Lake Valley and Kingston, the small country schools disappeared, and students attended either grade school or high school in more stately buildings in Hillsboro. Dwindling numbers of young families in Kingston and Hillsboro have more recently led to the closing of schools in these towns. The few remaining children are bused to Truth or Consequences. The Hillsboro grade school is now a residence, and the high school serves as a community center.

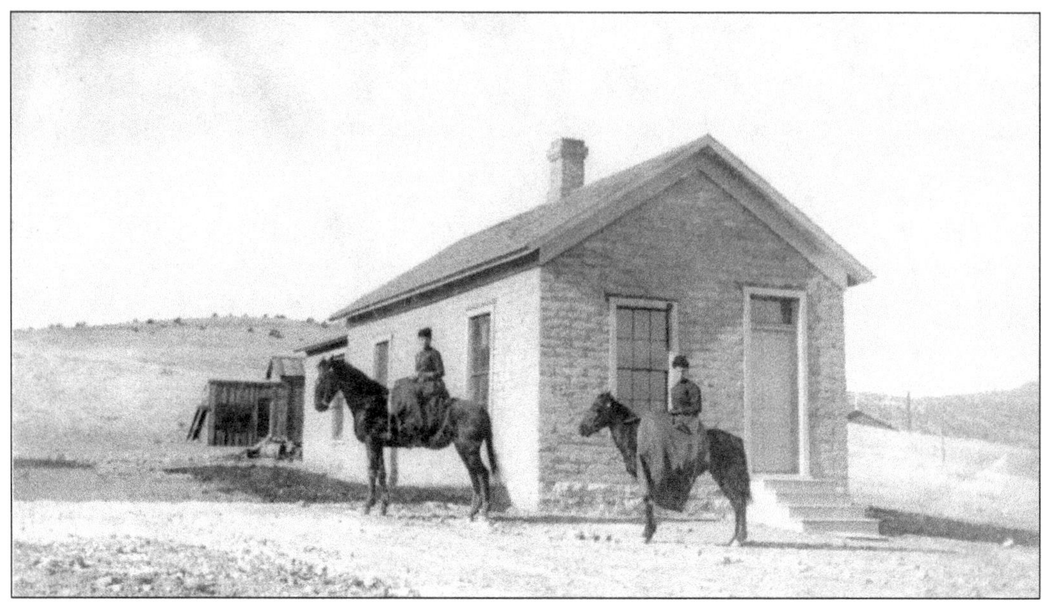

This is a photograph of one of the first Lake Valley schools. Its teachers are seated sidesaddle on their horses outside the schoolhouse. One of Lake Valley's early teachers was named Miss Dunn. This schoolhouse became the church of well-known preacher Hunter Lewis, "Padre of the Rio Grande." (DT)

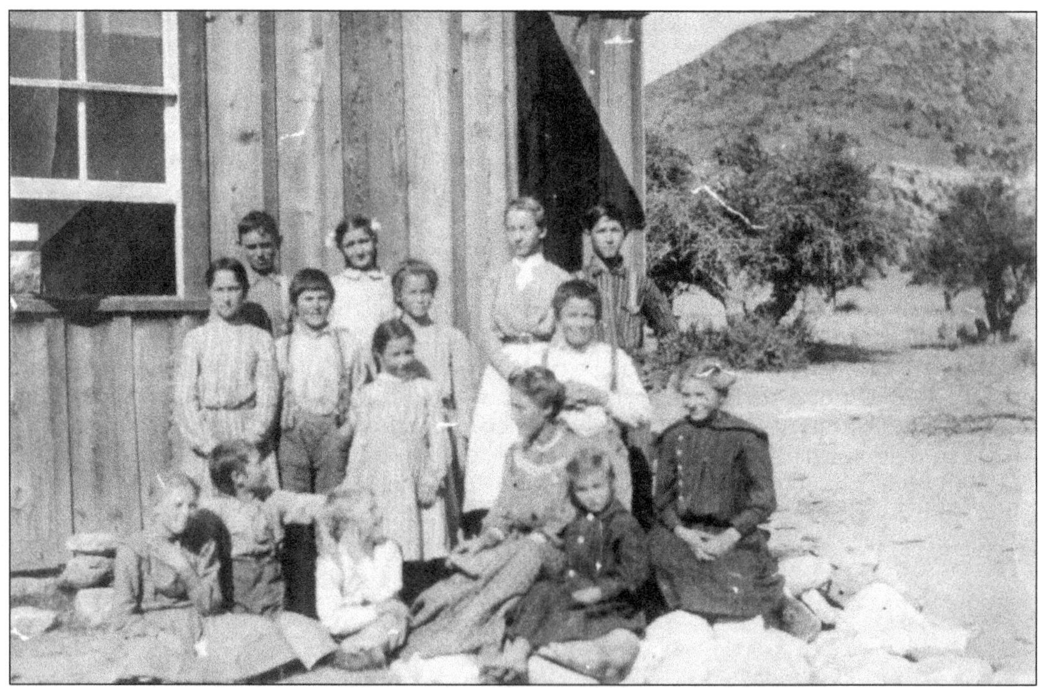

The one-room school on Tierra Blanca was built in 1905 by the Tierra Blanca residents. Students, from left to right, are Edgar May, Eva May, Willie Richardson, Dudley Lyons, Maggie Lyons, Pete Kinney, Carolyn Beals, Morel Beals, Eula Lyons, Minnie Richardson, Johnnie Lyons, Earl Richardson, Ida Kinney, and Elizabeth Kinney. The teacher was Addie Colson Richardson.

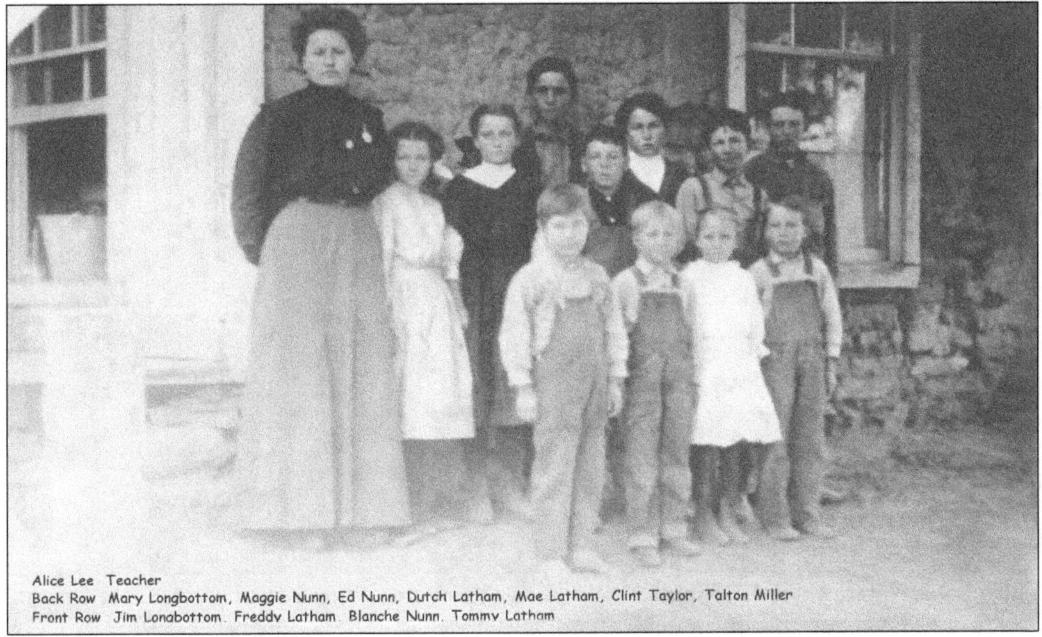

The teacher of the little adobe school on the Berrenda was Alice Lee, daughter of Civil War veteran and rancher Thomas Lee and his wife, Ann Benner Lee. The students in the picture are the sons and daughters of well-known ranch families on Berrenda Creek. The school term was only three months.

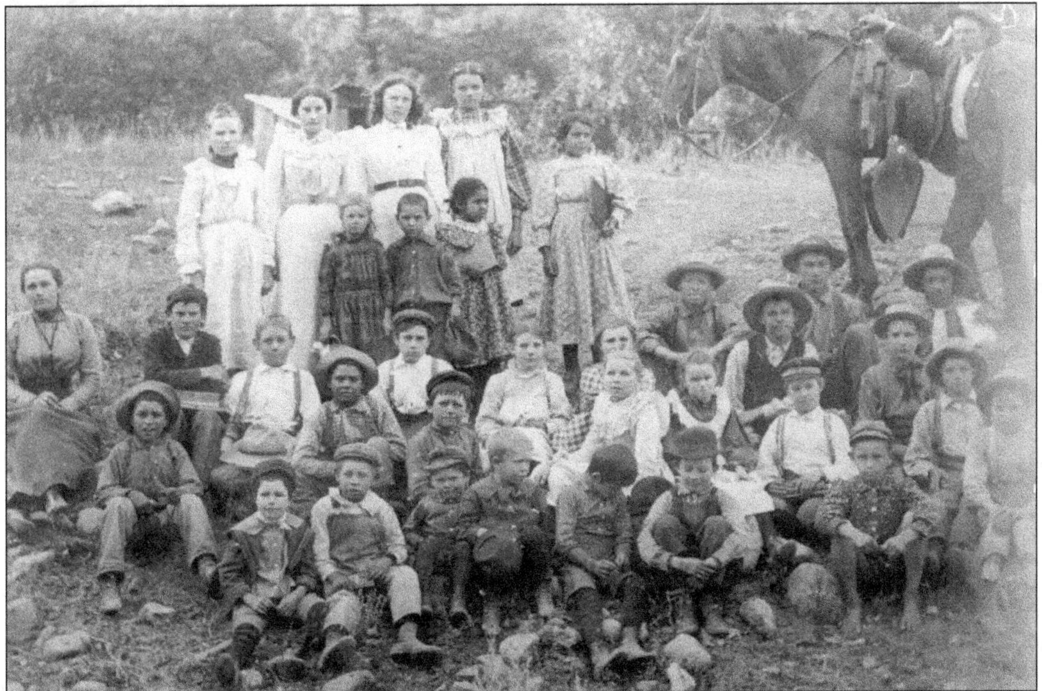

By the early 1900s, a large number of children sought education in Kingston. Typical of the times, a single teacher taught all grades, probably in a single-room school. The gentleman at upper right is Percy Pague and the teacher is Miss Randall. (PBM)

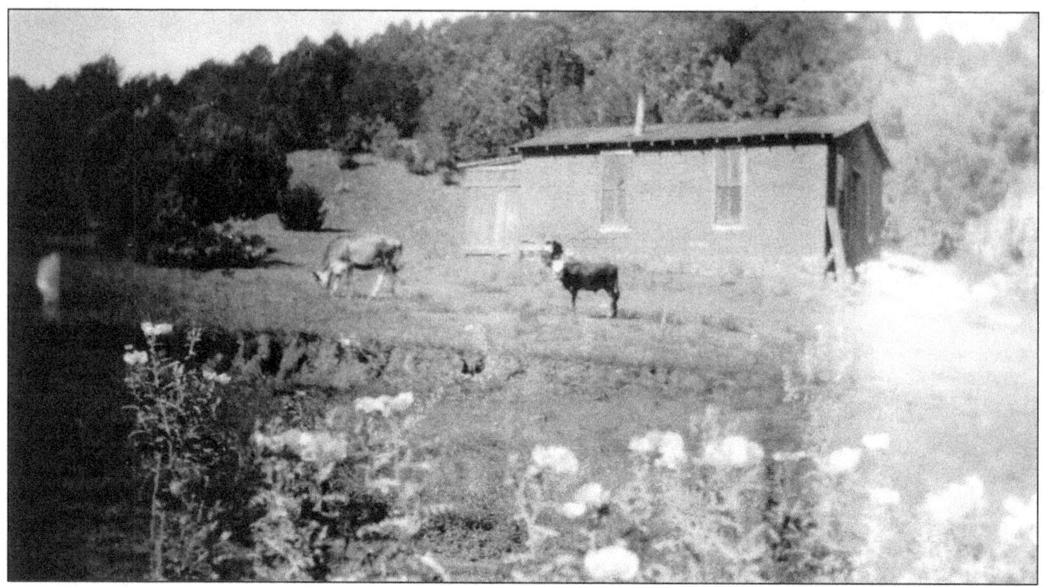

This photograph of the early Kingston school was taken after it ceased to be used. Made from adobe, it was probably a little more comfortable than some of the framed shacks used by more remote communities. This building has been refurbished and is now a meeting place for the Kingston Spit and Whittle Club, which carries on many community affairs. (MM)

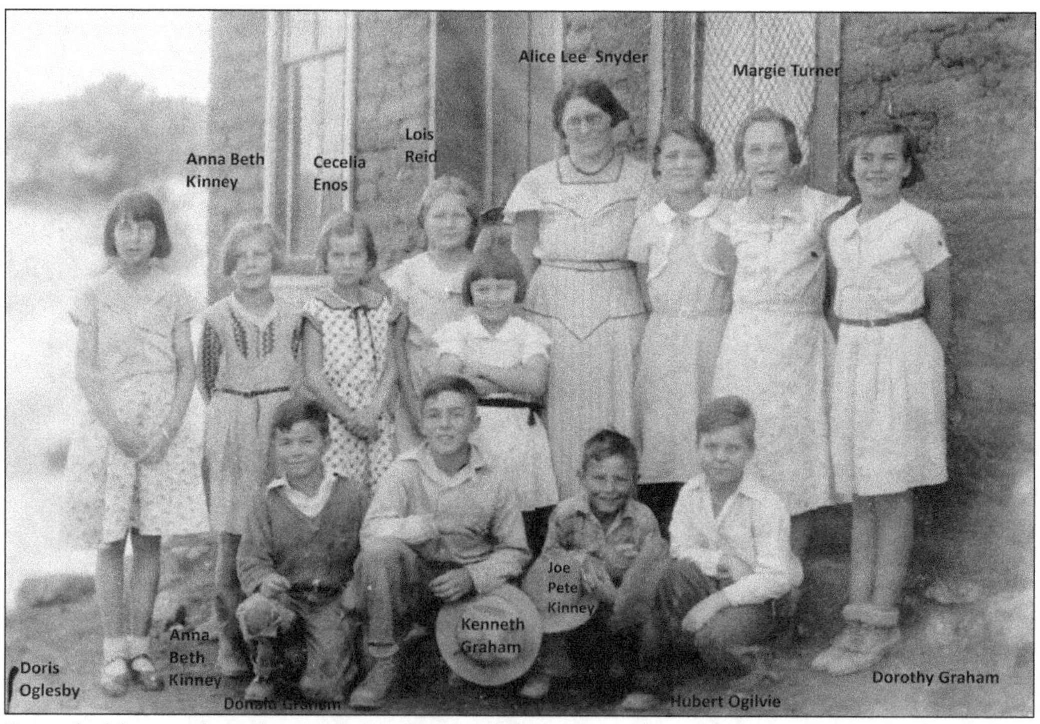

Several of the people in this 1934 photograph of Kingston students are descendants of early families. Donald Graham, shown kneeling at the lower left, has contributed photographs to this book. Alice Lee Snyder was one of the earliest teachers, having also taught on the Berrenda. (DG)

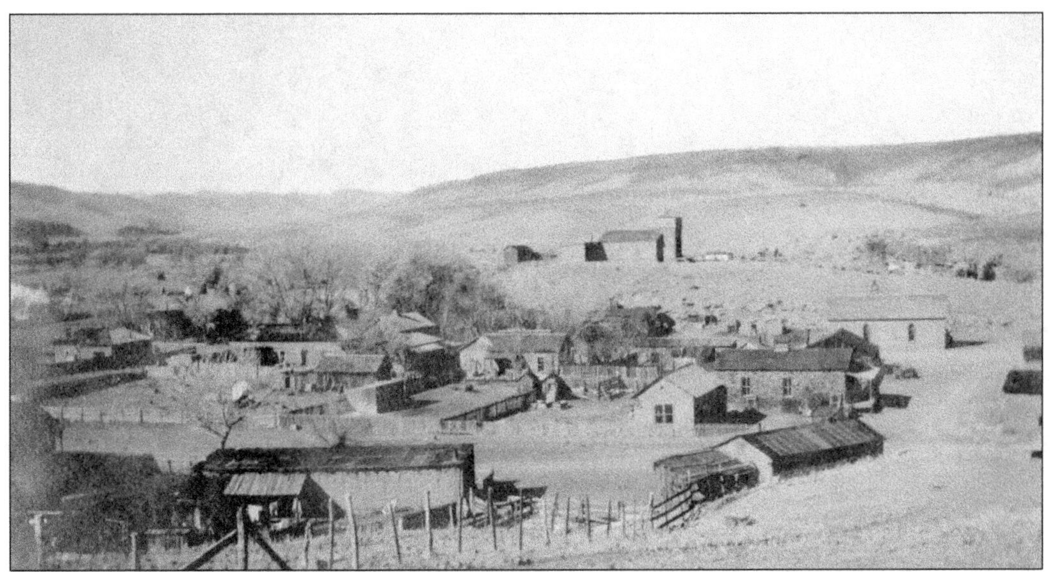

An article in the October 1883 *Rio Grande Republican* states, "The first object that attracts the attention of a stranger on approaching Hillsboro after a long and weary ride from Lake Valley, is the very pretty little school-house perched on the top of a high hill that overlooks the town." (IHSF)

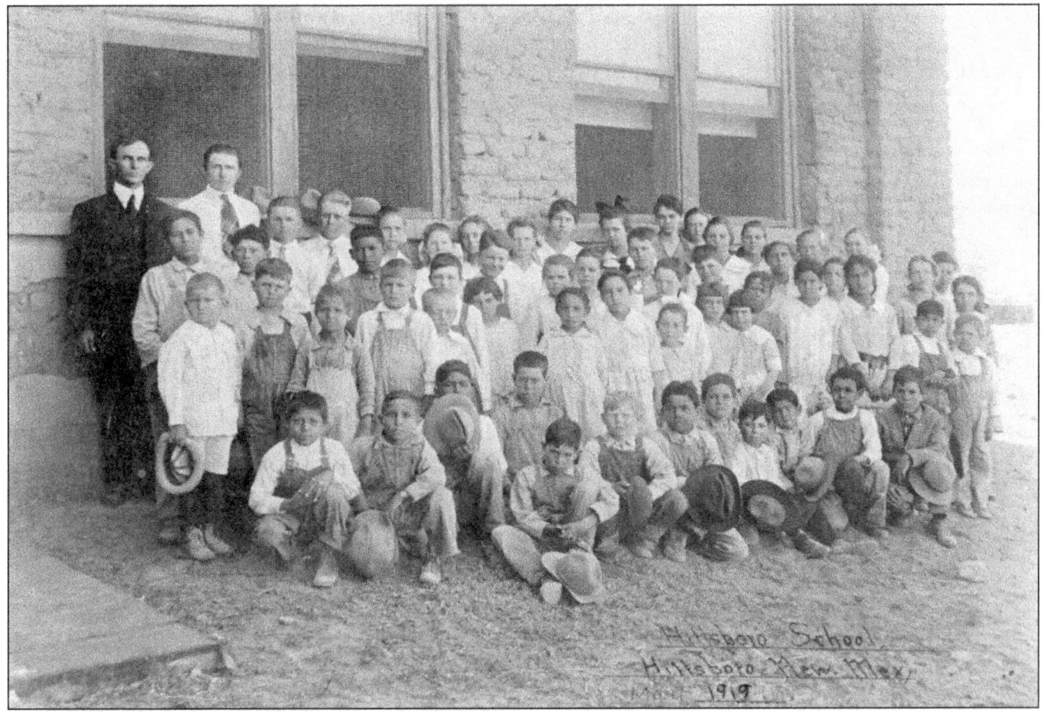

This is the Hillsboro School class of 1919. The teacher, top row left, was Mr. Foster. Beside him is George Miller. Students are Mike Montoya (kneeling), Olive Beal, Ruby Nave, Jody Latham, Walter Nations, Nelson Latham, Charlie Byrne, Myrl Robinson, Irene Hammel, Maggie Carbajal and Inez Carbajal, the Madrid boys, Carl Coalson, Lula Hirsch, Edna Mae Collins, Kathleen Kalks, and Frances Ringer. (GSM)

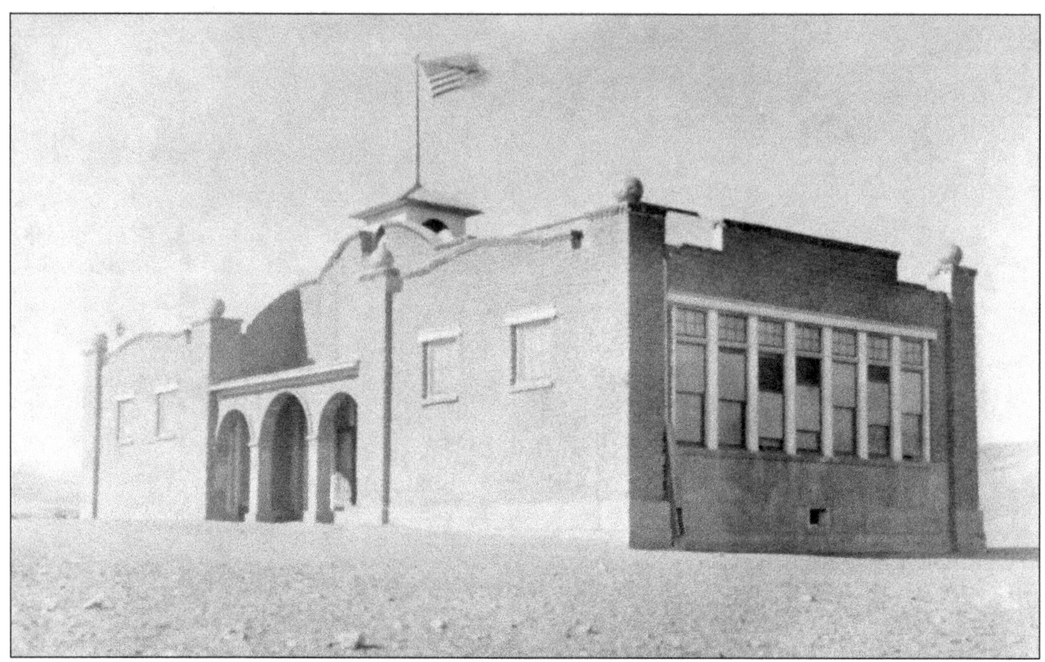

This is a picture of the second Hillsboro School, built around 1911 after the first school burned down. It has changed somewhat but is still in use as a fine private home. Hillsboro High School, built in 1929, similarly ceased to be used for education and in the last 20 years has become the busy Hillsboro Community Center and Library. (GSM)

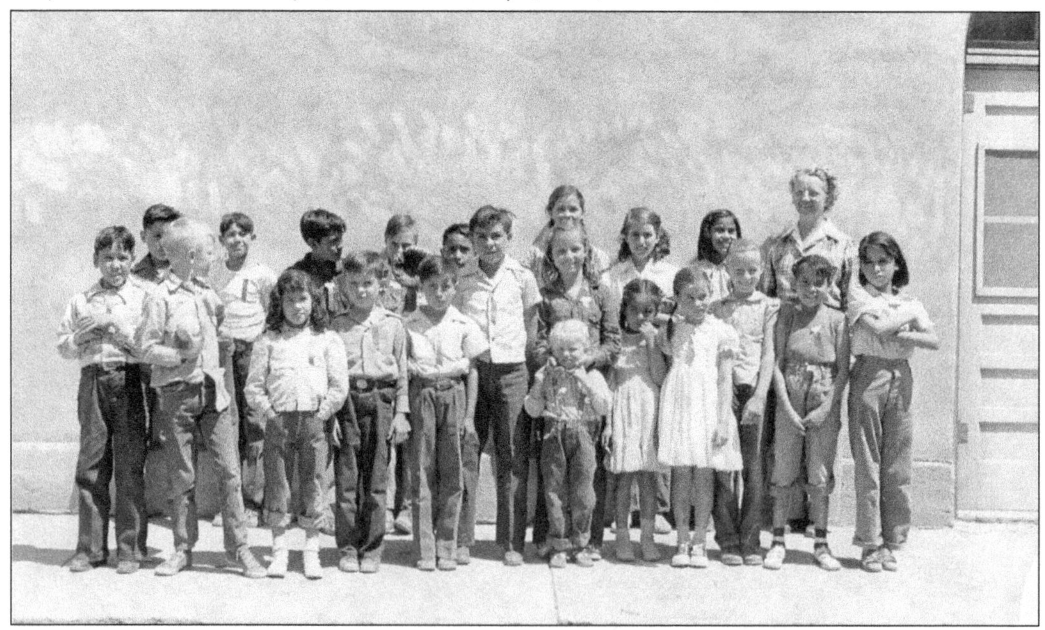

Here is the 1952 class at Hillsboro Elementary School. From left to right are (first row) Adrian Luna, Tuffy Nunn, Nelle Montoya, James Sullivan, Braulio Montoya, Paul Benavides (tall boy), Ethel Mackey (with hands on shoulders of unnamed youngster), Narcisa Garcia, Dorothy Mackey, Katherine Garcia, and Sandy Torres; (second row) Paul Torres, Eddie Montoya, two unknowns, Greg Torres, Shirley Mackey, Priscilla McCall, Inez Torres, and teacher Mrs. Kemp. (NM)

Seven

People and Places

The day-to-day lives of people who ran businesses and provided services to support the local industries of mining and ranching remain the untold history of the area. As is so often the case, only the sensational side of life—war, crime, disaster, politics—seems to persist, while the names and activities of those who simply held the communities together and avoided conflict fade. Hillsboro is fortunate that many pictures, if not stories, of these workaday individuals have been saved, and a sampling is presented here to try to portray the way people lived, which was not so different all in all from the way people live today. For many of these gatherings, only the pictures remain, so the authors and readers can only guess what has brought the people together.

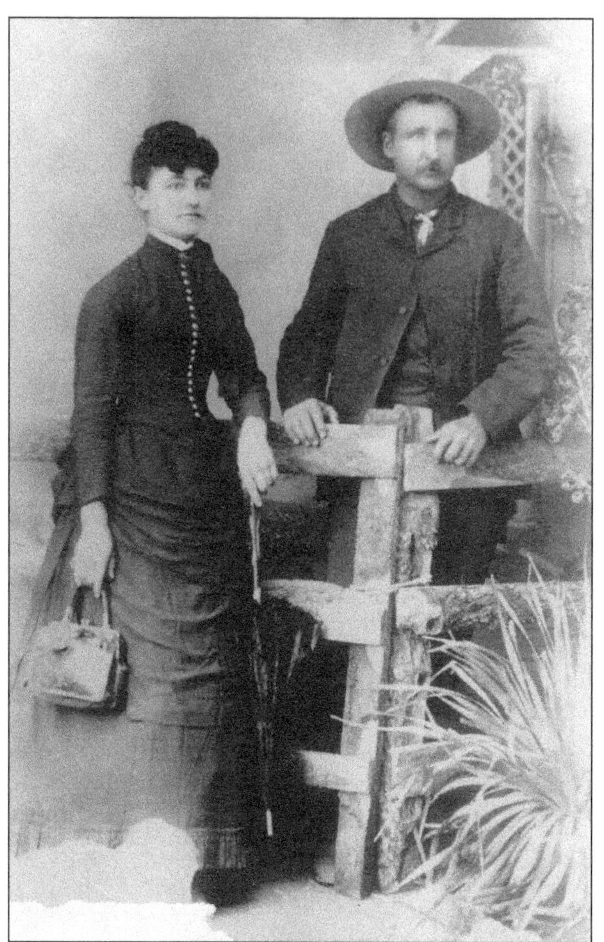

In her wedding picture, Bell Nunn looks tiny and delicate. Actually, she chewed tobacco, cleaned her teeth with a mesquite root, drove a wagon, rode sidesaddle, and lived for a time in a dugout. Nunn feared electricity and would use only oil lamps, but she taught herself to read and write.

Some early Lake Valley residents lived in dugouts at the second location of the town, called Sierra City. A dugout was a shelter dug into the side of a hill. They were temporary and were used as dwellings only until larger buildings could be constructed. After houses were built, dugouts were often used as cellars. (IHSF)

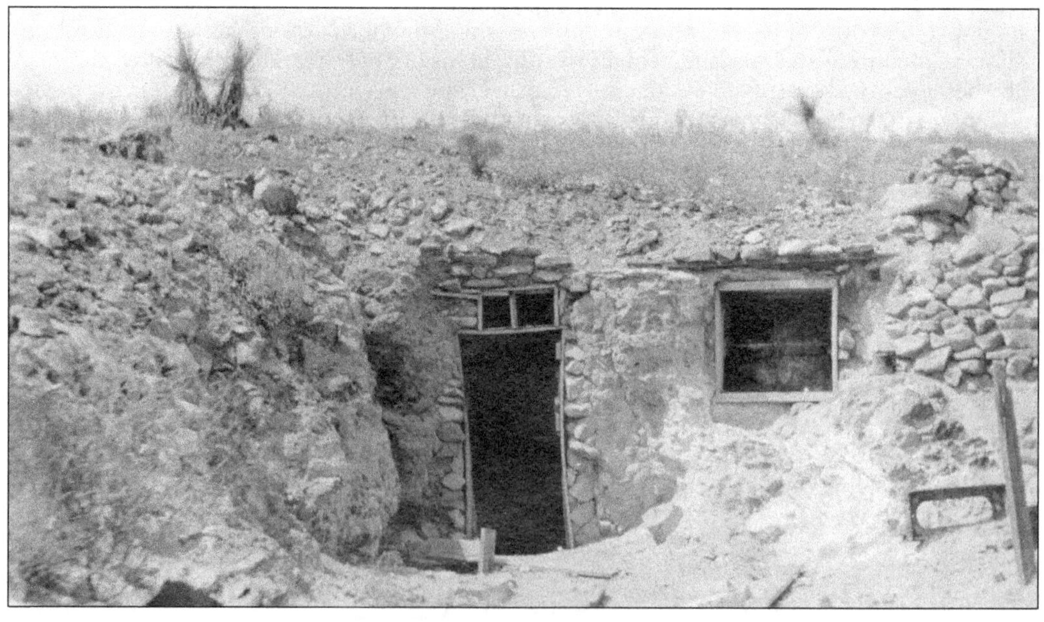

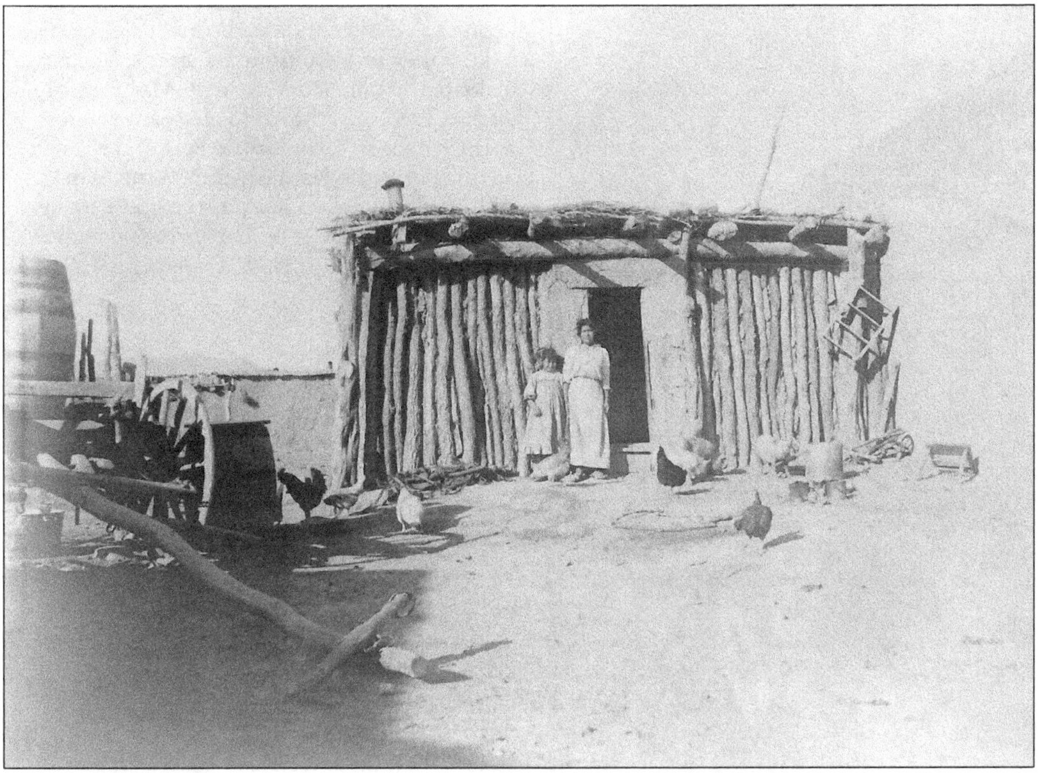

A jacal is a thatch-roofed hut with walls of close-set wooden stakes plastered with mud. This one is in an area near Lake Valley called Chihuahuaita by the Hispanic residents or Little Chihuahua by the Anglo residents. (DW)

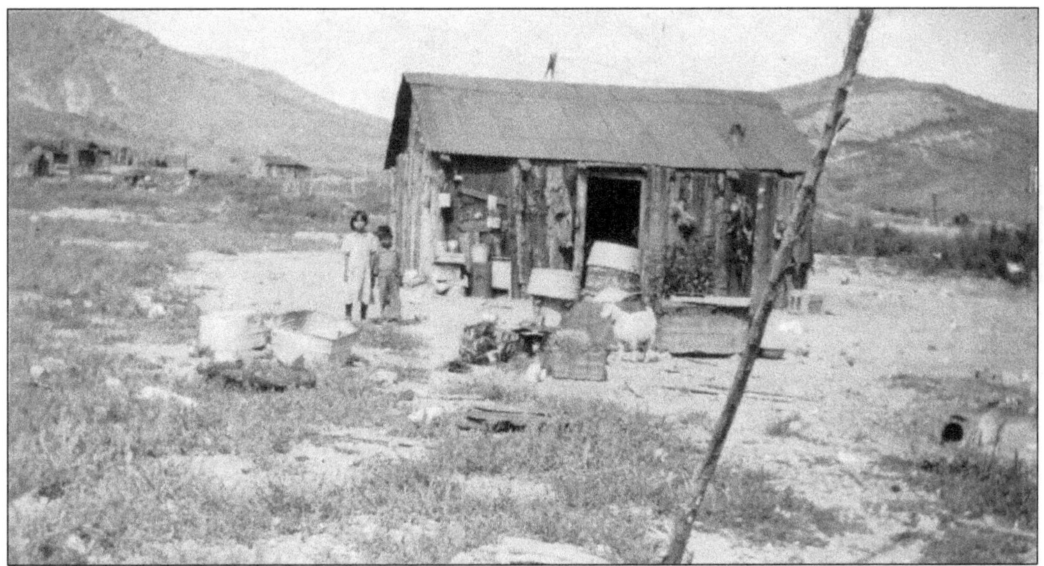

Some Hispanic women took in laundry while their husbands worked in the mines. Few other occupations were available to women. There are a number of washtubs, a clothesline, and a washboard outside this home in Little Chihuahua. Water was heated over a fire, and the clothes were washed by hand, using the washboard. (DW)

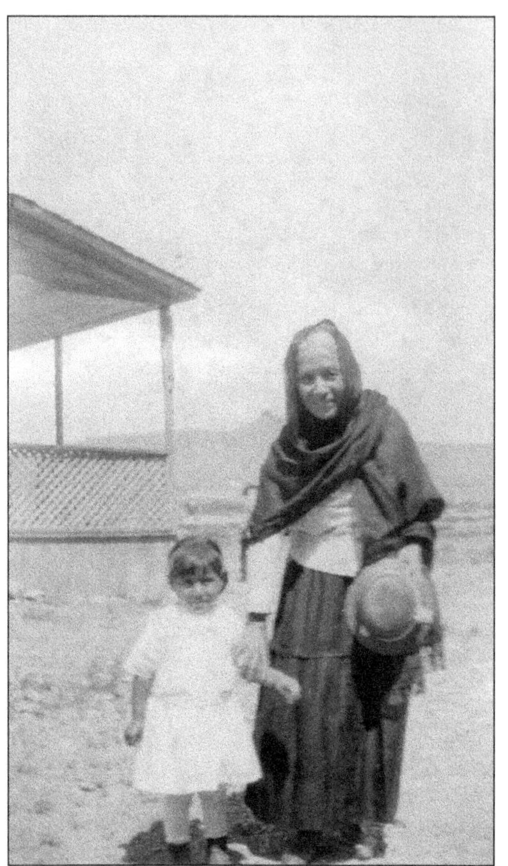

Leonides Chavez and son Pedro "Pete" came to Lake Valley in 1906 from Zacatecas, Mexico. In 1916, she married Margarito Martinez. He died in 1918, and she and Pete spent the rest of their lives in Lake Valley. Pete and his wife, Savina, were the last residents to leave, in 1991, making Lake Valley a true ghost town. The little girl here is probably Pete's daughter Alejandra, who died from a snakebite. (DW)

Most homes such as this one belonging to Elizabeth Bartle McLean were built of wood or scrap lumber on simple rock foundations. This may be one reason there are so few buildings remaining in Lake Valley. Shown here are McLean, her daughter Emily, and her grandchildren May and Arthur Glasson. Elizabeth came to the United States from Cornwall, England.

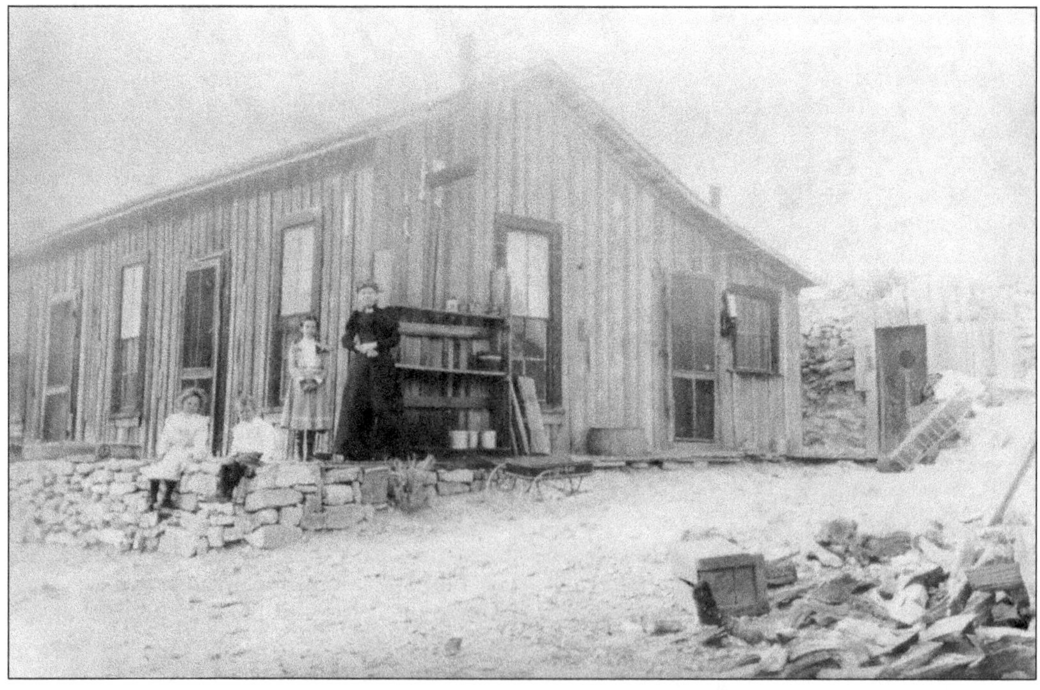

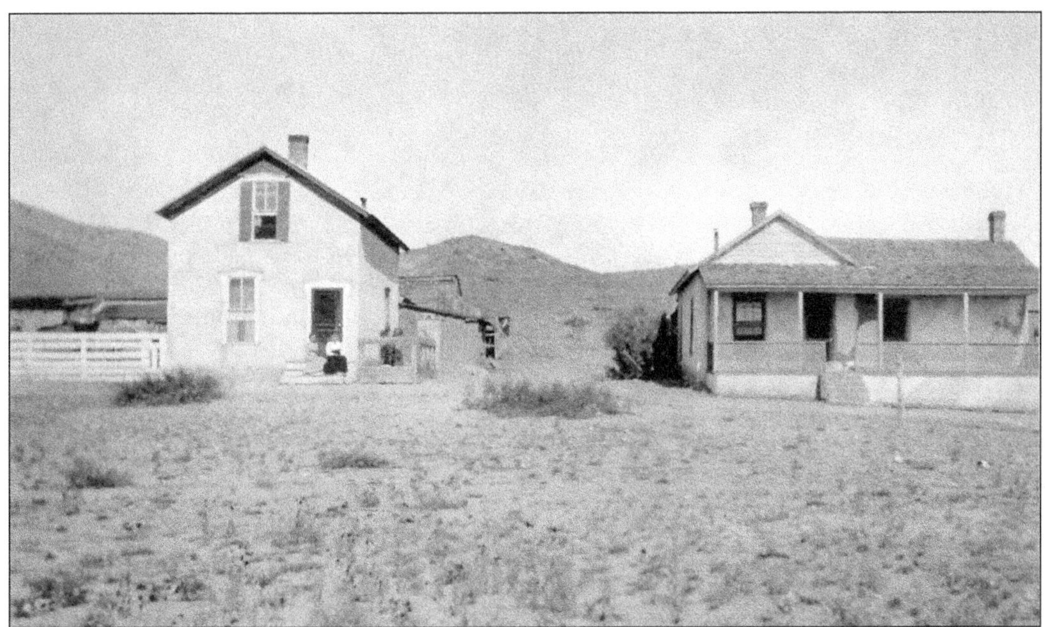

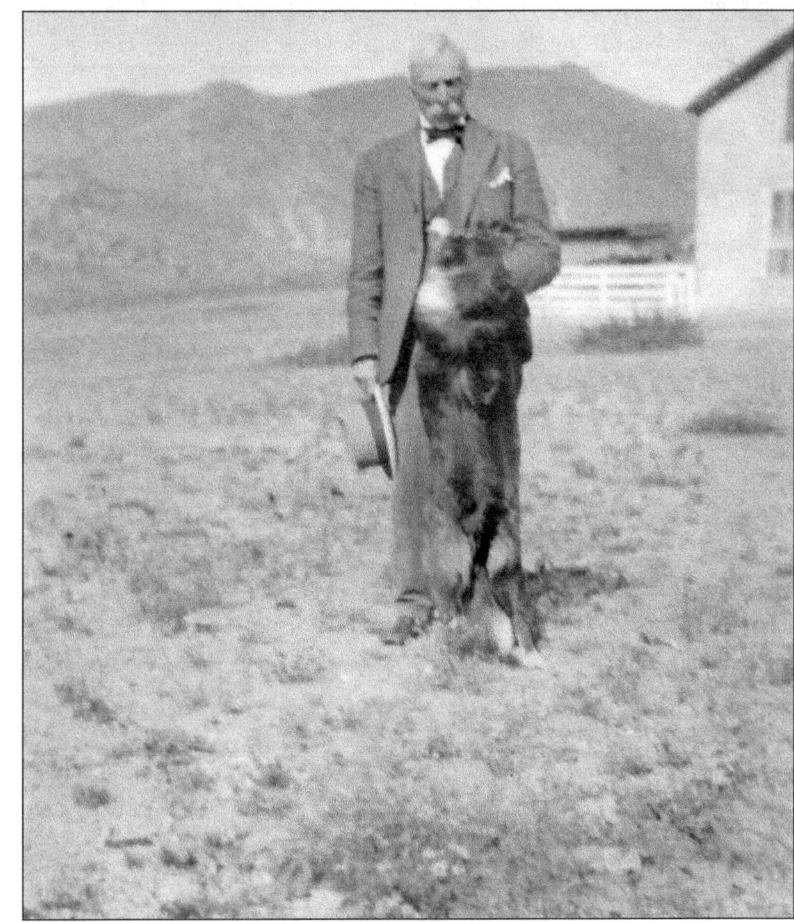

The better homes of Lake Valley's wealthier residents, such as those of Maj. Morgan Morgans and Jesse Stanley, were built of adobe or brick. Seated on the porch of Major Morgans's house are his sister–in-law Frances Moffitt and her daughter Minnie. This photograph was taken in the 1920s. (DW)

Morgan Morgans was a major in the 176th Regiment of the New York Infantry during the Civil War. Major Morgans was a principal loser in the Lake Valley Fire of 1895. He managed to escape with only one pair of pants and his coat. (DW)

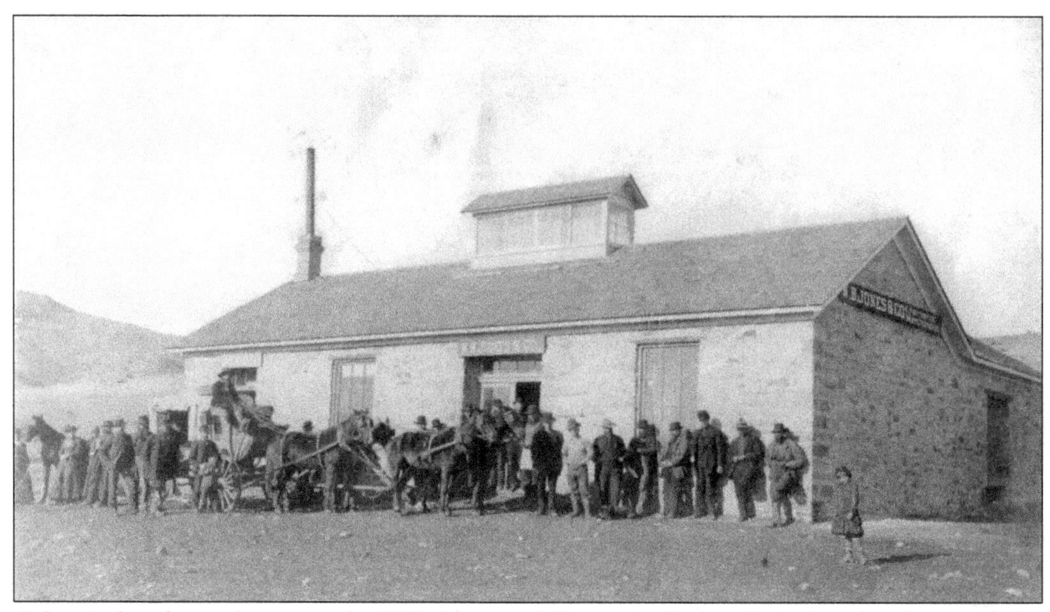

A four-in-hand stage has arrived at W.B. Jones and Company General Merchandise Store in Lake Valley. The store at one time served as a school and later as a Conoco station. It exists today as a run-down, boarded-up building. The cupola on top is gone. (DT)

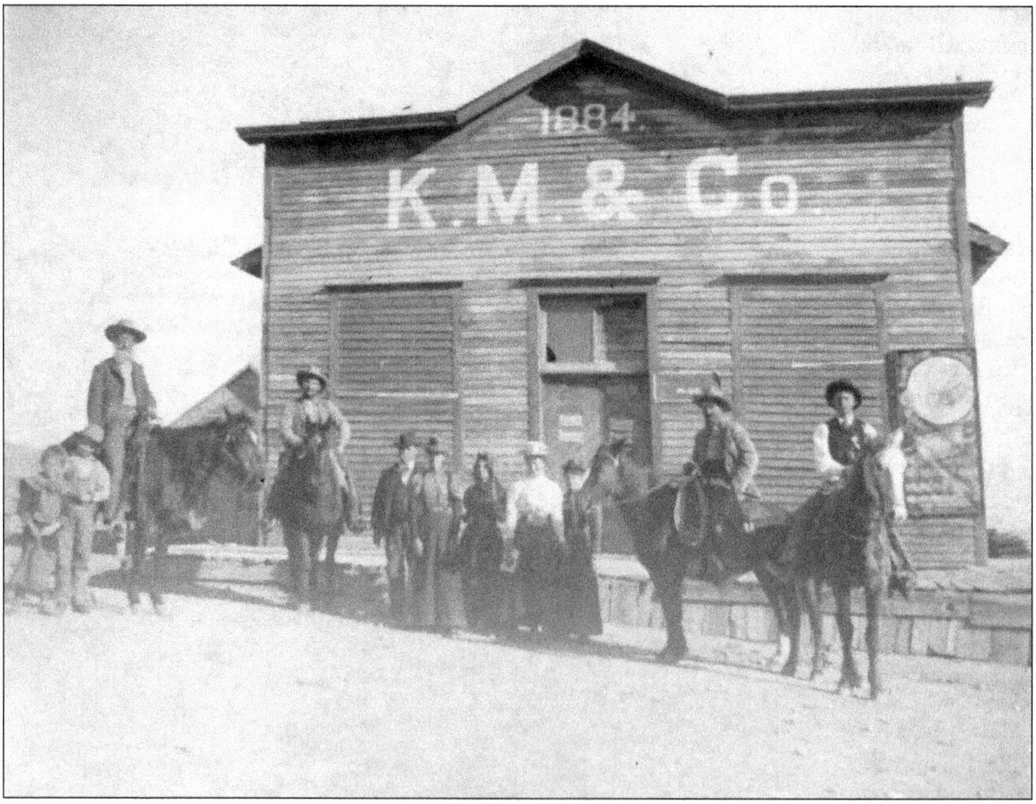

Keller Miller and Company lost its extensive stock of general merchandise valued at about $15,000 in the 1895 fire. This building may be the one that burned. (GSM)

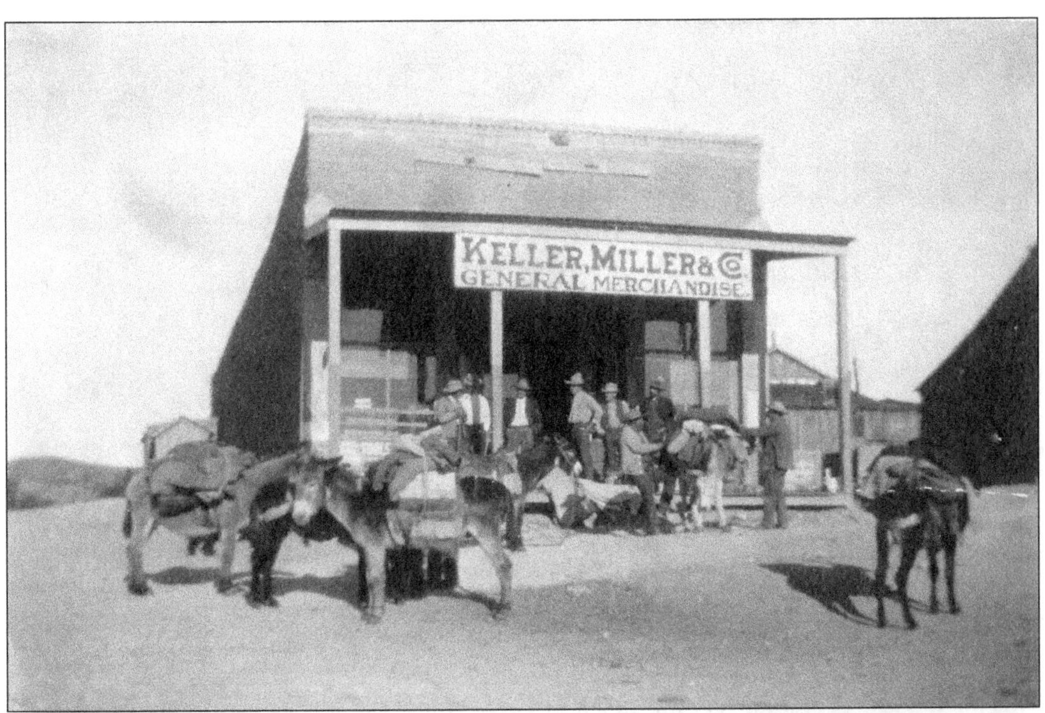

Keller and Miller opened stores in both Lake Valley and Hillsboro. Daniel S. Miller, one of the original owners, was born in Virginia and died in 1919 in Lake Valley. He married Lucy McFarland, who was also from Virginia. She died in 1937. Both are buried in the old Lake Valley Cemetery on the hill overlooking Lake Valley. (DW)

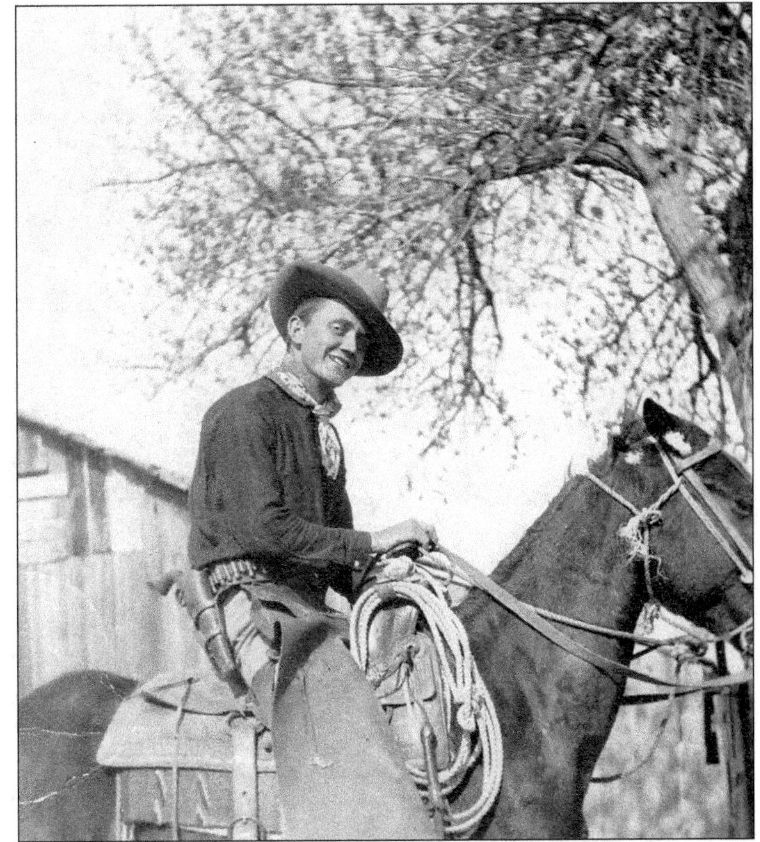

Daniel Miller, son of Daniel S. Miller, was also a part of Keller and Miller Company in Lake Valley. He lived his whole life in the town and never married. (DW)

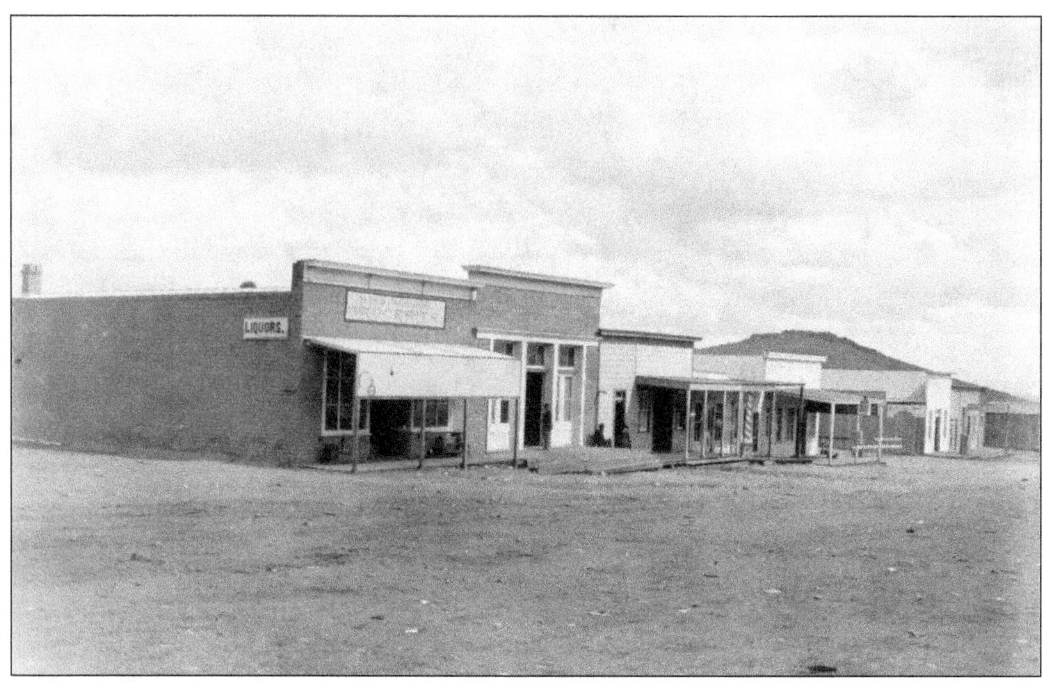

This photograph of Main Street was taken in 1885. This is the street that caught fire in 1895. A close look reveals a grocery store, a barbershop, a skating rink, and a drugstore. By 1895, Lake Valley was in a state of decline, so these Main Street businesses were never rebuilt. (DW)

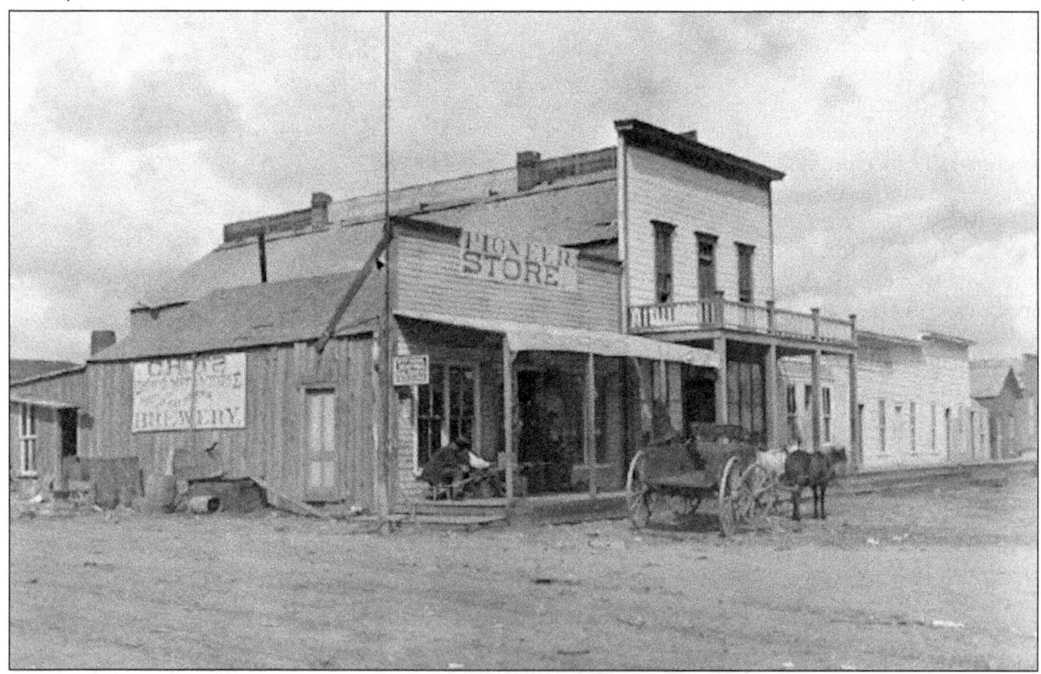

Shown here on Railroad Avenue are the Pioneer Store, the Sierra Grande Hotel (later named the Endicott), the Stage Office, Major Morgan's Boarding House (later the Christian Endeavor), an unknown building, and the *Sierra Grande Press* office. Beyond the newspaper office is the Keller Miller Store. (RGHC)

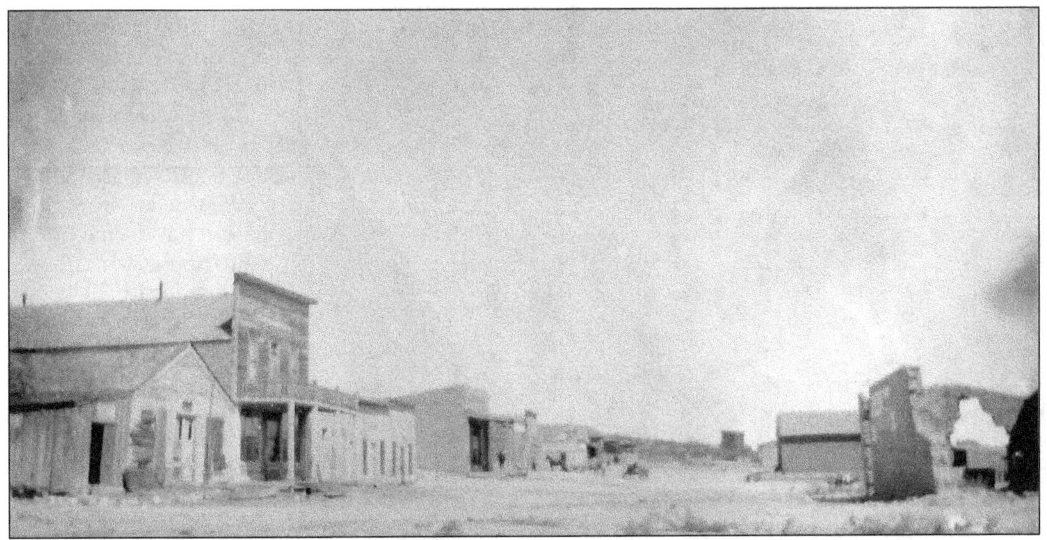

Lake Valley is becoming a ghost town. The Pioneer Store, minus its porch, and the Endicott Hotel remain. The Stage Office is no longer used, and Maj. Morgan Morgan's boardinghouse is occupied by the Christian Endeavor Society. The Keller Miller Store can be seen with a building beyond. On the right is what remained of the Sinclair Store after the 1895 fire. (DW)

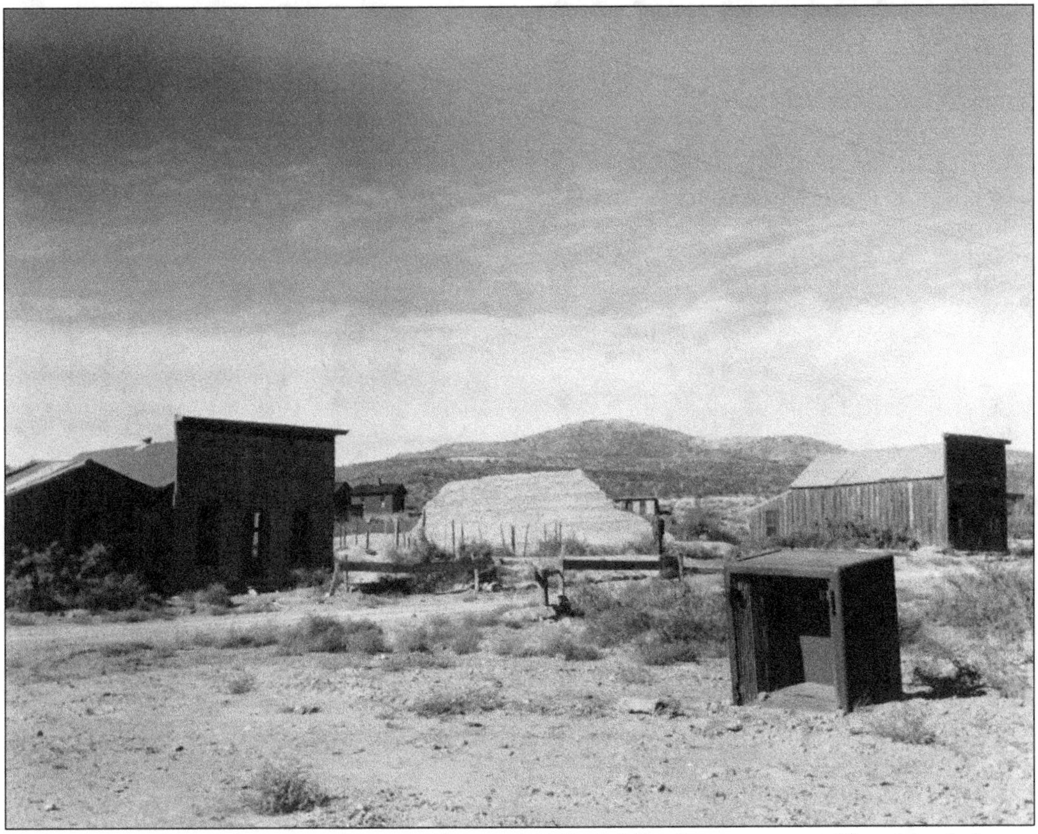

In 1952, the Pioneer Store, hotel, stage office, and Keller Miller Store are gone. The old safe shown in the photograph remains to this day. (DW)

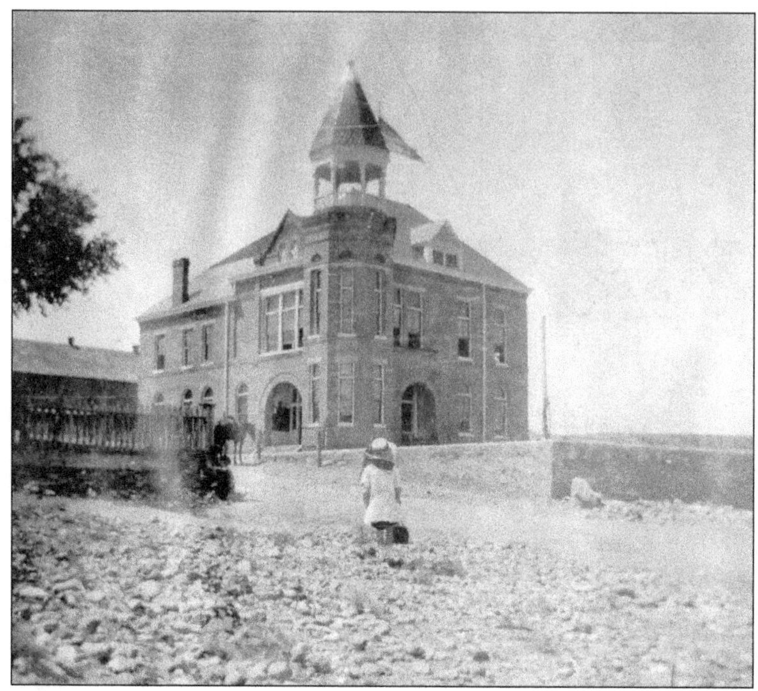

Hillsboro was a part of Dona Ana County until 1884, when Sierra County was formed and Hillsboro became the county seat. In 1892, the Territory built a handsome brick courthouse, which was used until 1936, when the county seat was moved to Hot Springs. The stately old building was sold and dismantled in 1939. Stories conflict as to what happened to the bricks.

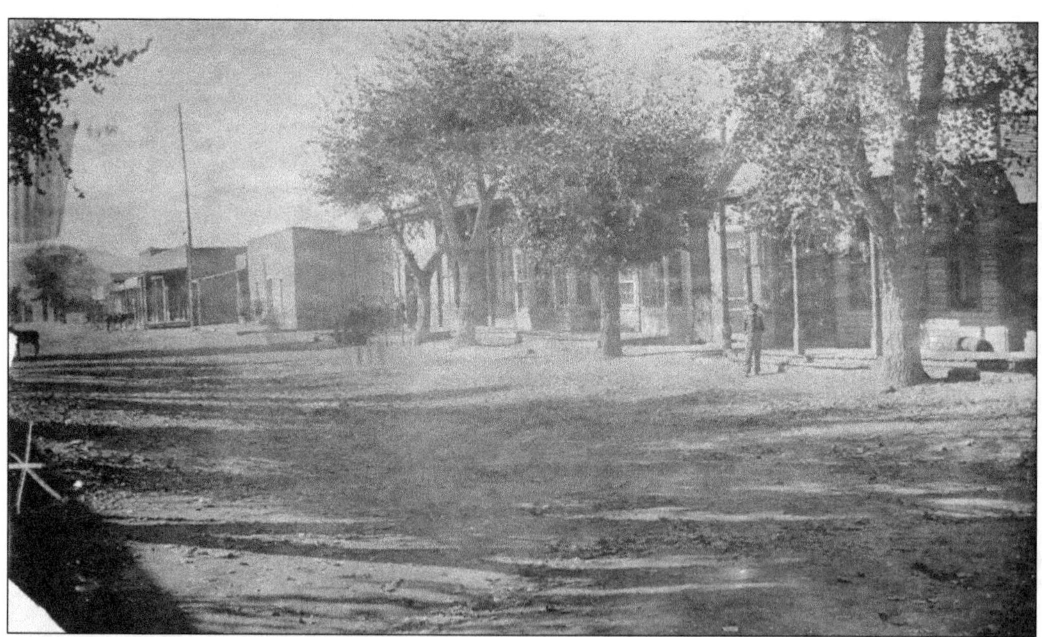

This very early photograph shows most of the north side of Main Street in Hillsboro, before the time of cars. A horse is tied to a hitching rail at the bar. Plank sidewalks existed, and burros roamed the streets. Floods have since destroyed all of the buildings shown on this side of the square adobe. (BRM)

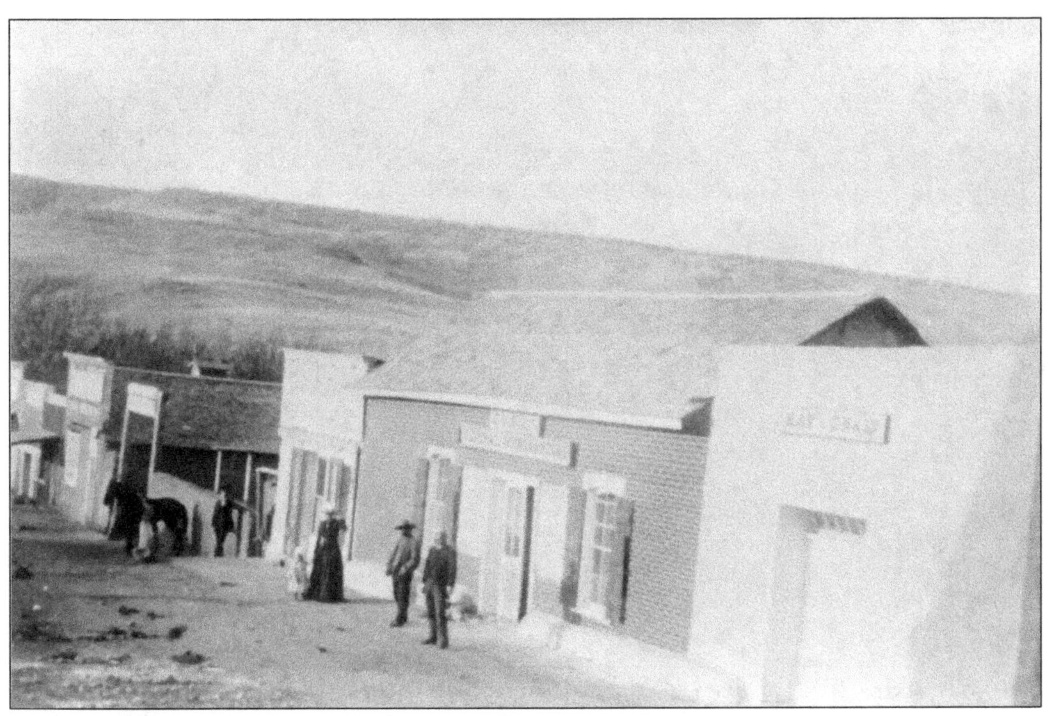

Shown here are two photographs of what was once Broadway Street in Hillsboro. Today, it is State Highway 27 coming in from Lake Valley. The E.M. Blum General Merchandise store later became Sadie Orchard's Hotel. This can be seen in the photograph below. Elias M. Blum appears in the 1880 census in Hillsborough. Living with him is John Smith, store clerk. Blum came from Germany to the United States in 1880. Sadie was a well-known madam in both Hillsboro and Kingston. (BRM)

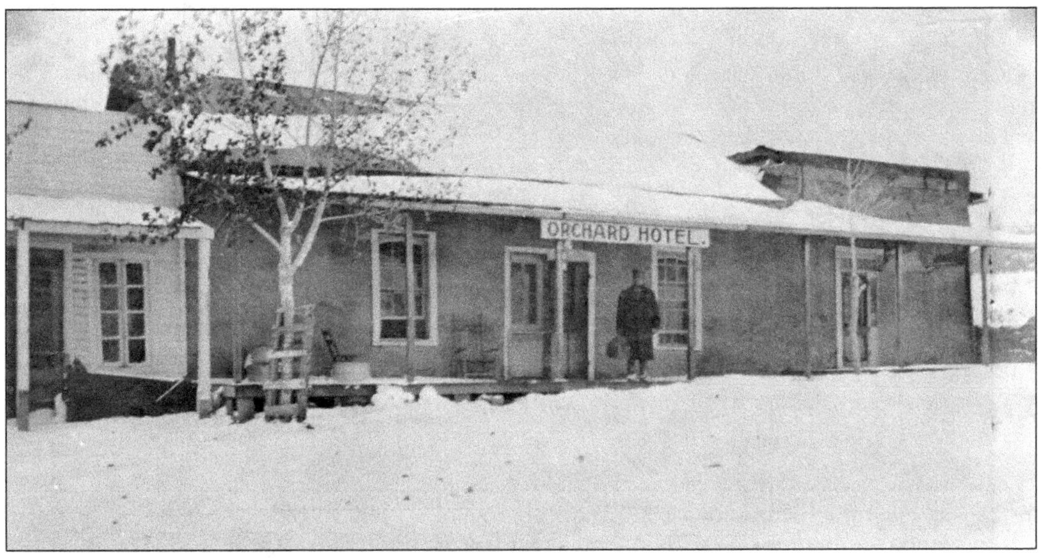

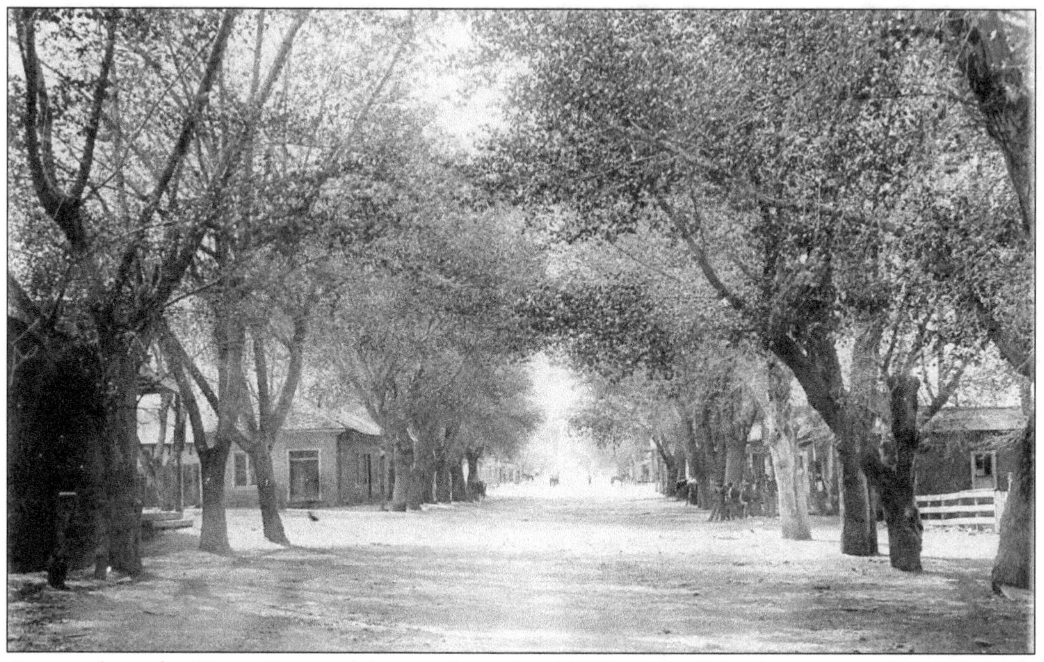

An article in the *Sierra County Advocate* from April 1888 reads, "The long rows of trees on both sides of the streets in Hillsborough give the town an artistic appearance of beauty that no other town in the territory can boast." (BRM)

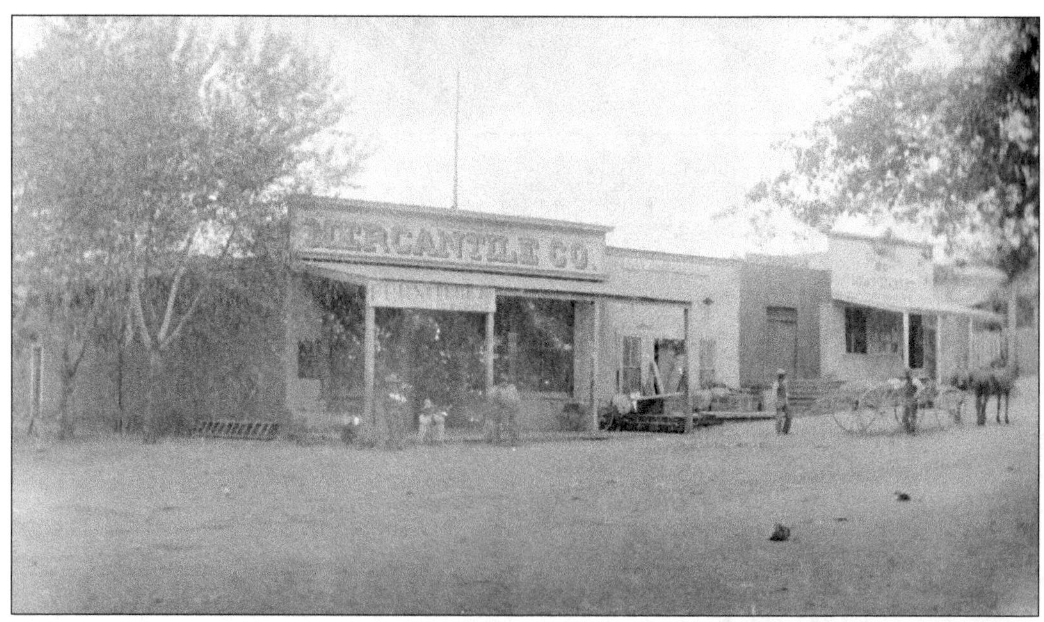

In this early picture, the original spelling, Hillsborough, is used. In 1884, the name of the town was shortened to Hillsboro. Little is known about this particular mercantile. (BRM)

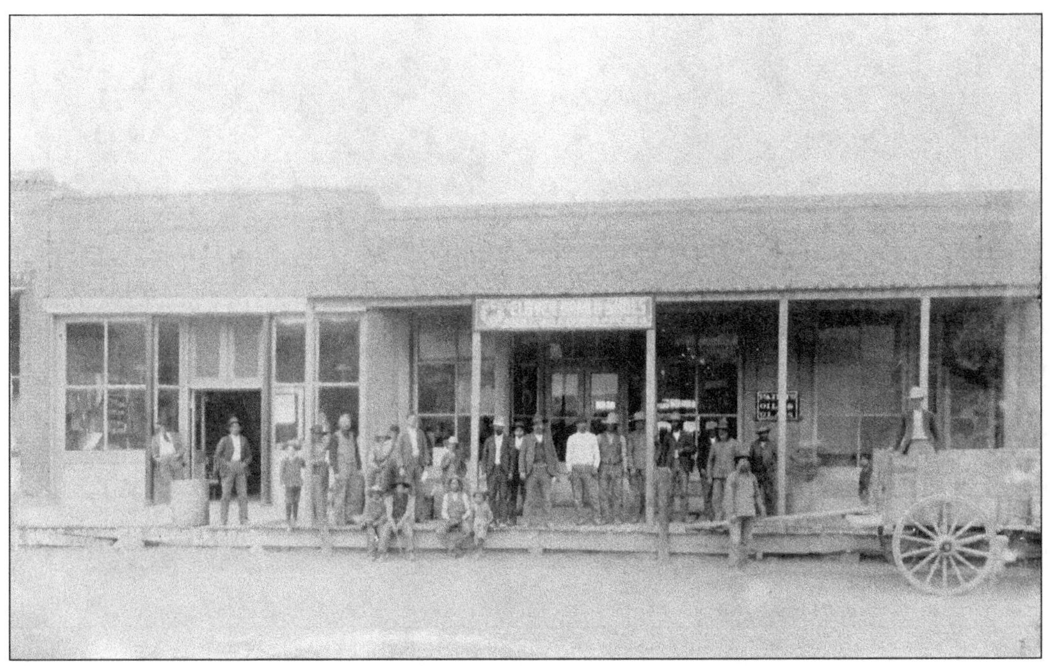

On the left is an early general store. Painted on the plank sidewalk are the words Merchandise Cooper Bros. Clover brand shoes, paint, oil, and glass are advertised on the signs. The building on the right looks like another store and may be the same building that is today's Barber Shop Café and formerly housed the S-X Saloon. (GSM)

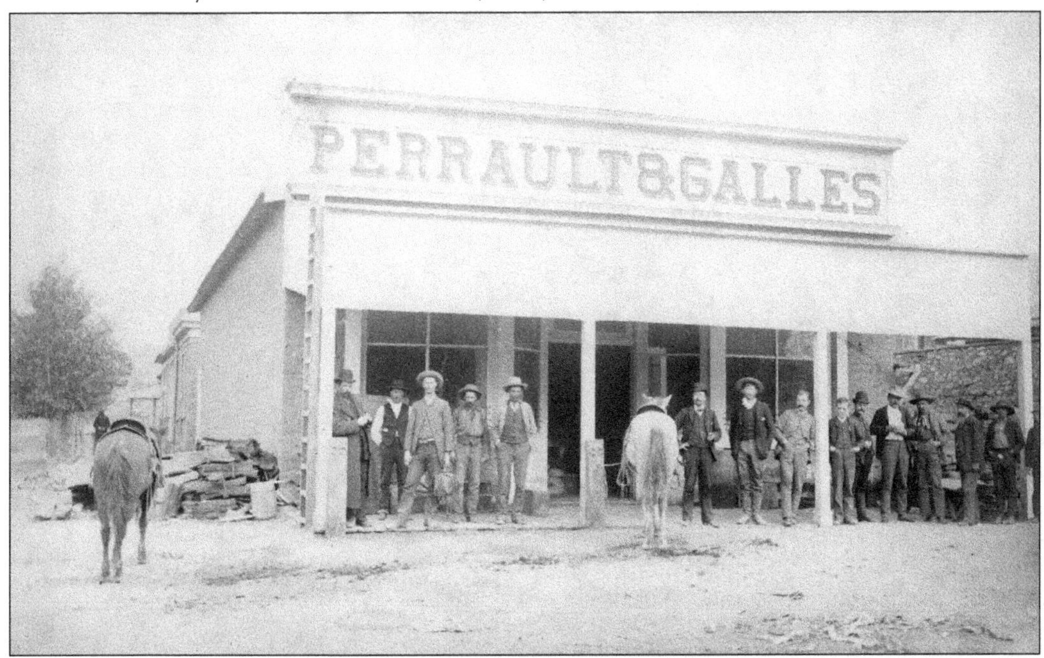

George Perrault, a native of Canada, came to the New Mexico Territory as a soldier with Company M, 1st California Cavalry. He opened a mercantile store in Hillsborough with Nicholas Galles. In 1879, Perrault married Adelaida Alert, daughter of Jose Alert, another of Hillsborough's early merchants. (BRM)

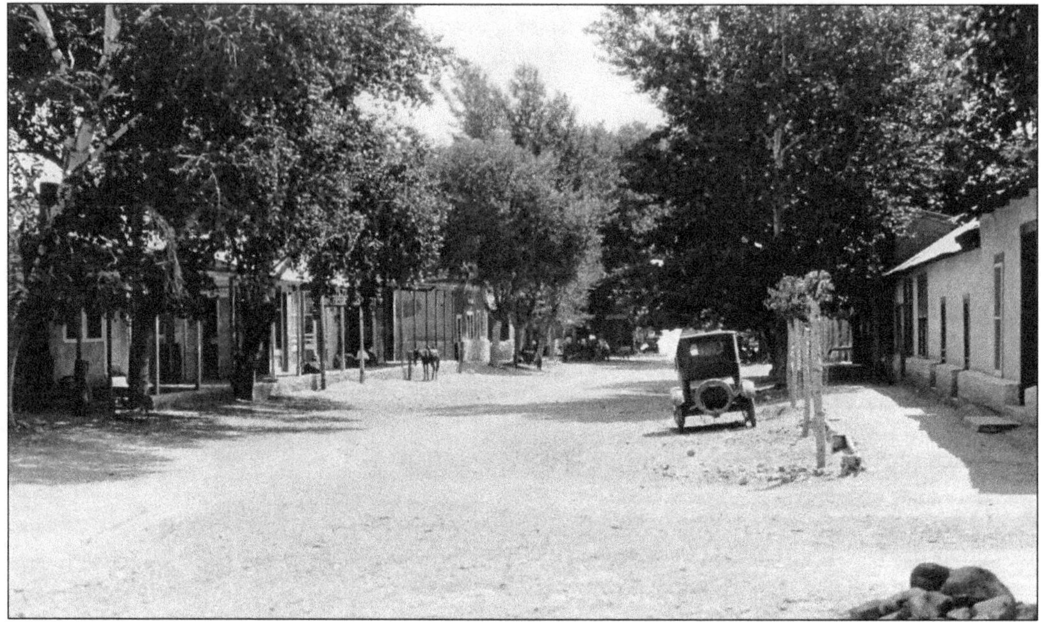

Looking west to east, the long building on the right began as the Alert Mercantile owned by Jose Alert, a native of Spain. This structure later became the Hatcher Hospital, owned by Dr. Octavius Hatcher. It was used during the flu epidemic of 1918. Nell Hatcher turned it into a hotel after Dr. Hatcher died. It is now a residence and a cooperative for local artists and craftsmen. (GSM)

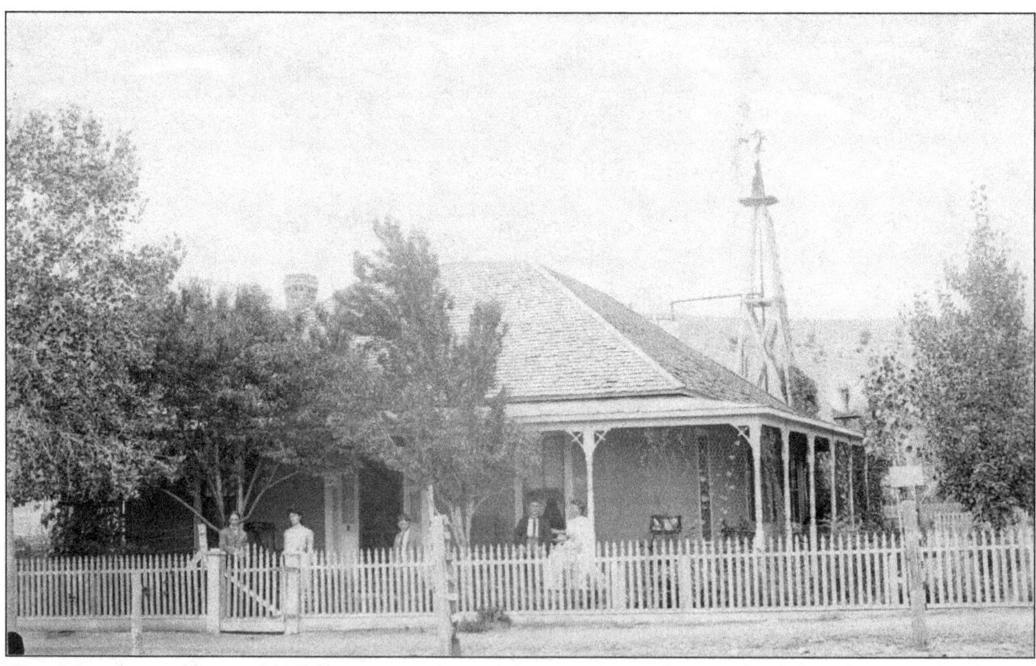

Tom Murphy and his wife, Nellie, are entertaining visitors on the porch of their home. This house with its wraparound porch still exists on Elenora Street in Hillsboro. Tom was a 1st Sergeant in the 15th US Infantry, Company G. He was later a saloon owner and Sierra County's first sheriff. (BRM)

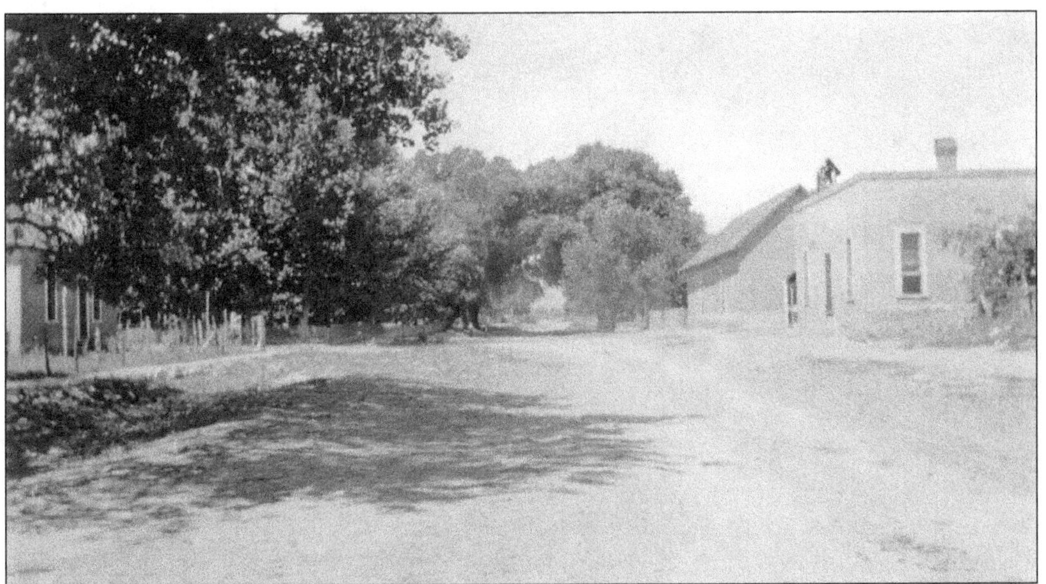

The house on the right started out as a two-room way station around 1879. It was here that the stage changed horses. The structure became the law office of Ed Tittman and his partner. Elias Padilla bought the building and sold it to Julia Hernandez Padilla, who made it her home. The house remains in the family. (GSM)

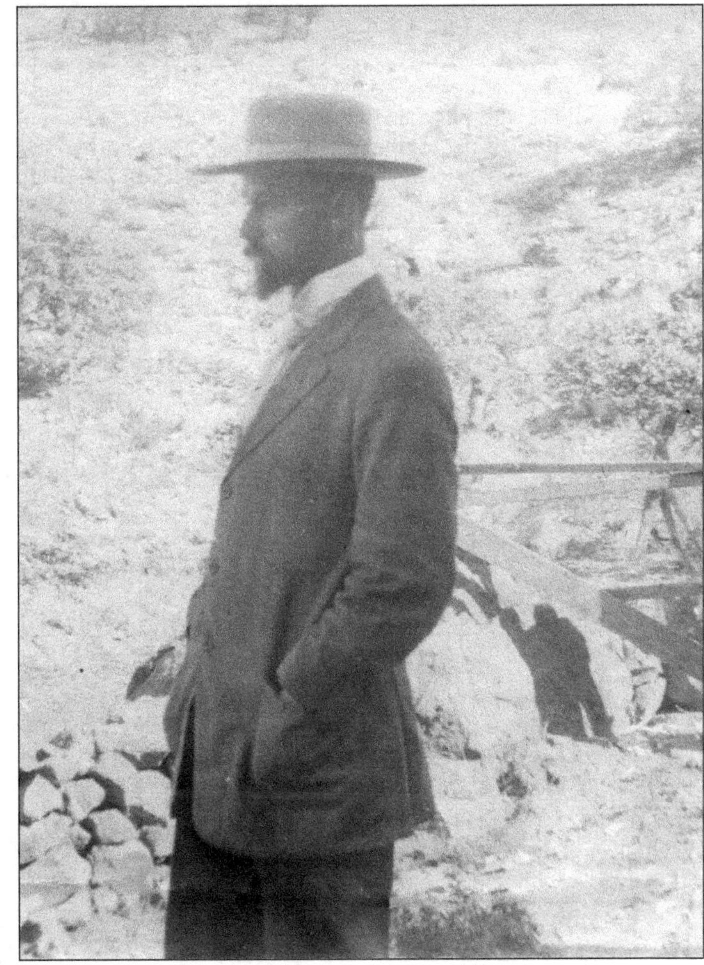

Edward Tittmann, editor of the paper that became *The Wall Street Journal*, came to Hillsboro for his health. He invested in the Ready Pay Reduction Co., practiced law, and started the *Sierra Free Press*. Tittmann played an important role in stopping the county seat from being moved to Cutter in 1909. He bought the Keller and Murphy houses and combined the two to create what is known today as the old Tittmann home. He is shown here in front of his mine. (Lynn Mullins)

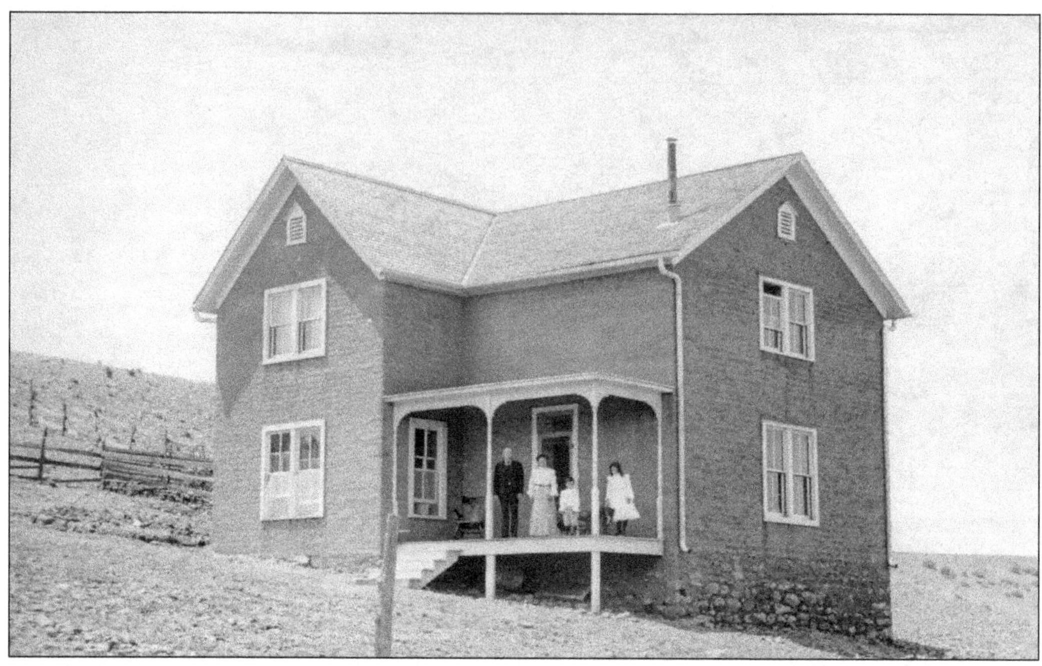

Overlooking the town of Hillsboro is a two-story Victorian home built by miner Jack Burke, who lived in it all his life. His son Bob grew up in the house but left for World War I and later sold the home. In 1920, Bob was living with his widowed mother and working as a carpenter. He was working as a machinist in an auto garage in 1930. The house still stands and belongs to a movie producer. (GSM)

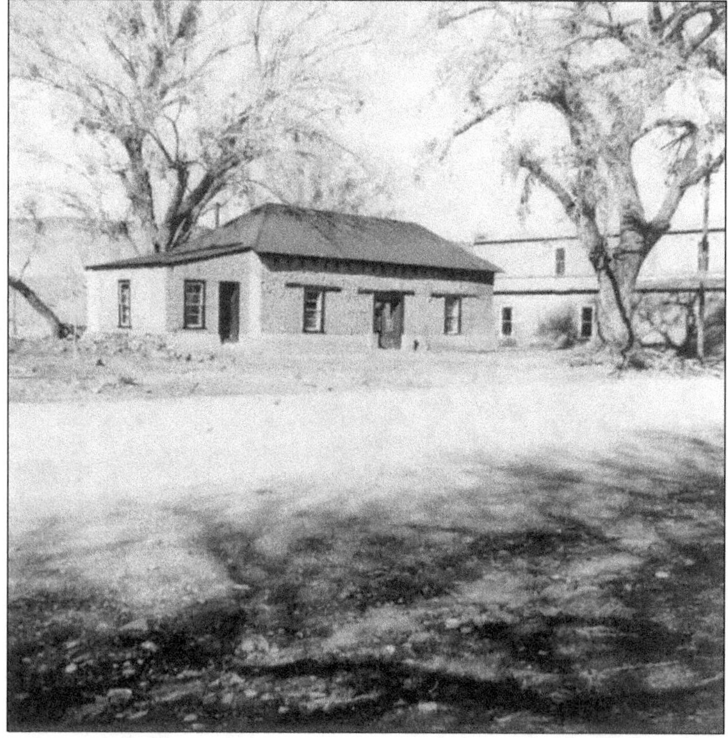

One of the first houses built in Hillsborough was the home of Confederate Brig. Gen. Charles Cotilda Crews and his wife, Mattie. Because the general was a doctor, the house also served as a doctor's office. The first two rooms in the house were used for this purpose. (GSM)

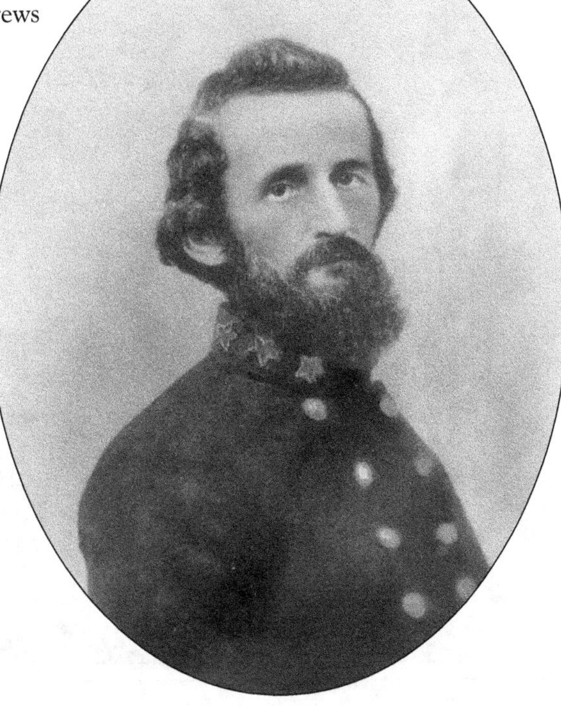

General Crews is the highest-ranking Confederate officer buried in New Mexico. He fought with the Army of Tennessee in Brig. Gen. Joseph Wheeler's cavalry, opposing Sherman's March to the Sea. Crews came to Hillsboro in 1879. (MC)

Martha "Mattie" Hampton, wife of General Crews, was one of only four Anglo women in Hillsborough in 1879. She organized the first Sunday school, learned to speak Spanish for her Mexican students, and was one of the founders of the Union Church. Hillsboro's Mattie Avenue was named in her honor. (MC)

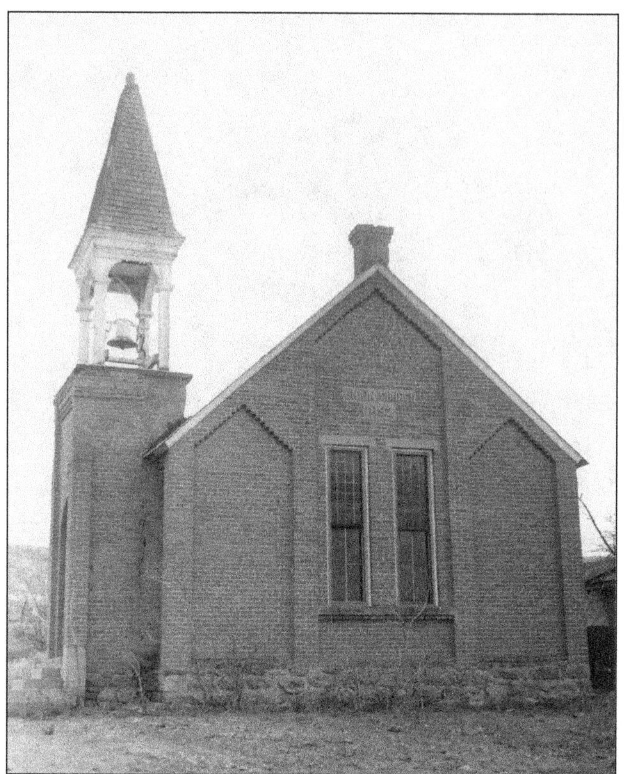

The Hillsboro Union Church was established in 1892. Frank W. Parker deeded the land as payment for his pledge of $25. A chandelier and opera chairs bought in 1893 are still in the church. The board of trustees included E.M. Smith, a Methodist; R.H. Hopper, a Baptist; J.M. Webster, a Congregationalist; Alex Story, a Presbyterian; and Nicholas Galles, an Episcopalian. Services are still being held every Sunday, as they have been for over 100 years. (Patricia Heydt)

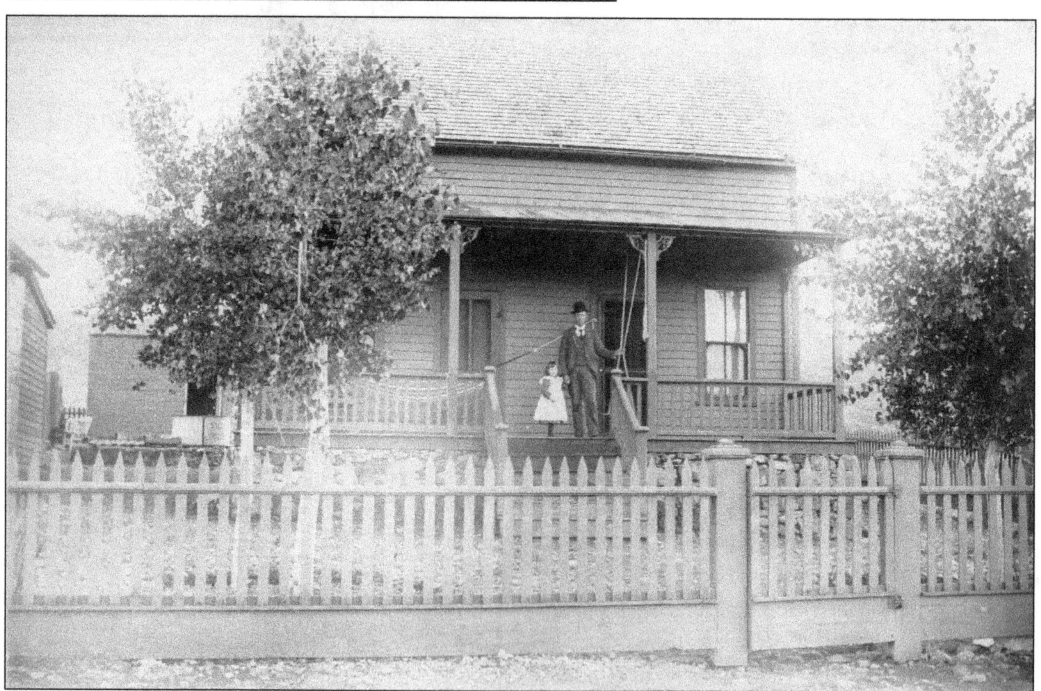

Frank W. Parker was the first owner of the home shown here, located across the street east of the courthouse. It was built before 1892 and has been continually occupied since. Parker was the judge at the Fountain Trial. (BRM)

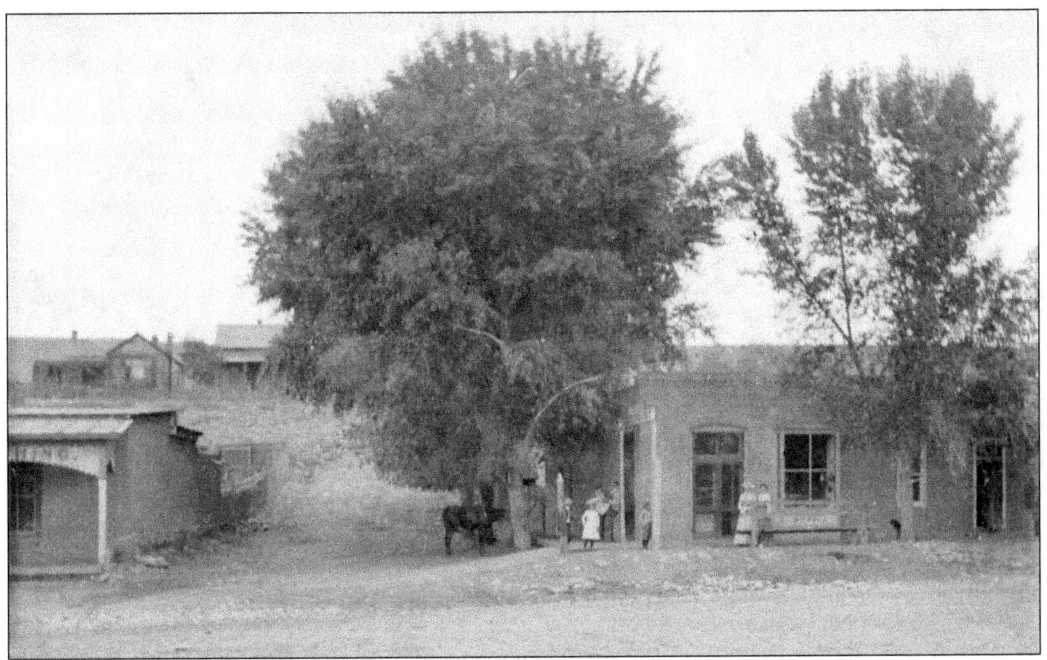

Seen here is a very early photograph of the George T. Miller Drug Store (now the General Store Cafe). In the background are the Miller home and the Frank W. Parker house. Miller moved the post office to his drugstore in 1898, when he became postmaster. The flood of 1914 caused this building to be rebuilt in its present form. (BRM)

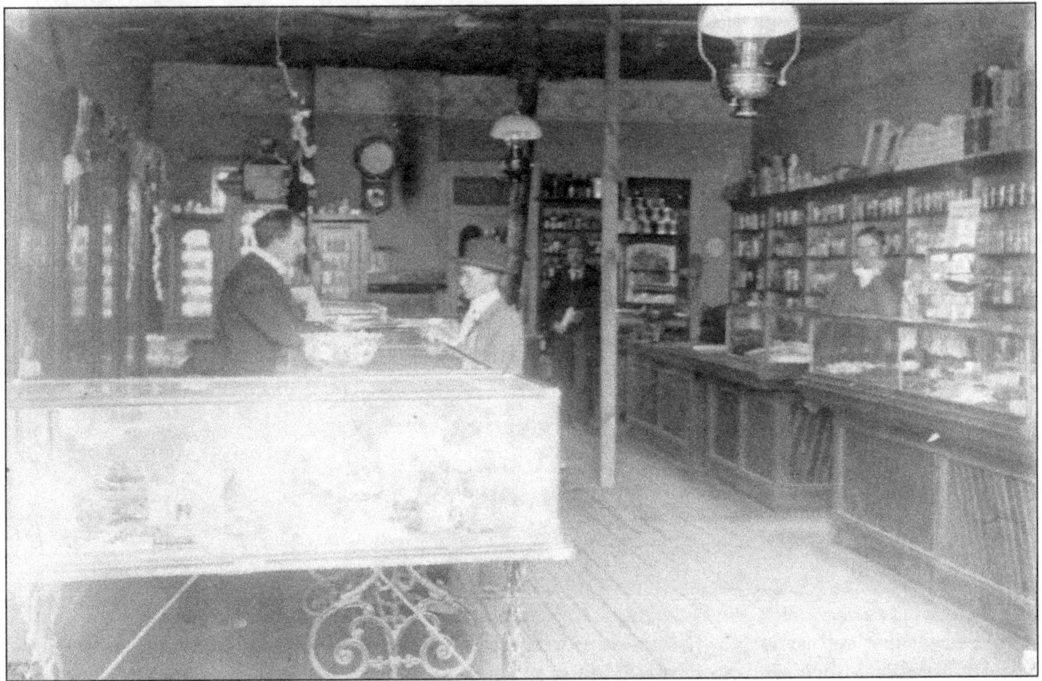

This photograph was taken in the early 1900s inside the George T. Miller Drug Store. George is behind the counter. After his death in 1909, George's wife, Ninette Stocker Miller, married A.L. Bird. She served as postmistress from 1909 until 1914. (BRM)

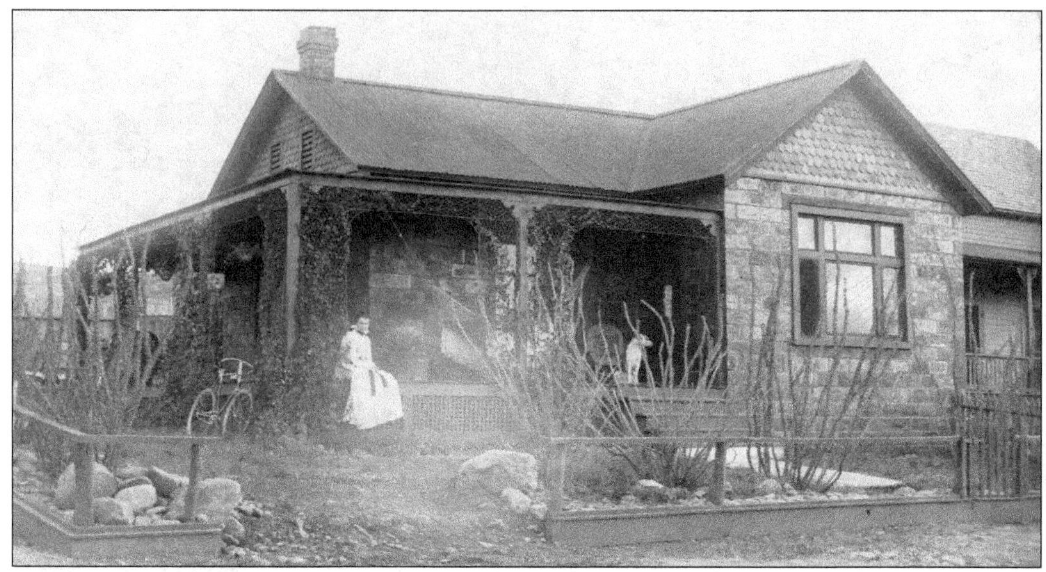

This home, made of molten gold slag poured into blocks, was built by brothers Nicholas and Peter Galles in 1894 for Nicholas's sister-in-law, Ninette Stocker Miller and her husband, George. Wood for the Victorian home came from the razed studio of photographer J.C. Burge in Kingston, as documented in a preserved contract. The home is in the National Register of Historic Places, and is a New Mexico Cultural Property. (BRM)

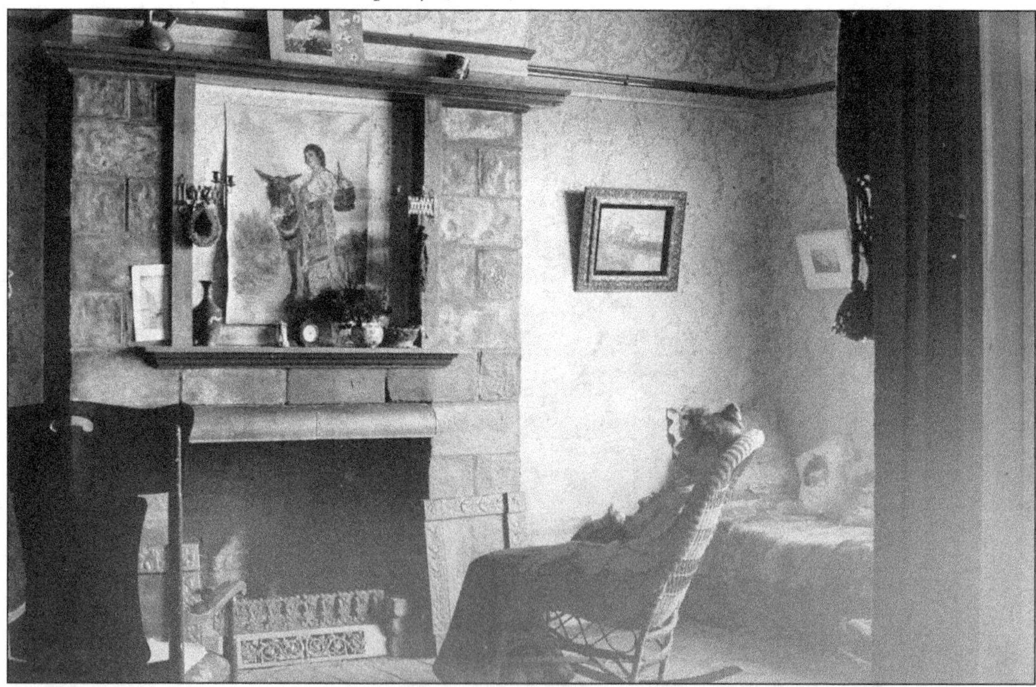

Future chief justice of the New Mexico Supreme Court Frank W. Parker sold this property to Ninette Stocker Miller, seen here in her living room. Ninette and her husband, George, operated the drugstore, purchased around 1896 from C.C. Miller, who would be murdered by Pancho Villa in Columbus, New Mexico, in 1916. George was Hillsboro's postmaster, a duty Ninette took over upon his untimely death in 1909. Ninette was a trained artist and prodigious painter. (BRM)

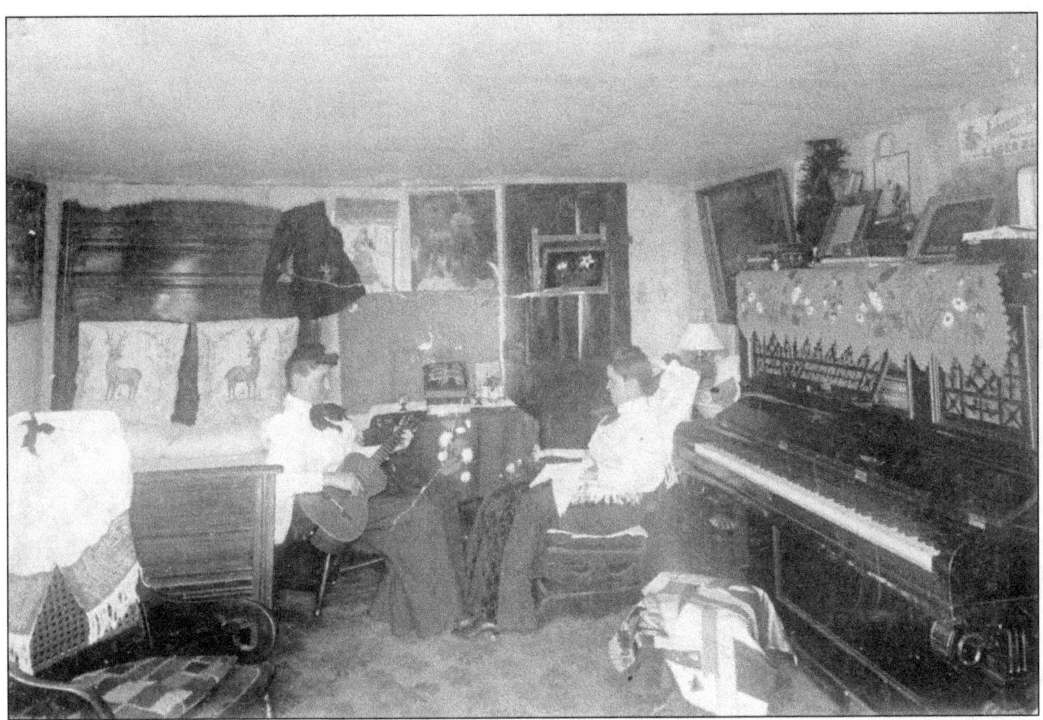

Sadie Orchard, Hillsboro's well-known madam, is in her bedroom/living room enjoying music played by an unidentified friend. It is not known if she is one of Sadie's girls or not. Sadie obviously lived well and had nice things. (BRM)

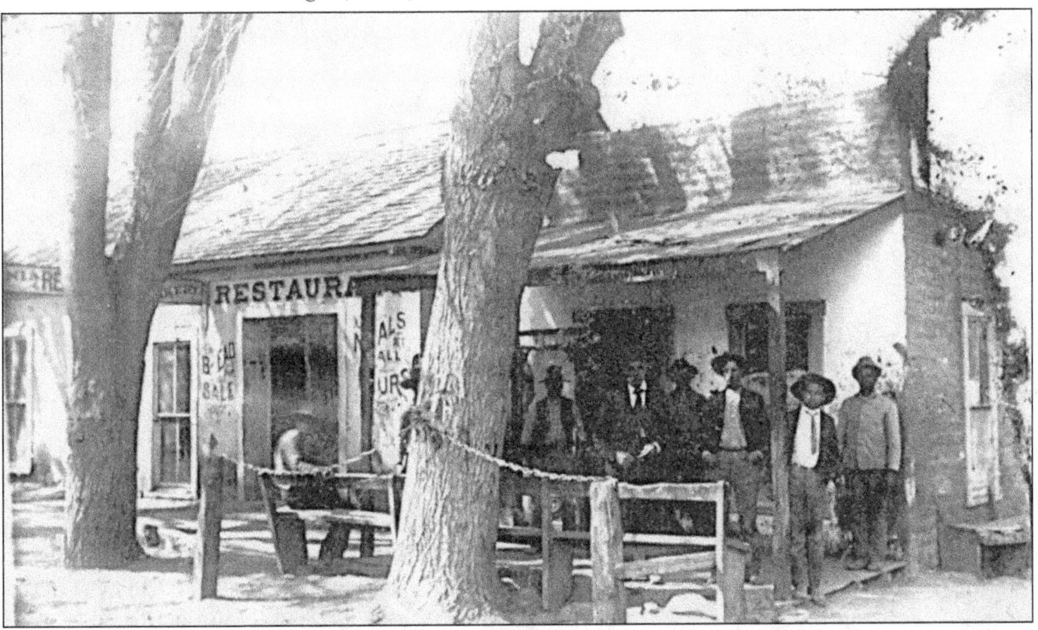

Of all the Chinese who came to work in the mines, one never left. Tom Ying opened a restaurant in Lake Valley and another in Hillsboro. He arrived in the United States from China in 1876. His restaurant in Hillsboro was in the Ocean Grove Hotel, which was owned by Sadie Orchard. Ying died in Hillsboro in 1959 and is buried in the Hillsboro cemetery. (BRM)

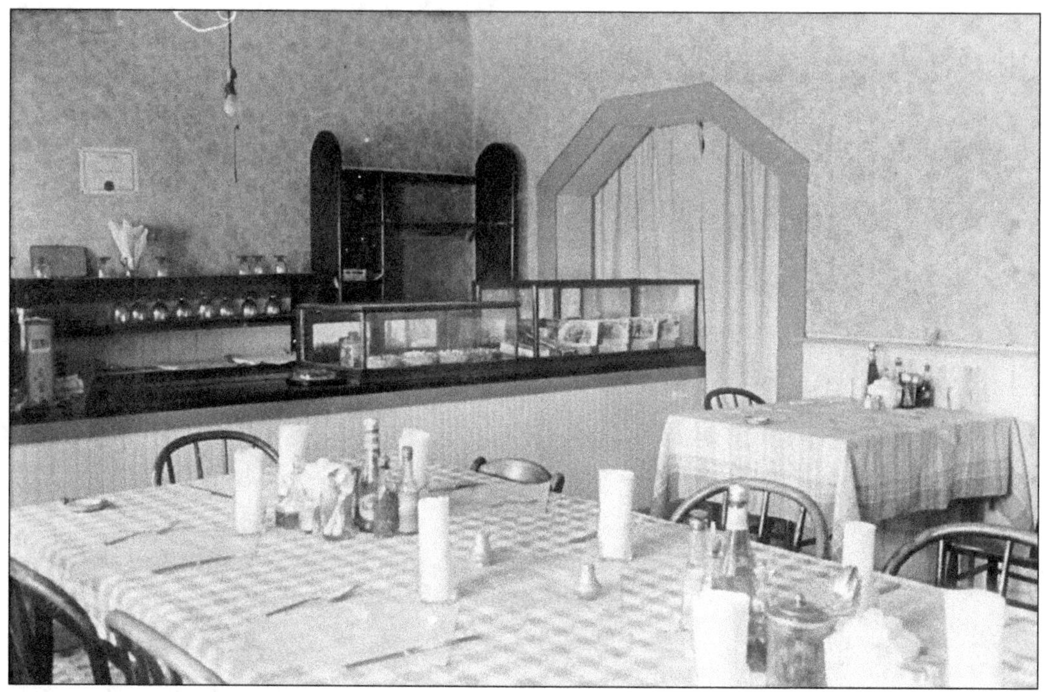

Tom Ying has turned the main room inside the Orchard Hotel into the seating area of his restaurant. The kitchen cannot be seen, but it still contains Tom Ying's old cast iron stove. This building is now the Black Range Museum and contains many items that belonged to both Ying and Orchard. (BRM)

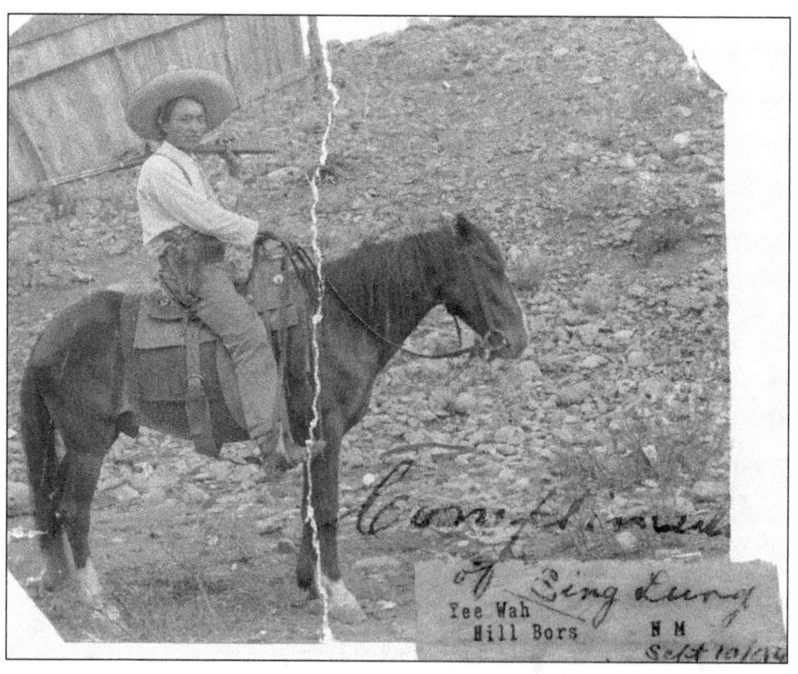

Chinese laborers came to the area to build the railroad, work in the mines, and farm. The November 1885 *Silver City Enterprise* reports the massacre of three Chinese truck farmers by Apaches near Lake Valley. This unidentified man appears to be posing for a picture to send back to China. (BRM)

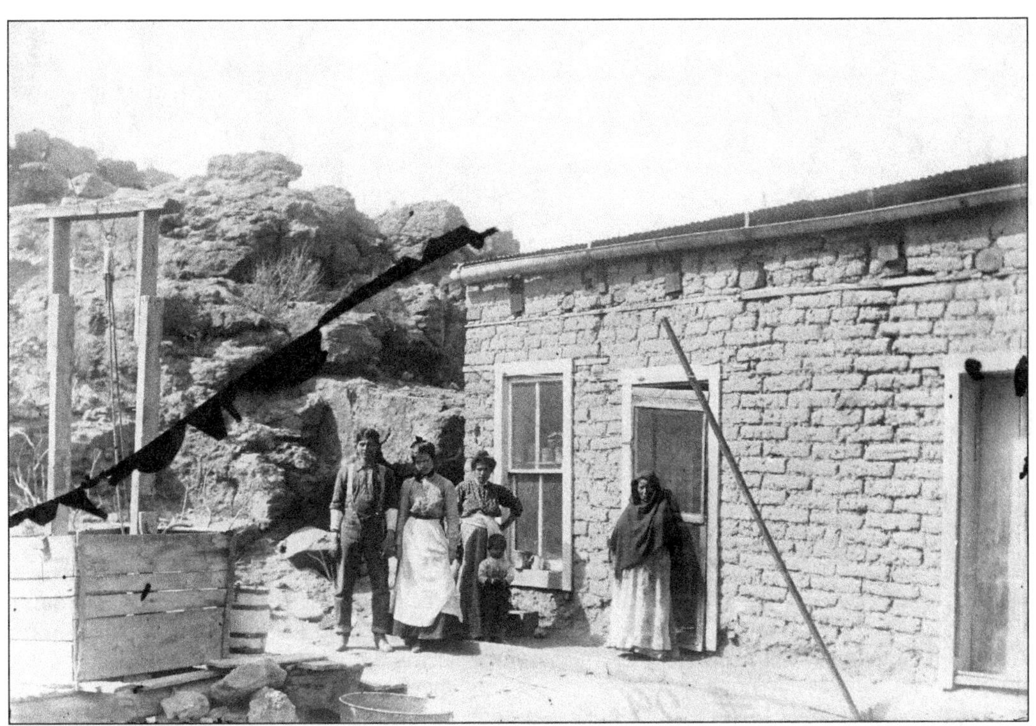

Many of these poorer shacks and adobes were built near Percha Creek and have long since been destroyed by major floods. This unidentified family lives where North Percha, Middle Percha, and South Percha Creeks converge. On the north side of Hillsboro, the area is called La Reserva. Adobe houses and hand-dug wells were used by all the residents in the area. This was where friendly Indian families lived. (GSM)

As a young girl, Rafaela Ortiz came in a wagon from Benson, Texas, to Kingston. She married Juan Hernandez, and they moved to La Reserva. Among the other families living in La Reserva were the Acostas and the Zamoras. In the photograph are Juan, Rafaela, and their daughter Julia Hernandez. Many of their descendants still live in the area. (GS)

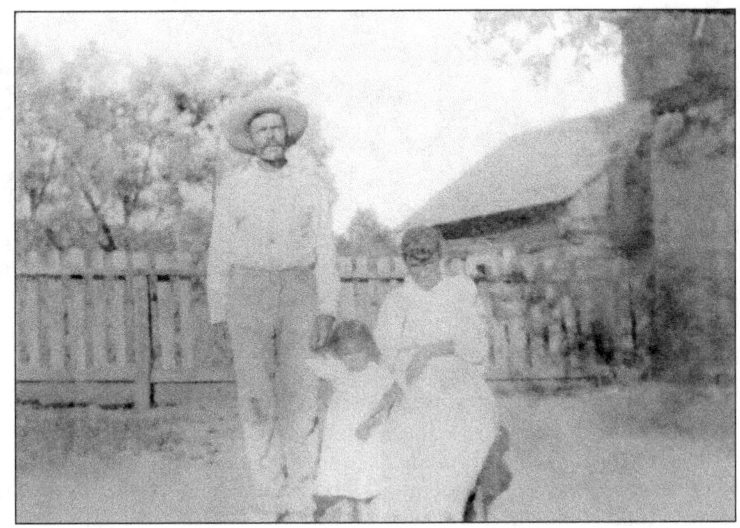

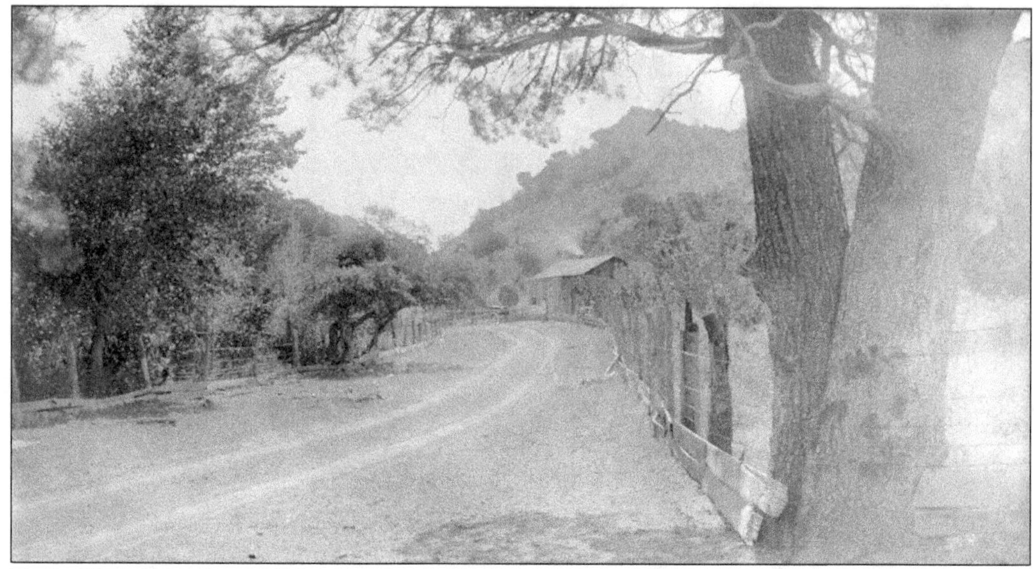

The toll road between Hillsboro and Kingston was constructed by Joseph David Whitham around 1890 and passed through the ranch property he homesteaded along Percha Creek, below Starr Peak. Whitham was a mining engineer and surveyor during Kingston's early days. (GSM)

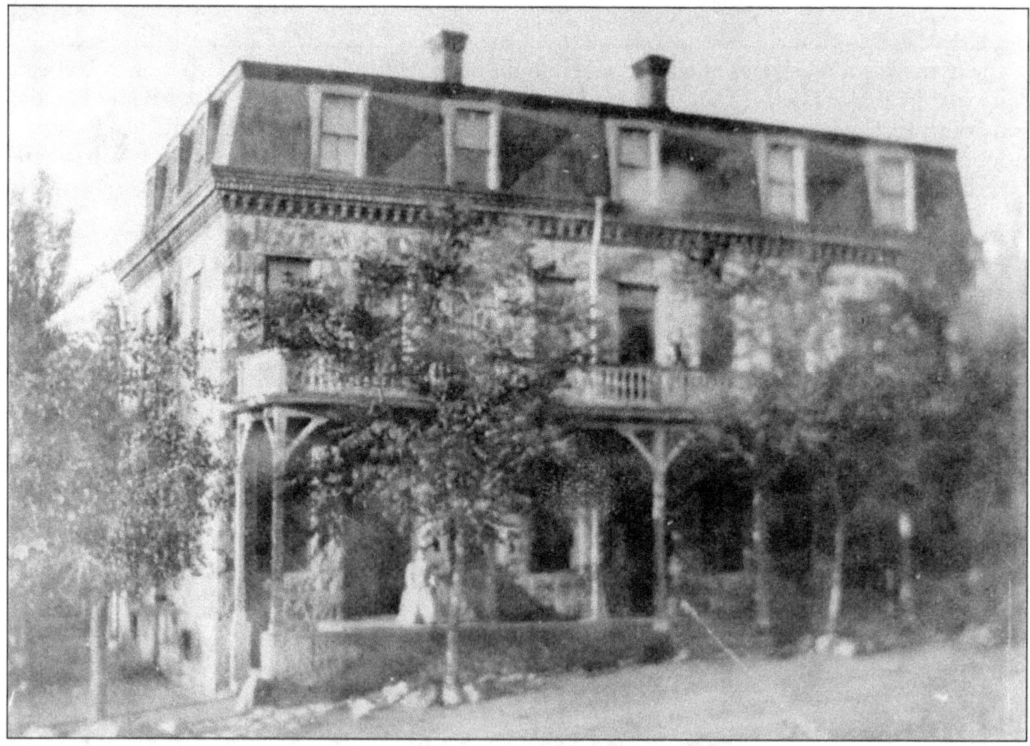

The original masonry construction of the Victorio Hotel in Kingston was done by Oliver Wilson, an immigrant from Sweden. The stone was quarried from a little gulch behind the hotel and close to a small spring, which provided water for the hotel. During Indian raids, women and children were taken to the hotel basement. The basement also served as a morgue in the winter, until graves could be dug in the spring. (DW)

Kingston's Percha Bank incorporated in July 1886 and did a vigorous boomtown business. This 1886 receipt documents a deposit of the Keller Miller Store in Lake Valley. The bank building is now a beautiful museum. (BRM)

THE PERCHA BANK.

JEFFERSON RAYNOLDS, President.

Kingston, N. M. 188

Your favor of ...... 12 ...... *received, with stated enclosures.*

WE CREDIT.

$109.63

Yr rem of $901.65 reached us on the 13th and was duly cr'd & advised. It made rather slow ... getting here

CHECKS ON OUTSIDE POINTS CREDITED SUBJECT TO PAYMENT.

WE DEBIT.

ENTERED FOR COLLECTION.

M & P | 250 —

WE REMIT FOR YOUR CREDIT AND ADVICE TO

Respectfully yours,

NORMAN C. RAFF, Cashier.

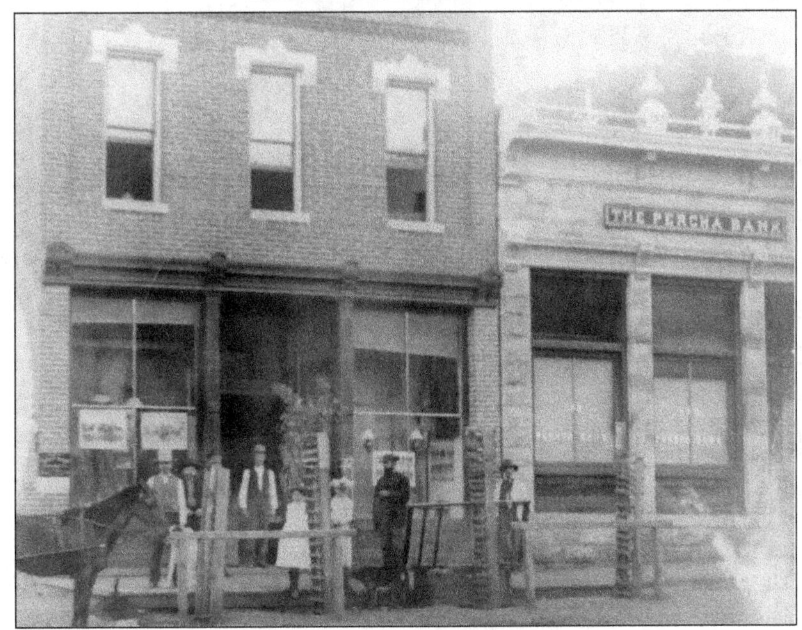

The Percha Bank president, Jefferson Raynolds, was a Canton, Ohio native and childhood friend of President McKinley. The 1886 Proceedings of the American Bankers Association reports the bank being flush with $30,000 in cash and $5,000 in securities. Bank cashier and Raynolds's associate, Norman Raff, was also from Canton. Oliver Wilson built the stone structure in 1885. (PBM)

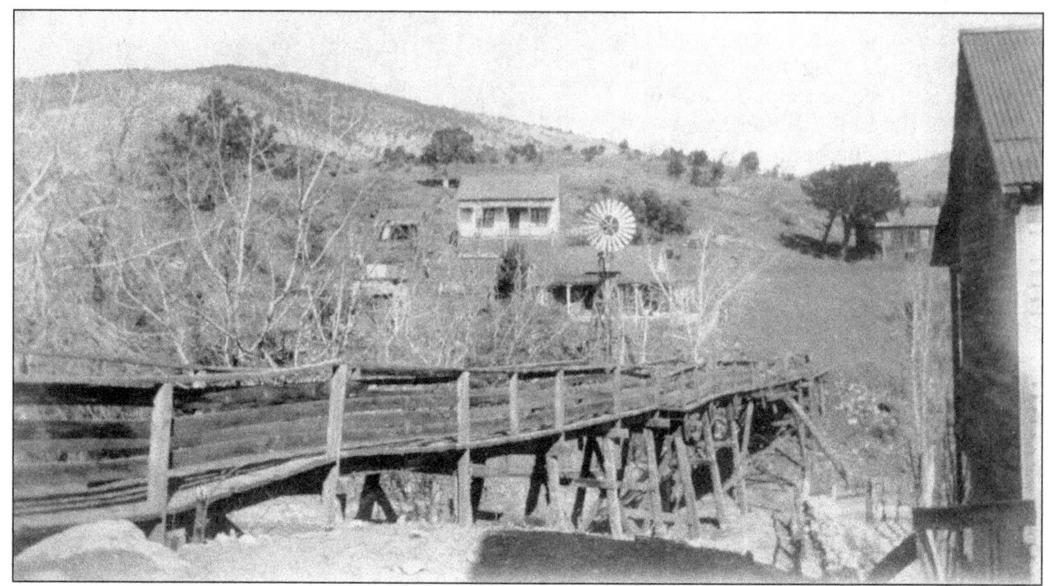

This is one of Kingston's footbridges as viewed from south to north. The Prevost windmill and house can be seen in the distance. Kingston was built on both sides of the creek, but footbridges have been replaced by bridges on road crossings for modern vehicles. (DW)

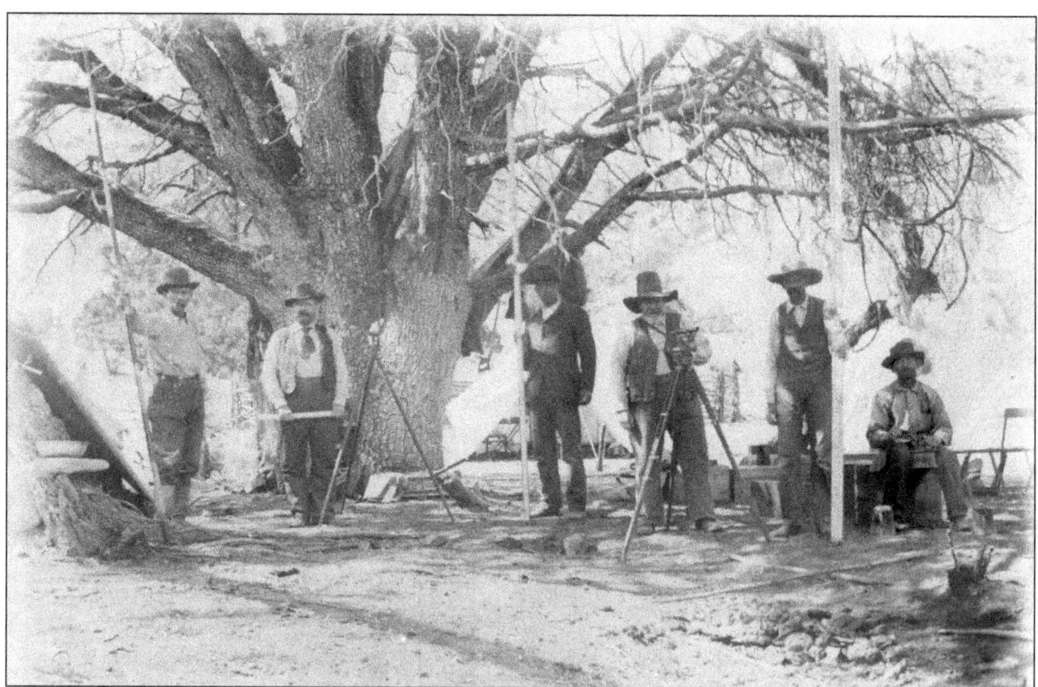

James Porter Parker, third from right, was the roommate of George Armstrong Custer at West Point and a first cousin of Mary Todd Lincoln. Parker joined the Confederate army and spent two years in Union prison camps. He later drifted to Kingston and became Sierra County's first assessor. Here, he is shown surveying the land for the initial layout of the town of Kingston. (GSM)

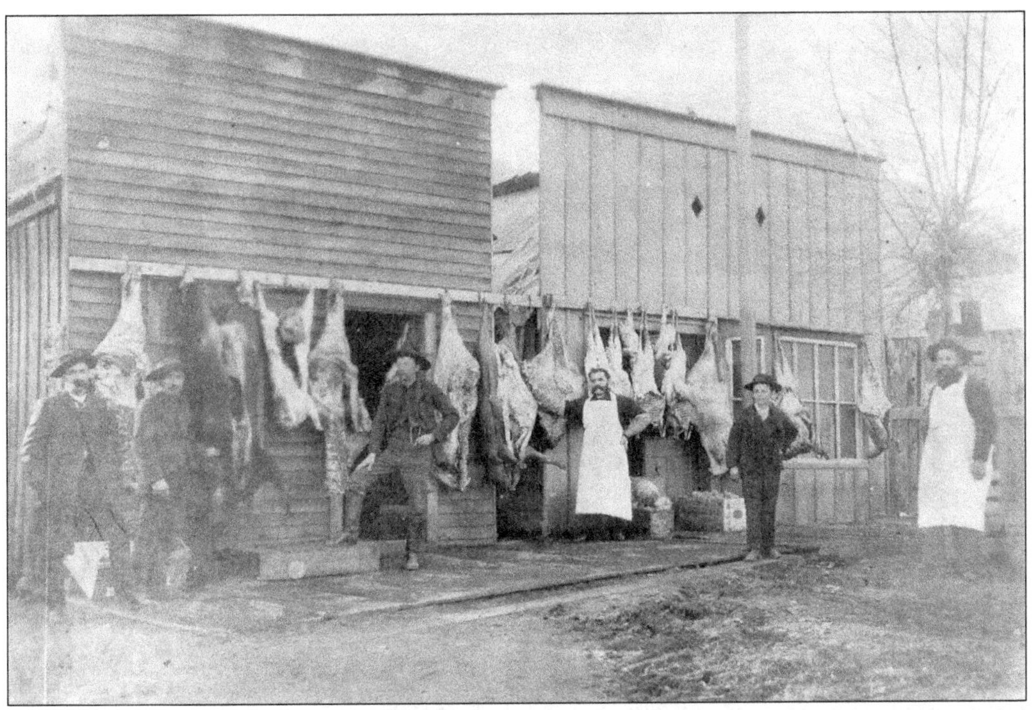

Kingston butchers in 1883 were not particular about what they sold. A bear and a bobcat are included in this photograph. Other animals include cow, antelope, goat, deer, and turkey. (GSM)

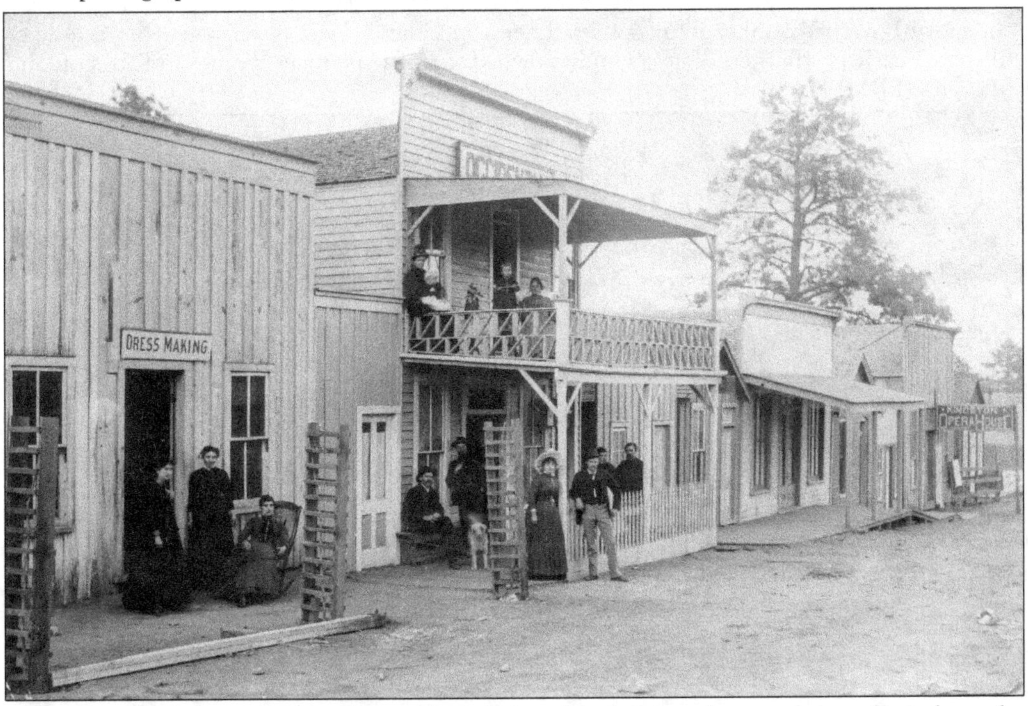

Shown here is Kingston's Main Street. Included in the photograph are a dressmaker's shop, the Occidental Hotel, and, further down the street, the Kingston Opera House. Lillian Russell is said to have performed here and to have been a good friend of Sadie Orchard. (BRM)

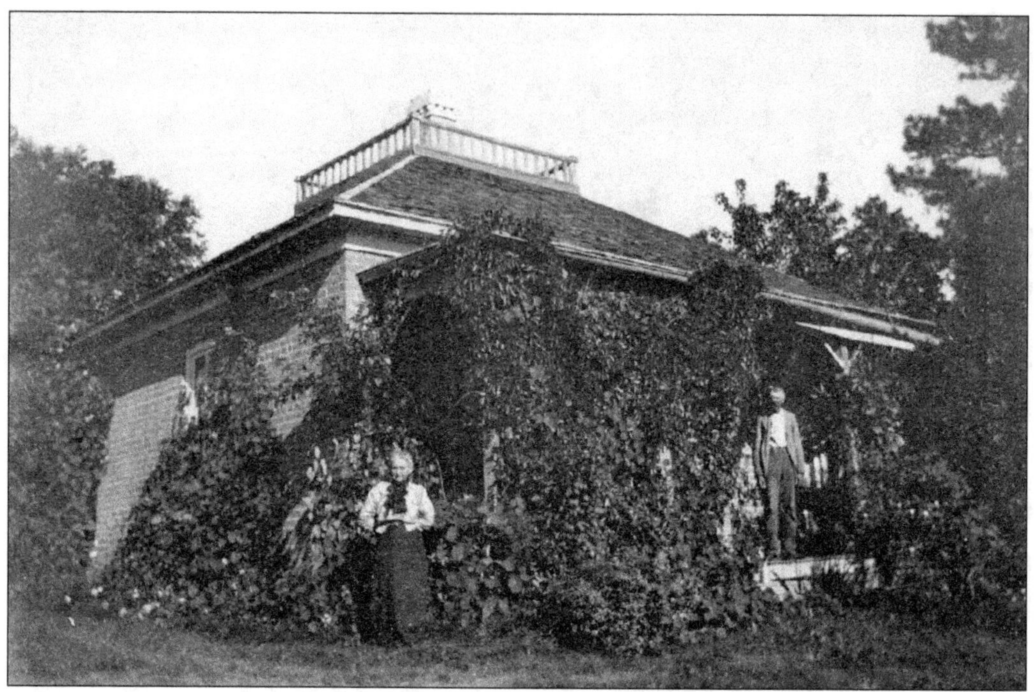

These two photographs taken in 1898 show the Robert West family at their fine brick home in Kingston. West came to Kingston from California sometime after 1880. Daughter Carrie married banker William Bucher, and daughter Anne married rancher Willard Hopewell; daughter Gertrude (not shown) married banker John Zollars. Their son Charles, who never married, was one of Hillsboro's early postmasters. These families owned some of the nicest homes in Kingston and Hillsboro. (BRM)

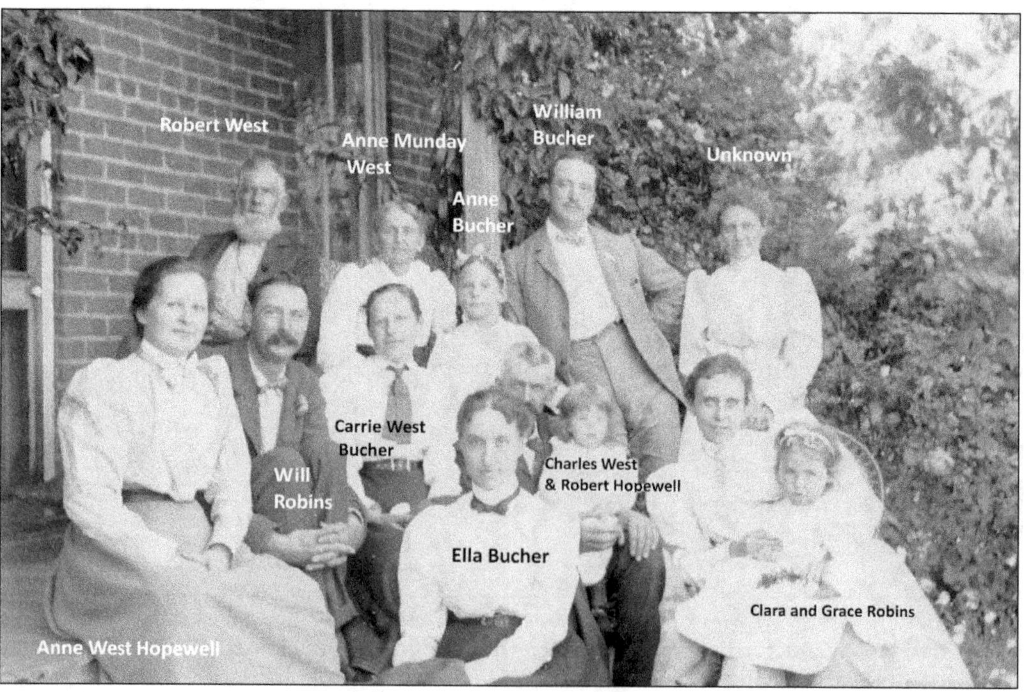

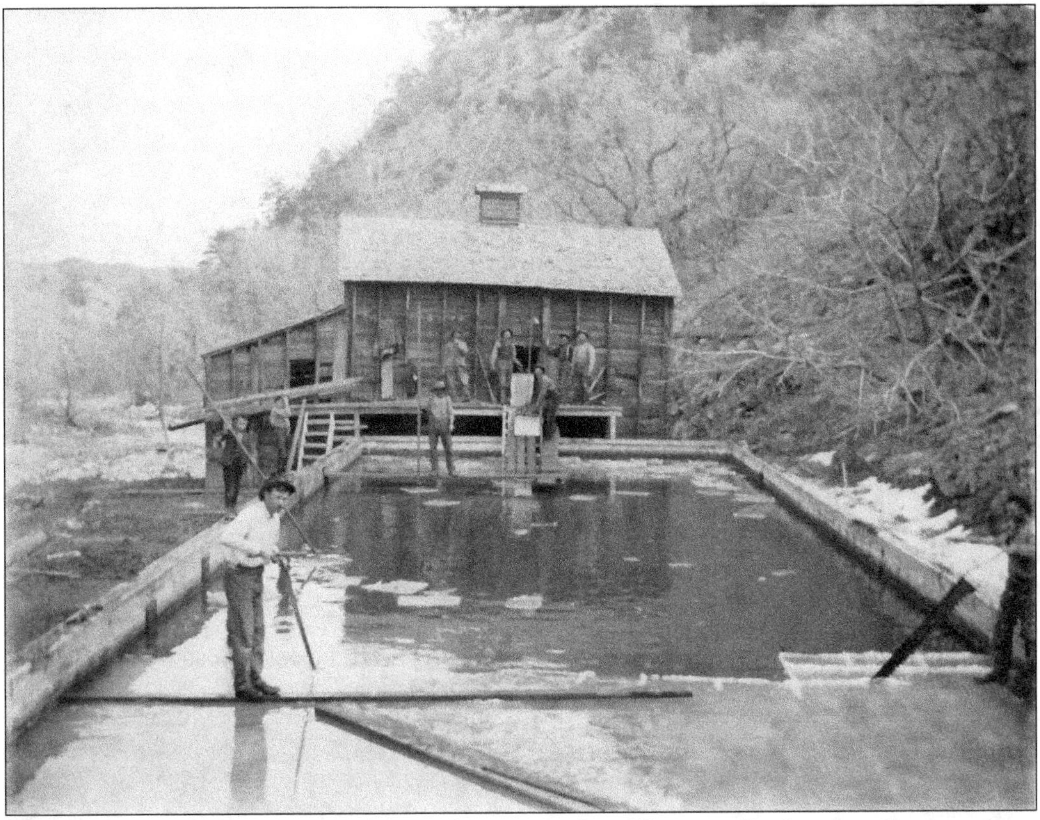

This ice plant was located on Percha Creek upstream from Kingston. Production of ice must have been an extremely uncertain enterprise in this climate. (PBM)

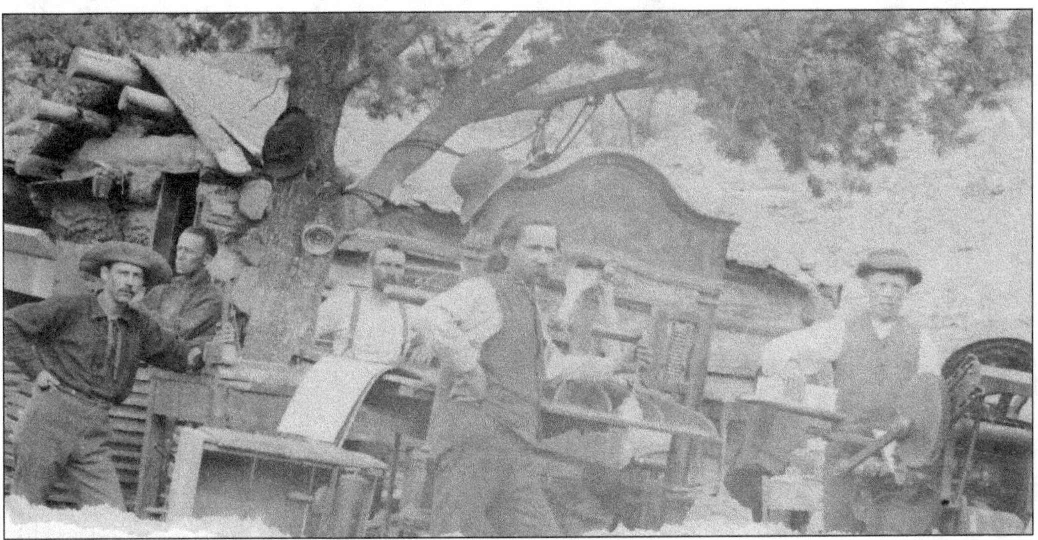

This photograph fragment demonstrates how important the printed word was from the beginning of the three towns. Here, aspiring journalists have set up shop outdoors while awaiting completion of a building for their newspaper. (GSM)

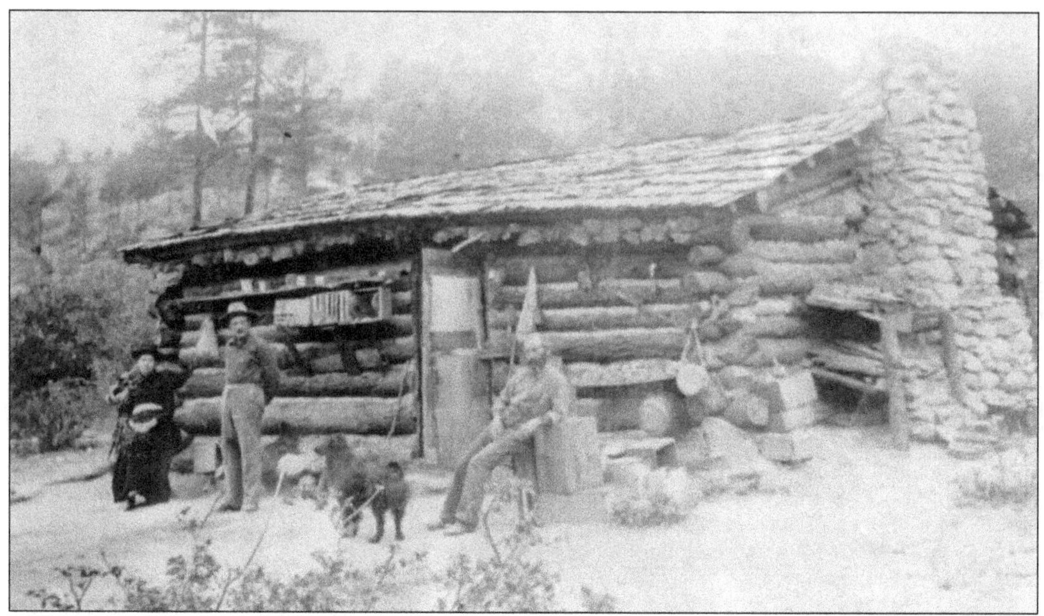

Percha City, another small mining boomtown that sprang up in the early 1880s, was located in the Black Range on Carbonate Creek about 12 miles west and north by wagon road from Hillsboro. John W. McCuiston was its first merchant and only postmaster. The post office closed after ten and a half months. All that remains is this small cabin, which was once the saloon. (PBM)

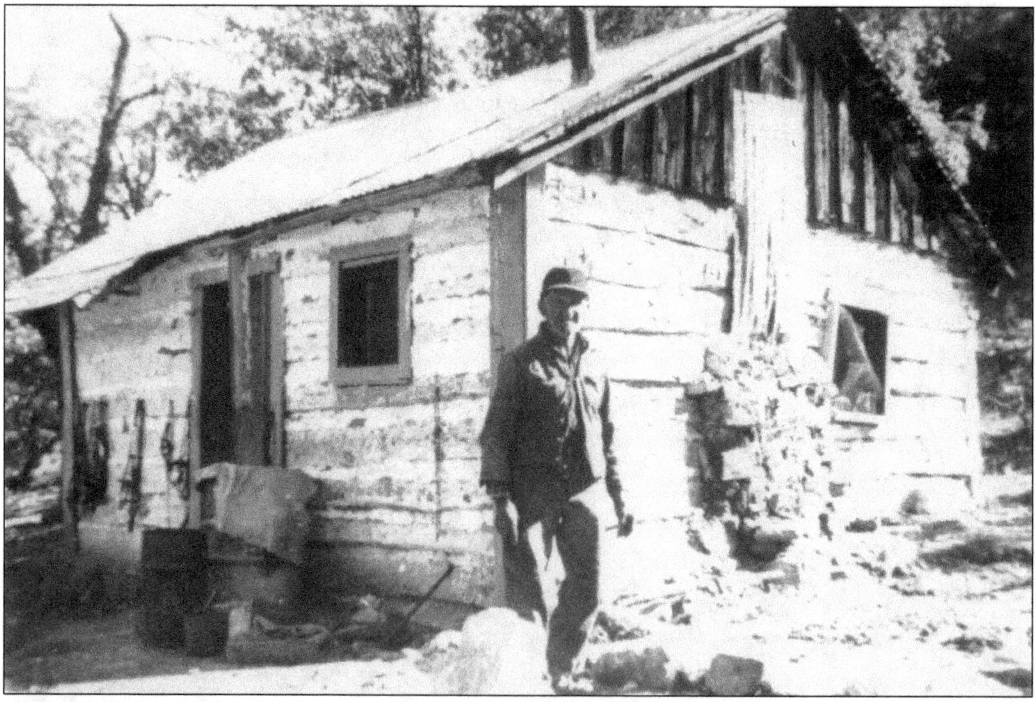

News of gold and silver finds brought people from all over the world to the Black Range. This cabin on the Tierra Blanca was built around 1889 by Sofas Hoisinger from Denmark. In the 1900 census, he is shown as a miner. In the 1920 census, he is a mine manager. The man in the photograph is Jeronimo "Chief" Sedillo.

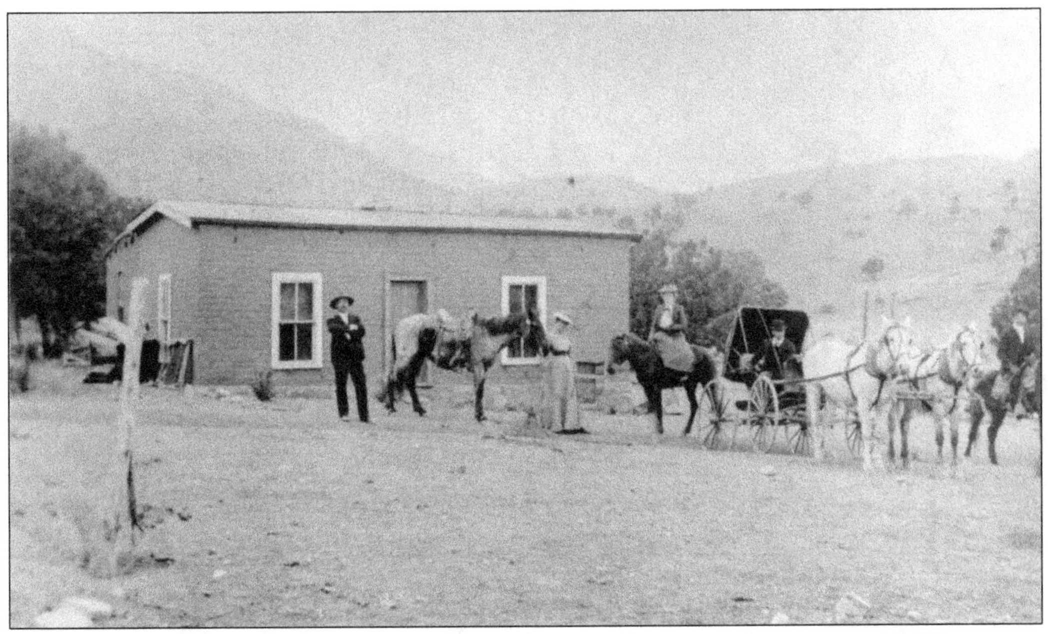

Carl Beals was one of the first homesteaders on Tierra Blanca Creek. He patented 120 acres in 1893, built the small adobe house shown in this photograph, and raised goats. A letter written by his sister Jessie in April 1899 states, "Carl and Archie are in the mountains with the goats. They come down very often. C. has had three rooms of adobe added to his house." Though modified, the house is still there and still in use.

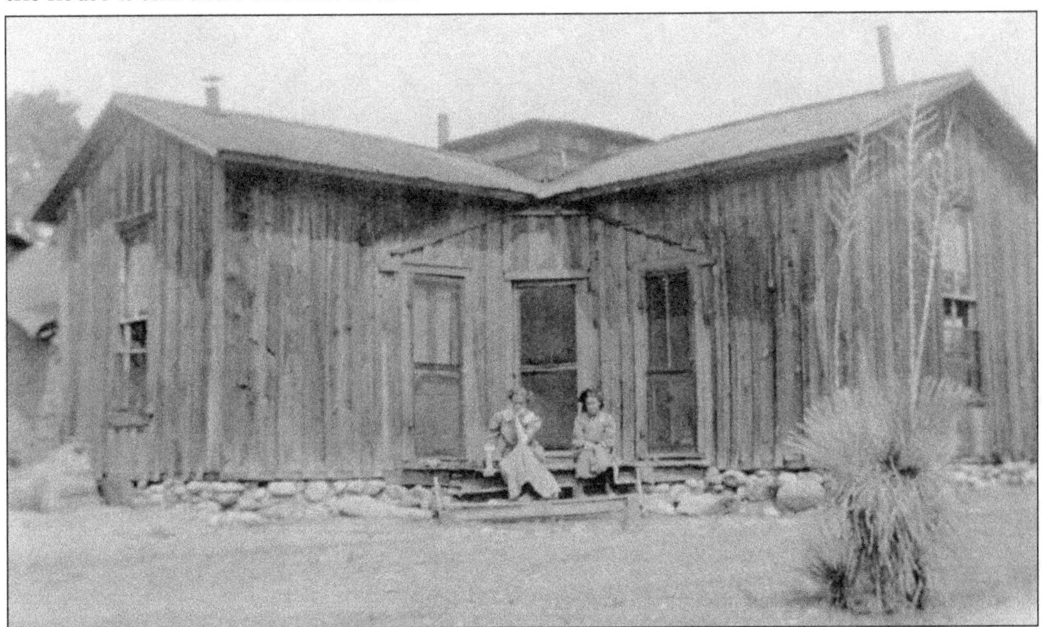

Dr. Guy Beals came to New Mexico from Michigan with the dream of starting a tuberculosis sanitarium. He found the ideal location on Tierra Blanca Creek, in the small mining community of Tierra Blanca. Beals patented 120 acres across the creek from his brother Carl and built his sanitarium. He had a few patients, but with the decline of the area due to the economic conditions in 1893, he had to abandon his clinic. Beals was also Tierra Blanca's first and only postmaster.

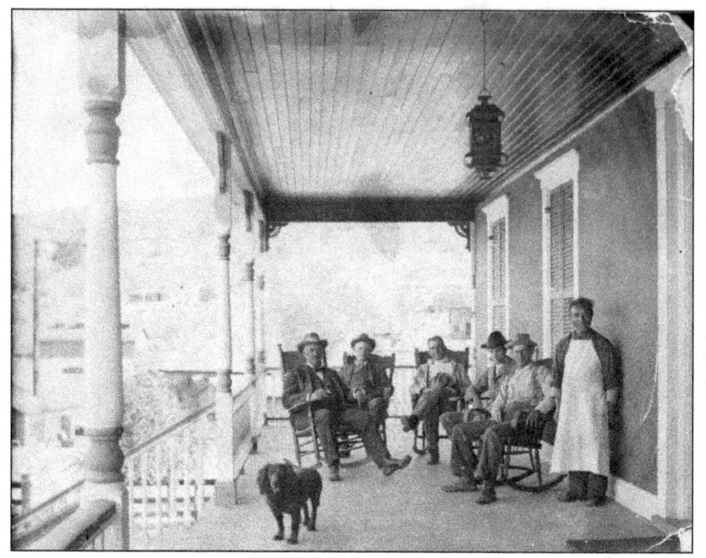

The town of Andrews was named after William "Bull" Andrews, who moved to New Mexico from Pennsylvania in 1902. He served as New Mexico's territorial delegate to Congress from 1905 to 1911 and was influential in obtaining statehood for the territory. Bull Andrews is seated on the left on his front porch in Andrews, a small mining town founded in 1898. In 1905, it boasted 100 residents, two stores with saloons, and four mining offices. (BRM)

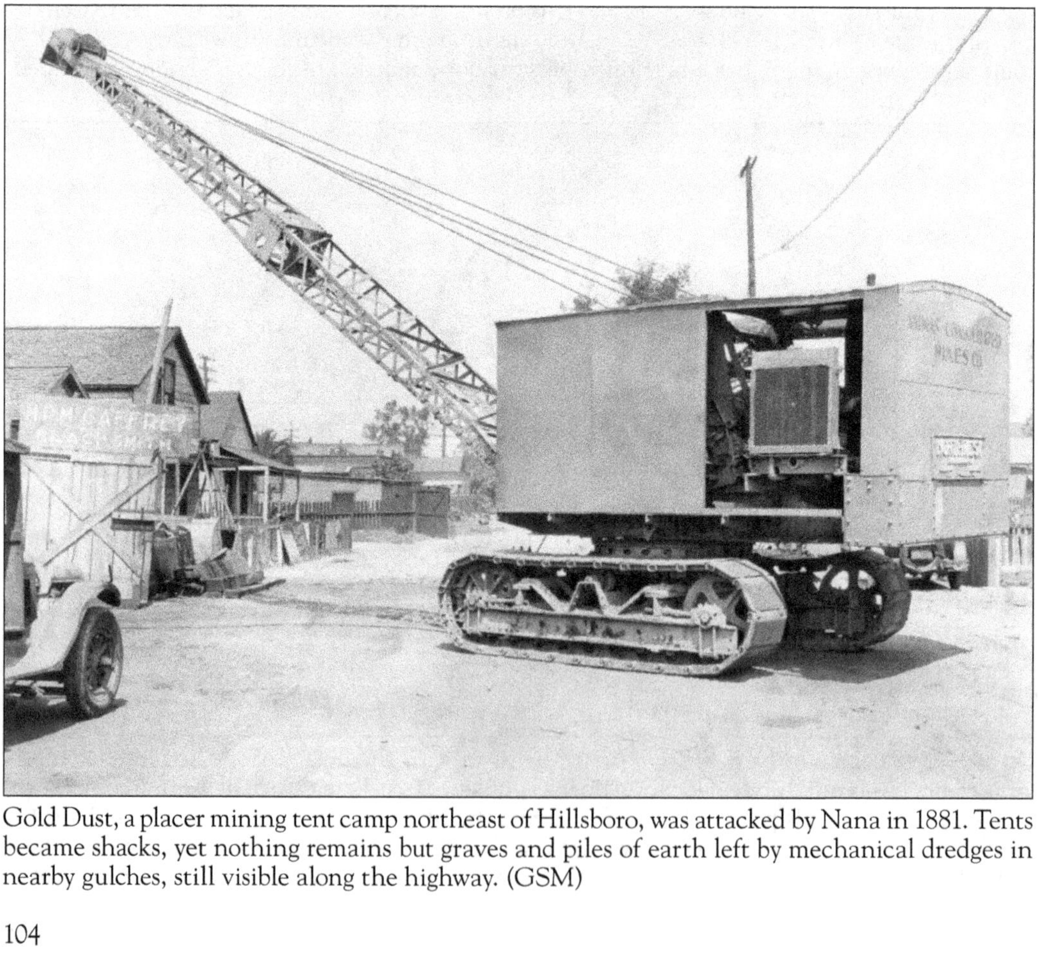

Gold Dust, a placer mining tent camp northeast of Hillsboro, was attacked by Nana in 1881. Tents became shacks, yet nothing remains but graves and piles of earth left by mechanical dredges in nearby gulches, still visible along the highway. (GSM)

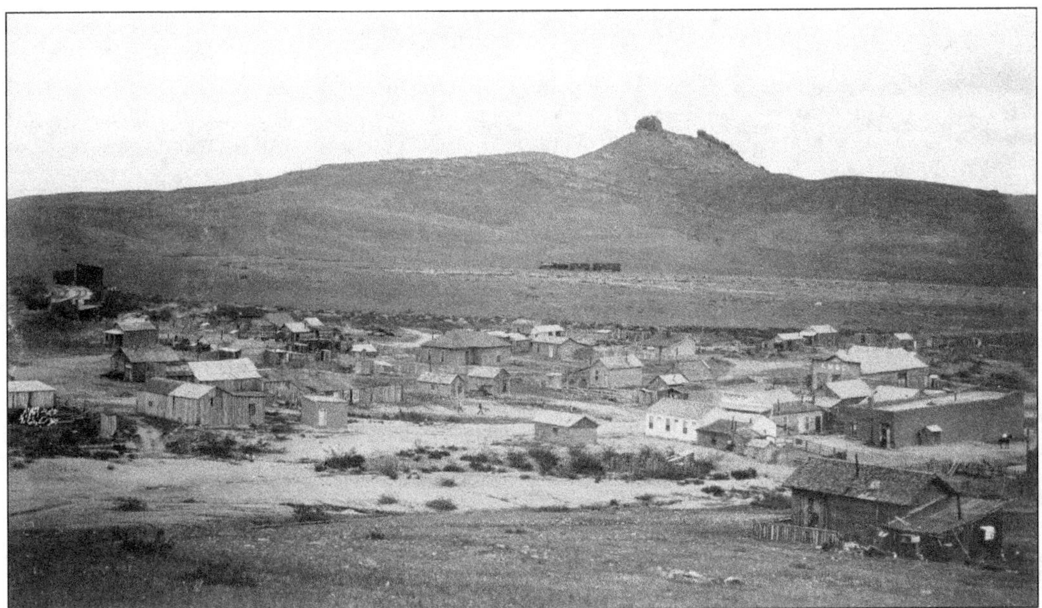

This is Lake Valley after its heyday and in a more peaceful time. The old town had the typical reputation of a lawless Old West boomtown, including Indian raids, cattle rustling, and gunfights. Colonel Fountain and the cavalry were called in several times. "Long Hair" James Courtwright from Fort Worth and Jim McIntyre were both needed as marshals. (RGHC)

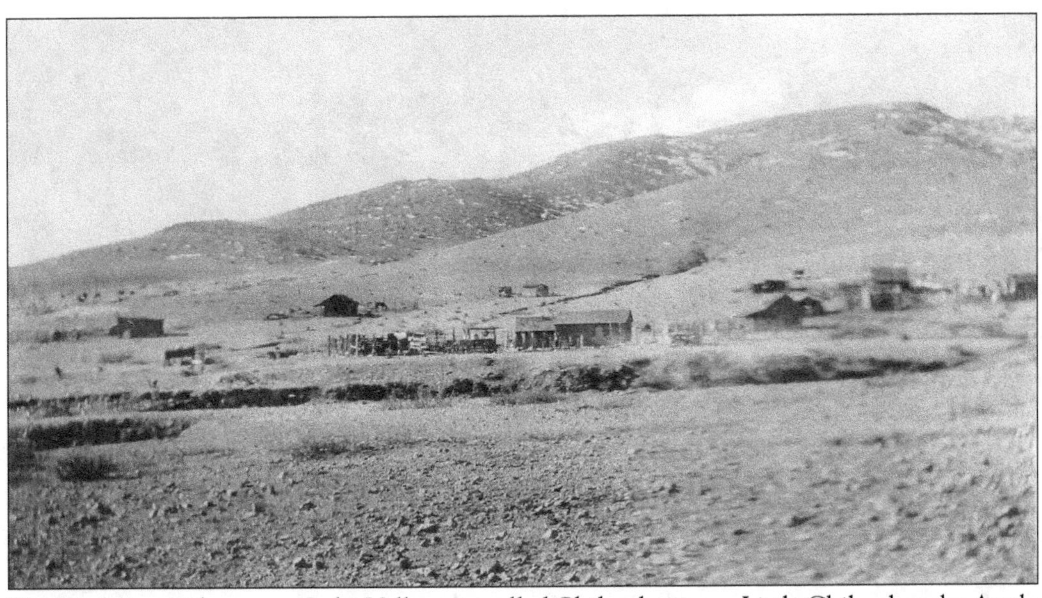

The Mexican settlement at Lake Valley was called Chihuahuaita or Little Chihuahua, by Anglo residents and Rinconada by Hispanics. The Martinez family came here in 1906. Other settlers were the Montoyas and the Arrelins. Many are buried in unmarked graves in the cemetery on the hill south of town. (DW)

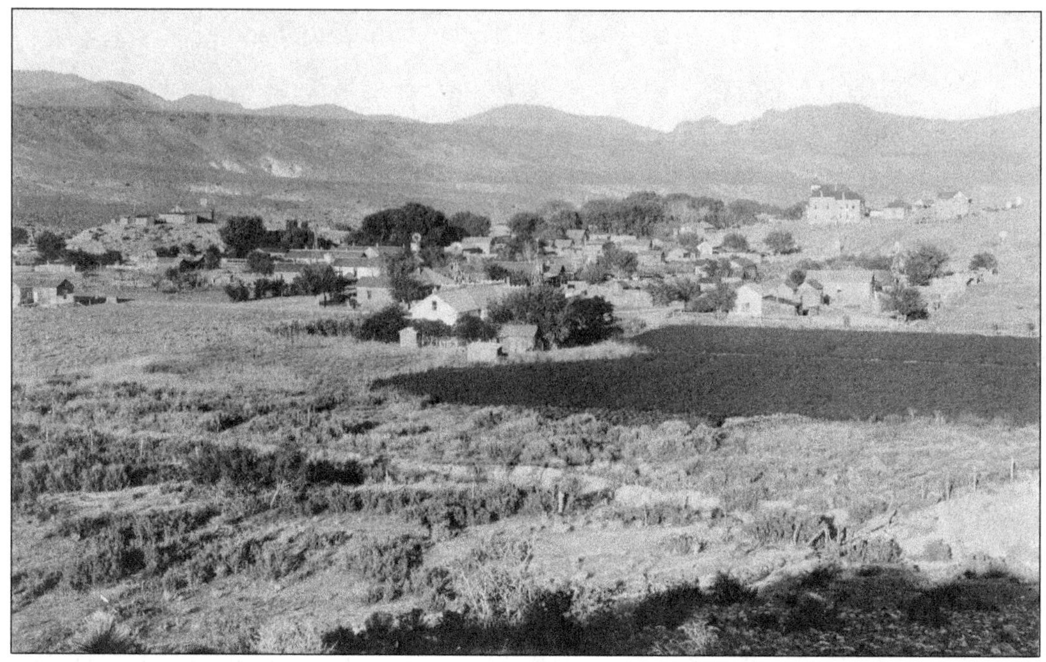

This panorama of Hillsboro from the southwest was taken between 1893 and 1909. In 1884, Hillsborough was designated the county seat of Sierra County and the name changed to Hillsboro. The first courthouse was on Main Street. By 1890, there were over 700 people, a public school, a church, four hotels, three stamp mills, a newspaper, and a number of saloons and stores. (BRM)

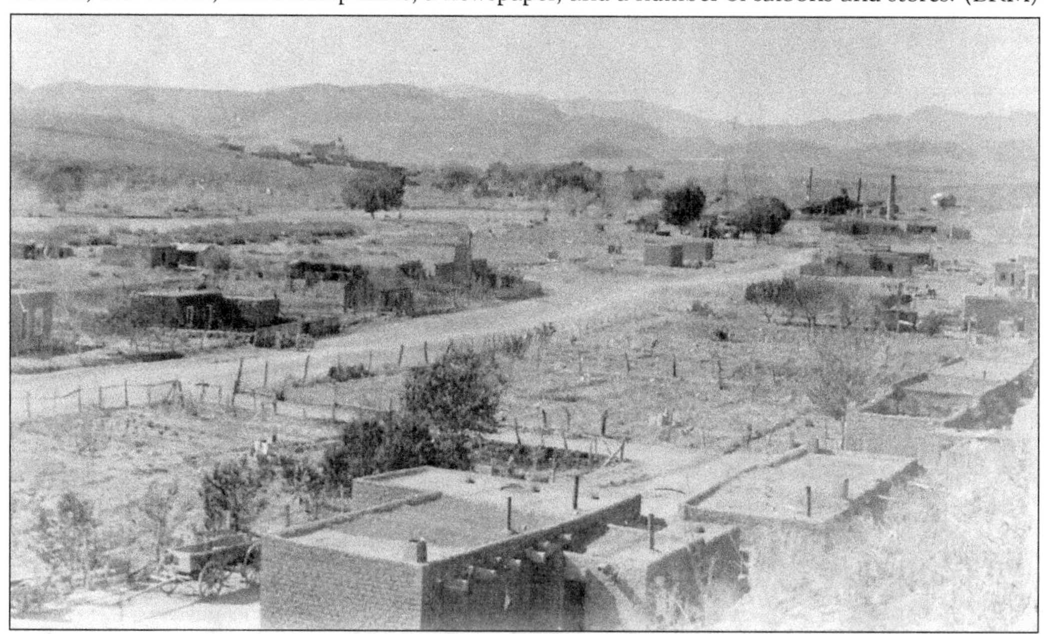

That portion of Hillsboro east of the main part of town and north of Percha Creek was called Tavalopa by its Hispanic settlers and Happy Flat by Hillsboro's white residents. Each adobe home and its adjoining lands where gardens were grown and animals were kept was called a *rancheria*. The old Spanish mission with its bell tower can be seen in the middle of the photograph. The Hillsboro smelter is in the upper right. (BRM)

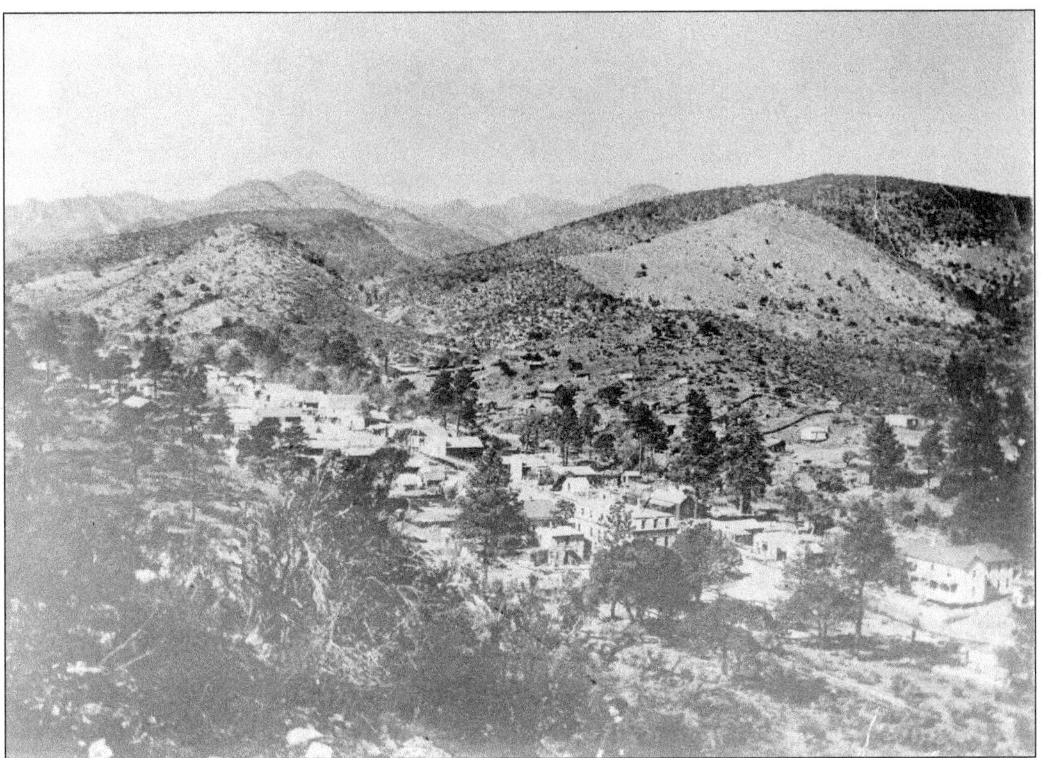

On November 2, 1882, an article in *The Rio Grande Republican* stated, "Kingston is only two months old. A day beyond that time its present site was a narrow ragged gulch. Now it is two miles long and has 2000 inhabitants. The mountains are filled with prospectors and at night fires gleam from every hill." This photograph shows Kingston around 1890. (DW)

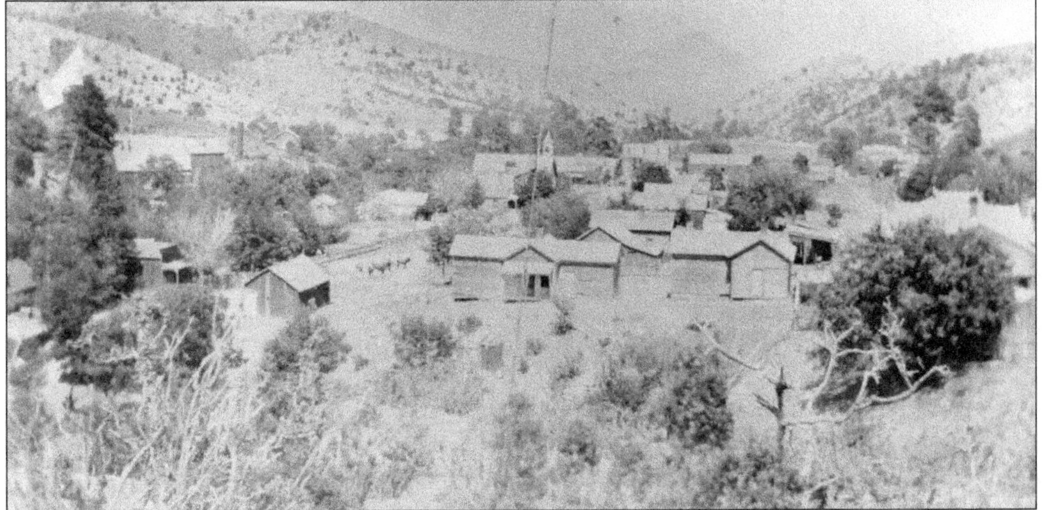

This early-1900s view of Kingston looks from west to east. The house on the left with a porch is the Steiner home. The smelter is near the smokestack. Sofia Hansen's Hotel is on the other side of the church. The long building is the Wohglemuth Livery Stable and next is the two-story drugstore. The wooden building in the foreground is the Ed Cahill Store, and Johnny Moffit's house is on the extreme right. (DW)

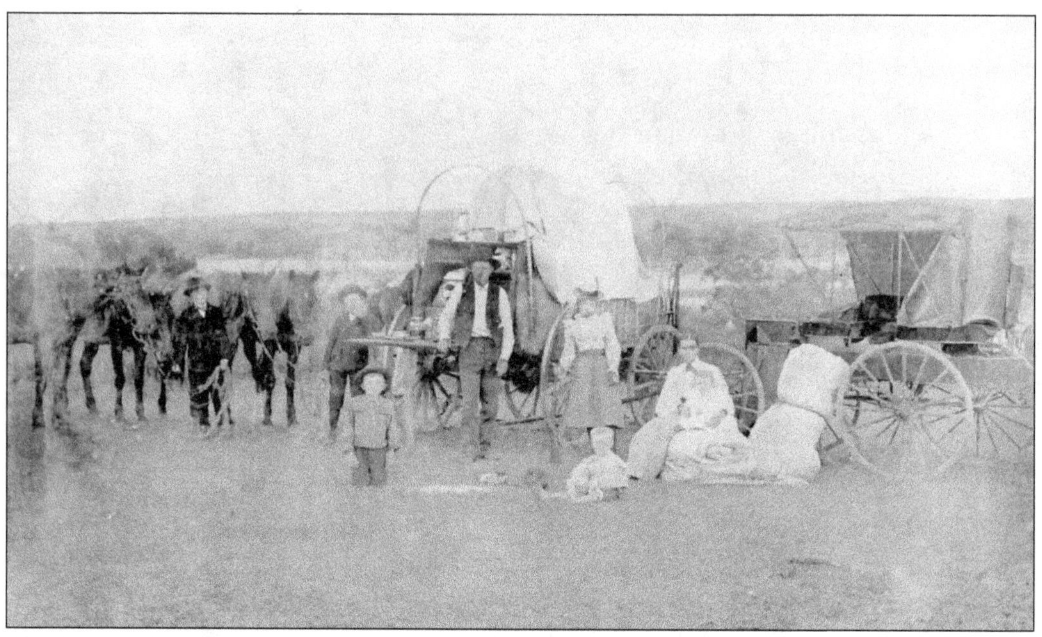

The Ortizes, Fergusons, Faulkners, Lathams, and many other families all tell of having first arrived in covered wagons, usually from Texas. Some came with herds of cattle. Many people walked, since the horses or mules pulled the wagons. Settlers primarily used farm wagons with wooden bows that arched from side to side. Here, the wagon is used to transport goods, and the people ride in a buggy or walk. (BRM)

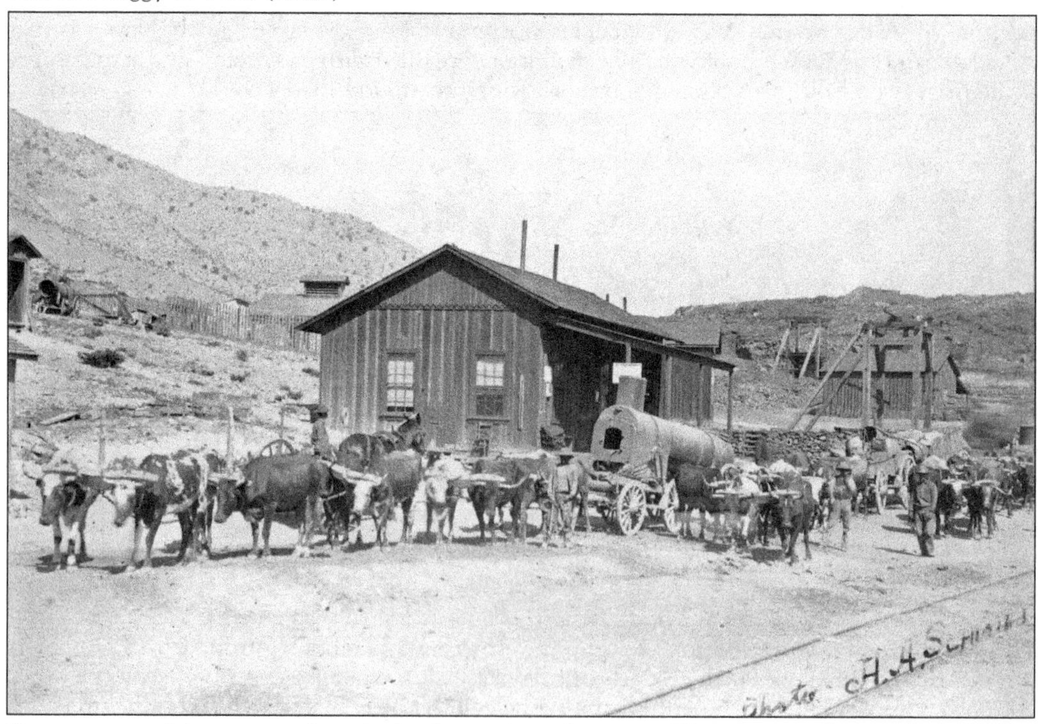

Oxen were used to transport heavier loads over long distances. This is a team leaving Lake Valley pulling what looks like a boiler for one of the mills. (RGHC)

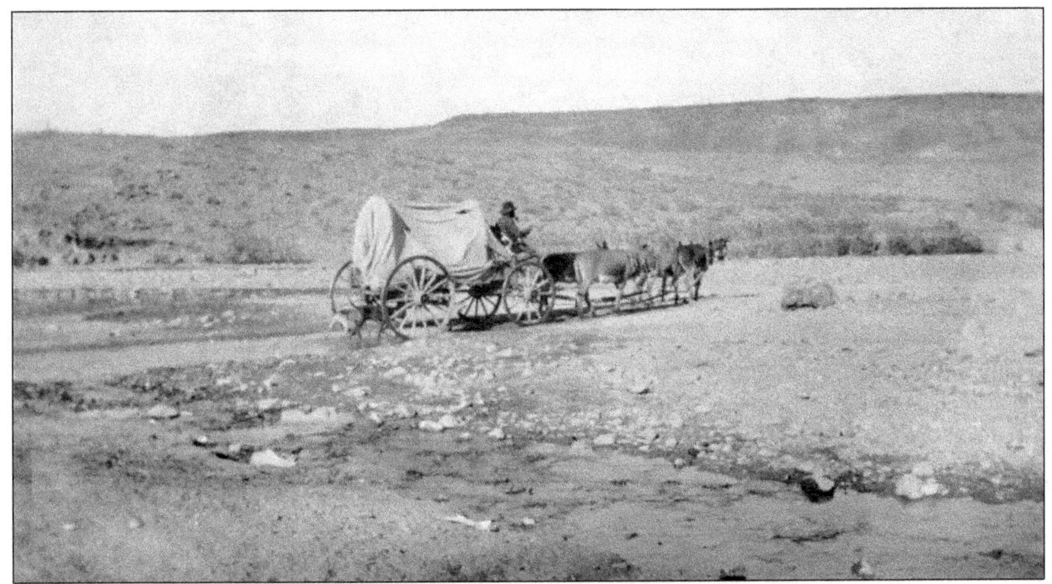

Bill Coalson homesteaded near Hillsboro in 1916. He raised a truck garden and sold milk, butter, eggs, chickens, and vegetables to people in Hillsboro and Gold Dust. Coalson was known as Uncle Billy, and children clamored to ride with him in his wagon. (BRM)

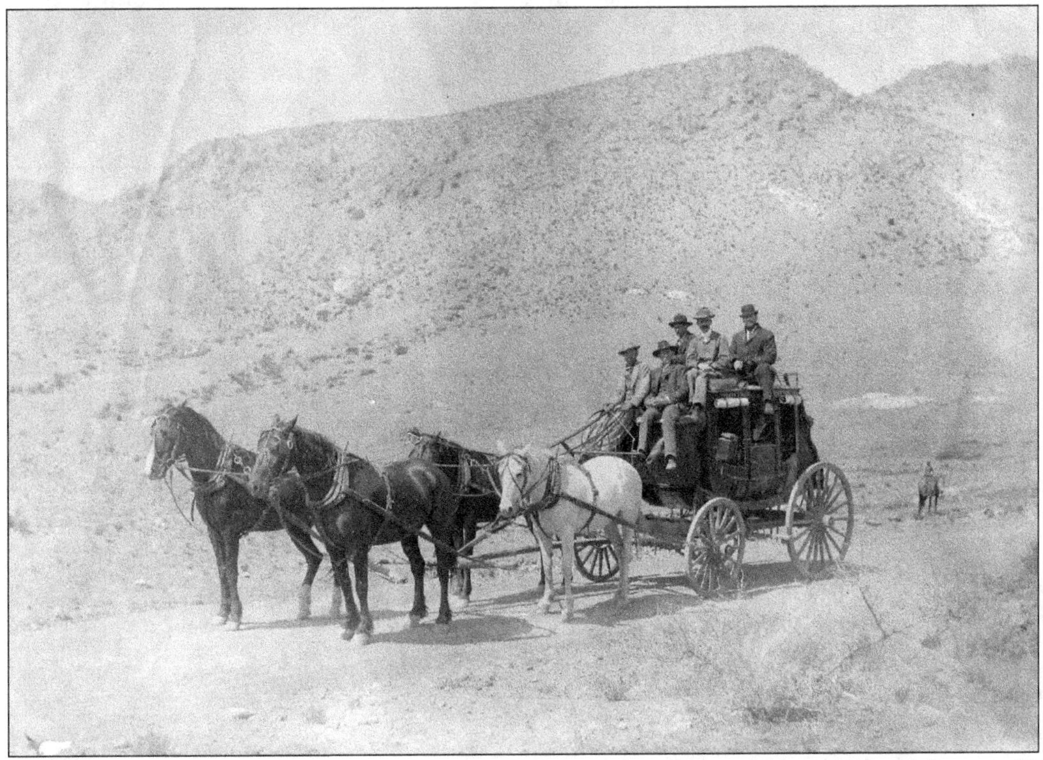

The November 1882 *Las Vegas Optic* reported that fare by stage from Nutt to Lake Valley was $2 and that the route was splendid, but the dust was terrible. The entire road was filled with loaded wagons, and hotel accommodations were scarce. When the weather was good, passengers often chose to ride outside of the coach, where they could view the passing landscape. (DW)

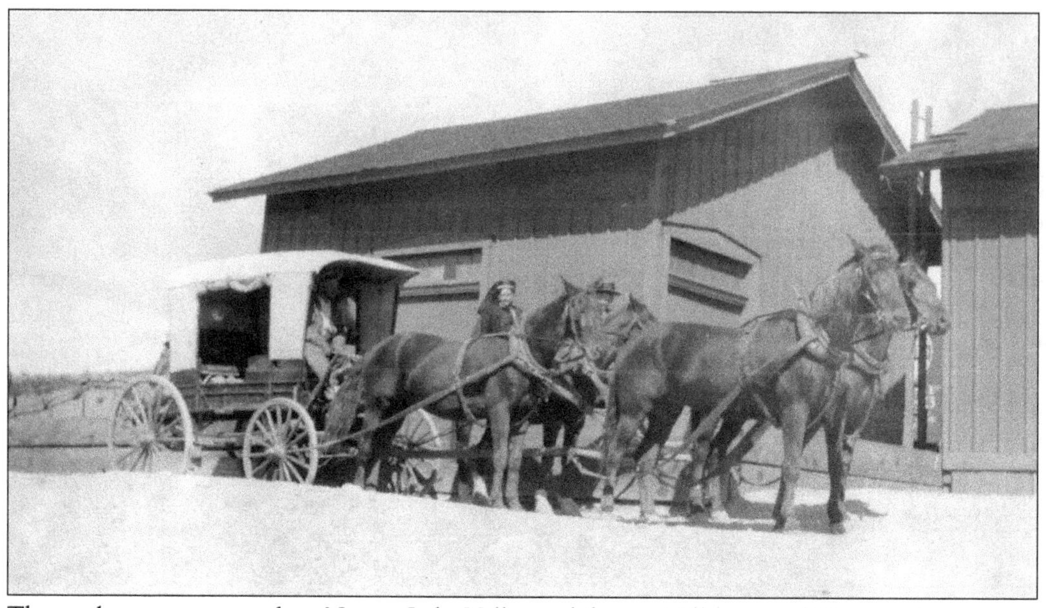

The mail wagon en route from Nutt to Lake Valley and then to Hillsboro and Kingston has stopped at the railroad depot in Lake Valley. In 1879, the Hillsboro Post Office opened, creating a mail route. With the arrival of the train at Lake Valley, the stage or the mail wagon had only to go as far as Lake Valley. The Lake Valley train depot remained standing until the early 2000s. (DW)

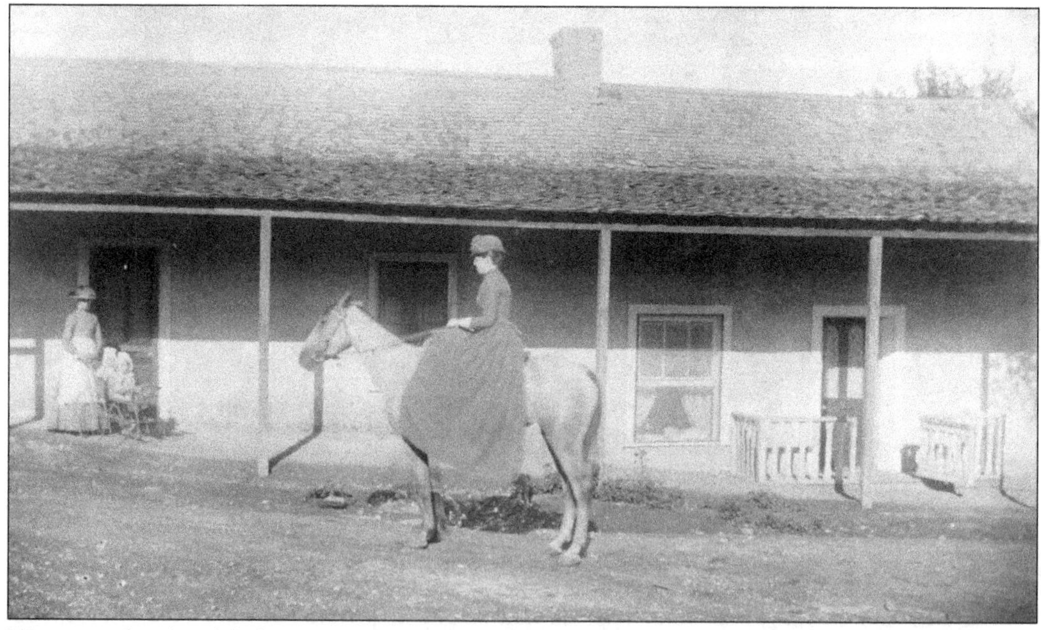

Women rode sidesaddle because it was considered improper to ride astride and was impossible to do in a long dress. Harriet Stocker Galles, wife of Nicholas Galles, stops to visit with an unidentified lady pushing a baby carriage. (Pam Thompson)

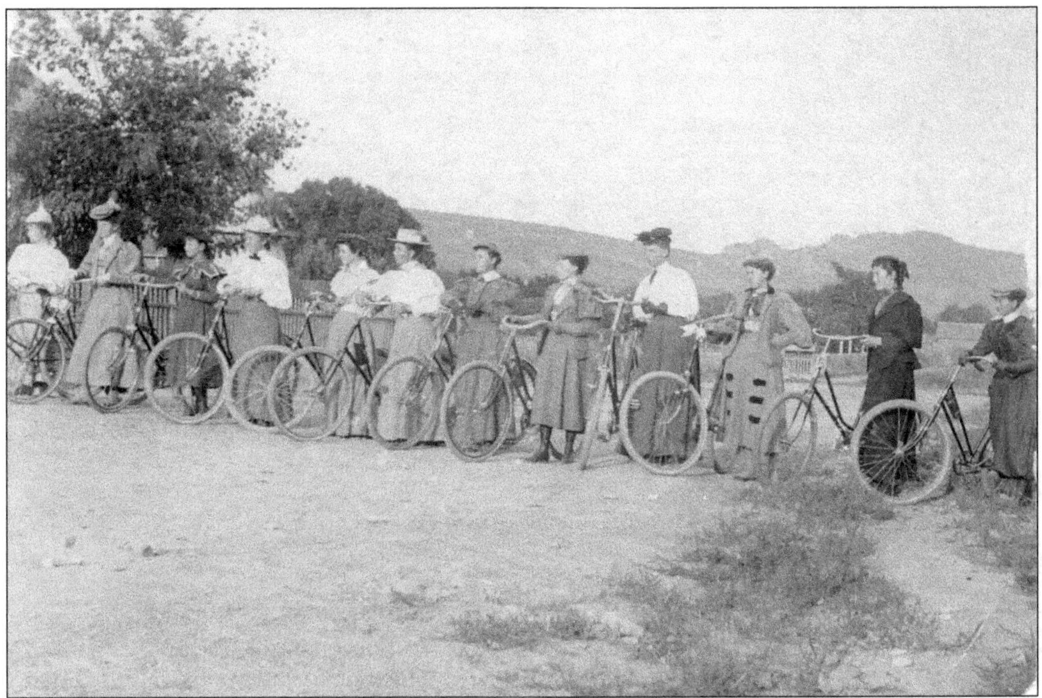

Susan B. Anthony said in an interview in 1896, "I think the bicycle has done more to emancipate women than anything else in the world." The bicycle craze in the 1890s led to a movement for rational dress, which helped liberate women from corsets, long dresses, and possibly even the sidesaddle for horses. These women are in Hillsboro, but the event is unknown. (BRM)

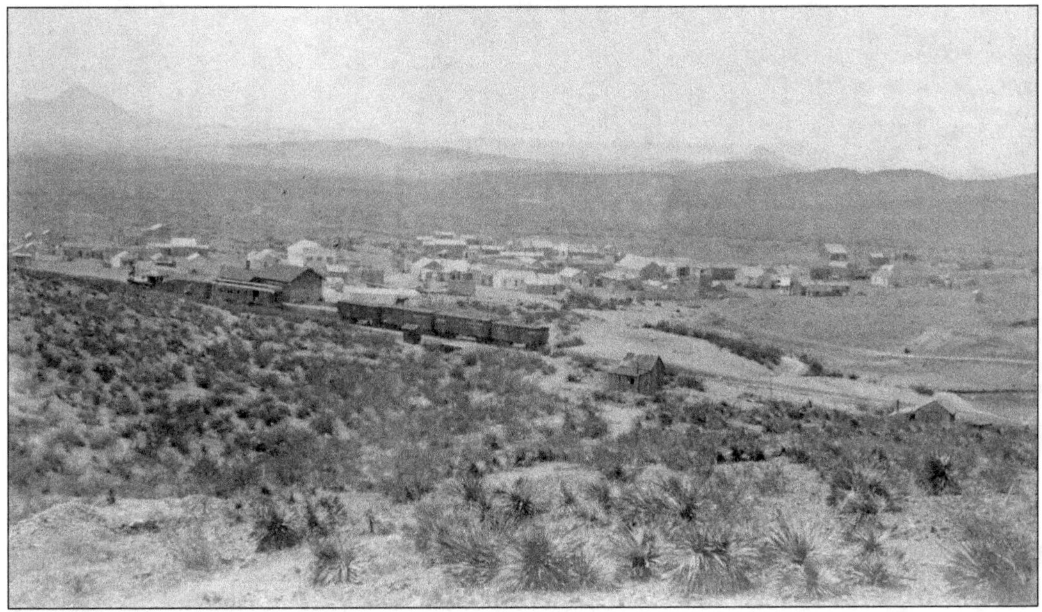

The Lake Valley Railroad was incorporated in 1882 as a branch of the Santa Fe. The Santa Fe Railway put in a branch from Nutt to Lake Valley because of the number of laborers and the amount of silver being shipped. It was dismantled in 1934. The little train here pulls two passenger cars, a flatcar, and four ore cars. (RGHC)

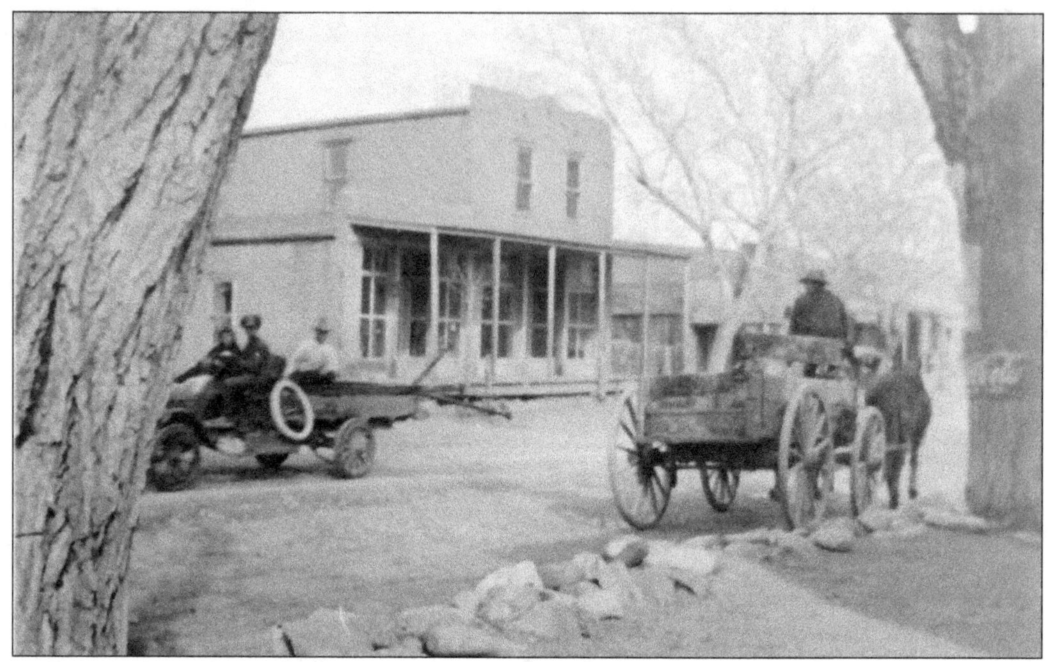

In this photograph, old meets new on Main Street in Hillsboro. One wagon has an engine and the other a horse. In other words, the newer version of horsepower encounters the older version. (BRM)

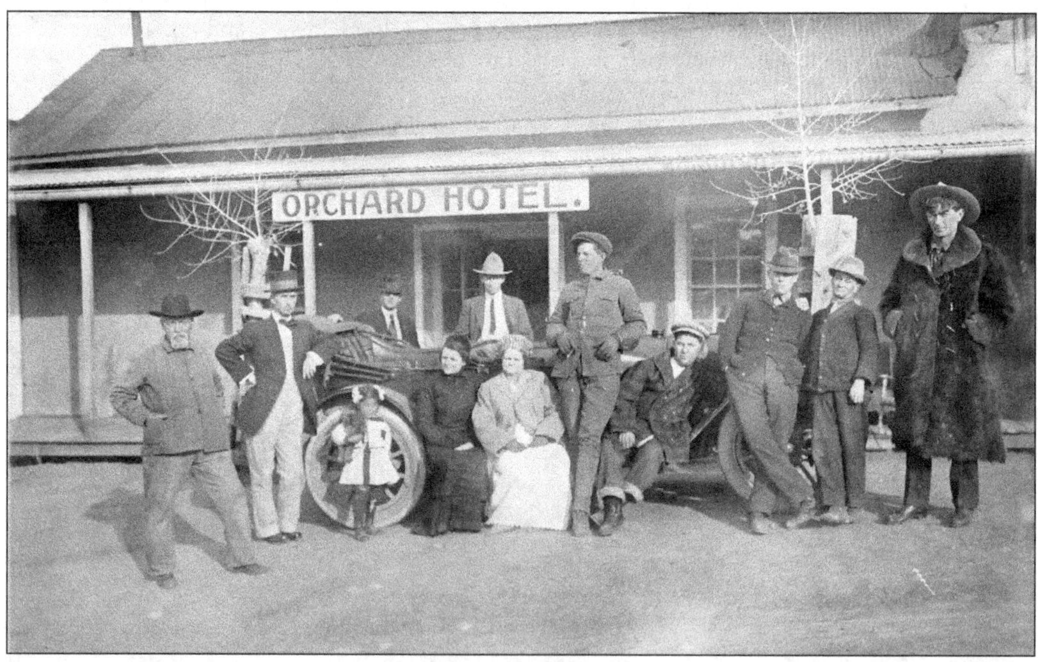

Posing on the first automobile to travel the stage road from Lake Valley to Kingston are, standing from left to right, Tom Lannon, unidentified, John Disinger, Phillip Kelley, Daniel Carbajal, Frank Harris, Gus Saline, and Frank Fink. Seated on the running board are unidentified (possibly Sadie's sister), Sadie Orchard (who once owned the stage line), and unidentified. The small girl is Josefita Montoya. (BRM)

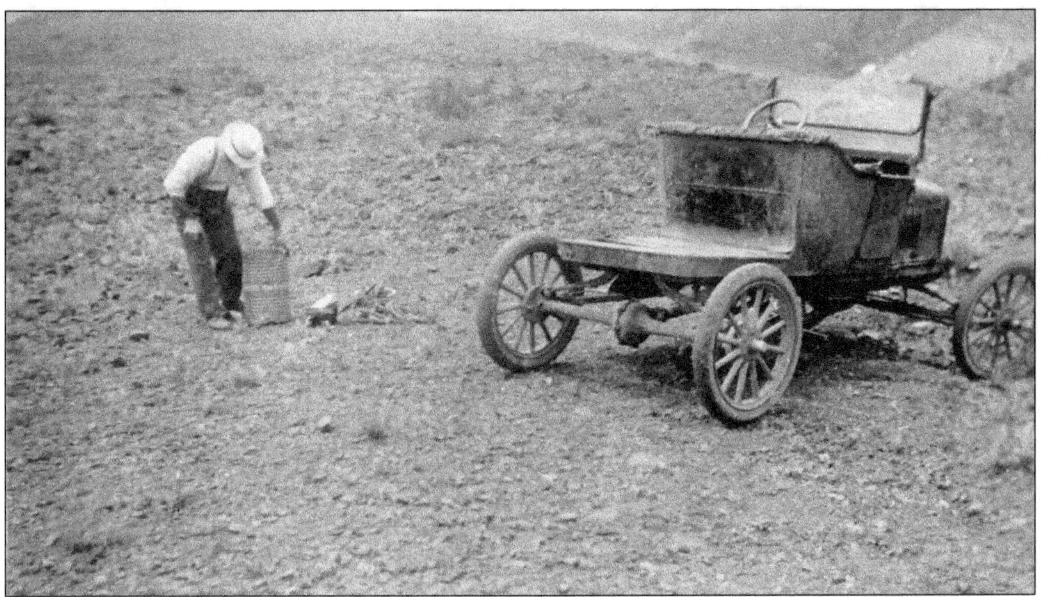

This is an early Ford Model T truck. The man appears to be loading a can of blasting powder. These old trucks received their gas via gravity flow. Therefore, if they were low on gas, and came to a hill, they had to turn around and go up backwards. (BRM)

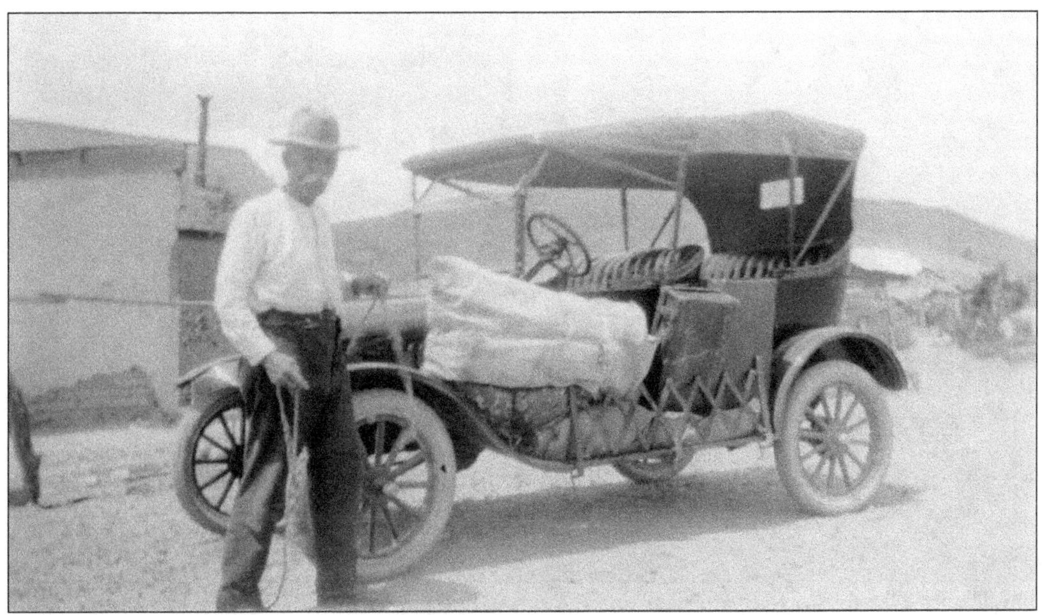

Pack mules and/or wagons were used early on to carry a bed when traveling. With the advent of the car, a fender functioned for the same purpose. Before the time of motels, many people camped by the side of the road.

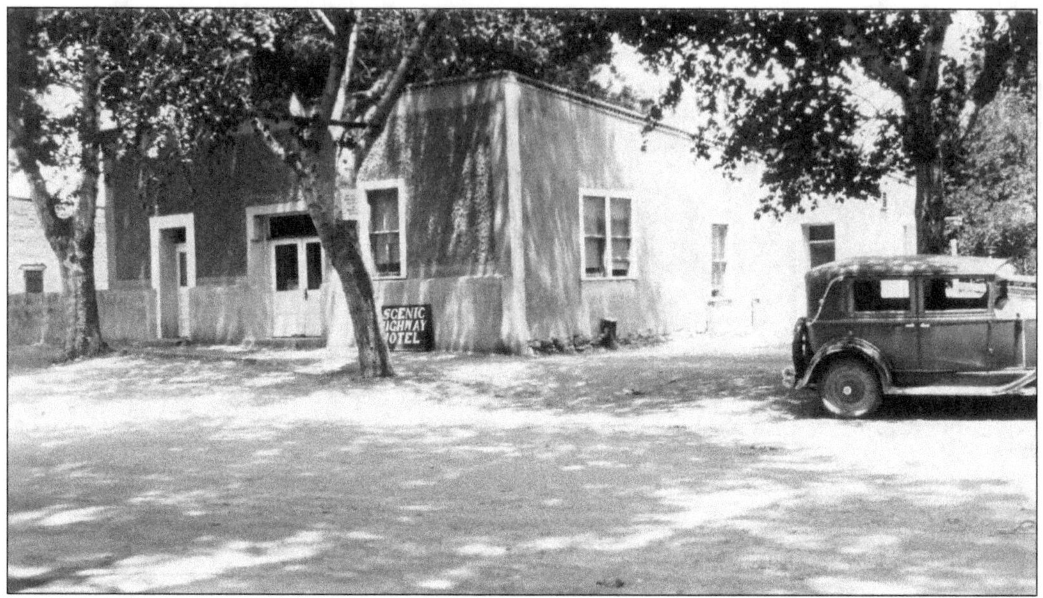

By the 1930s, travel by automobile was common and motor hotels (motels) began to appear. This one was probably opened to accommodate travelers using the new scenic Black Range Highway, built in 1935. This building has also served as a bank, a bar, a café, a store, and a home. (BRM)

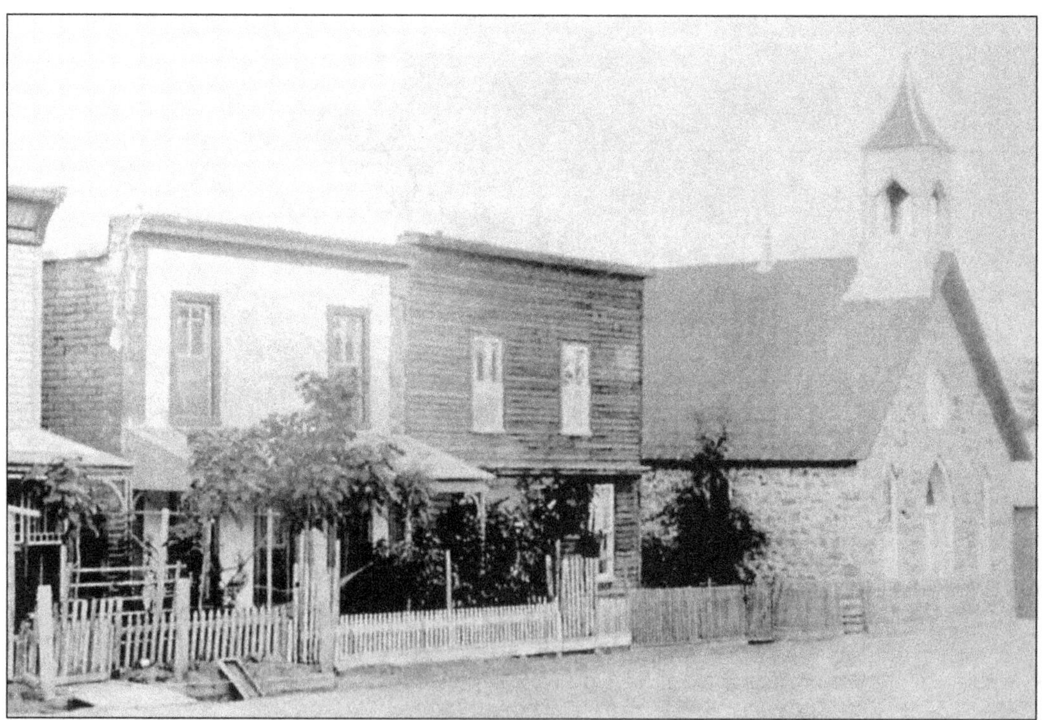

The Union Church in Kingston, shown here, was built around 1887 by gamblers and saloon owners. The people of Kingston thought the town needed some religious element. Citizens hired Reverend Chase from back East as the minister. Prior to 1899, the building was used mostly as a school. A Mr. Wolford, who came to Kingston for his health, was the schoolteacher. (DW)

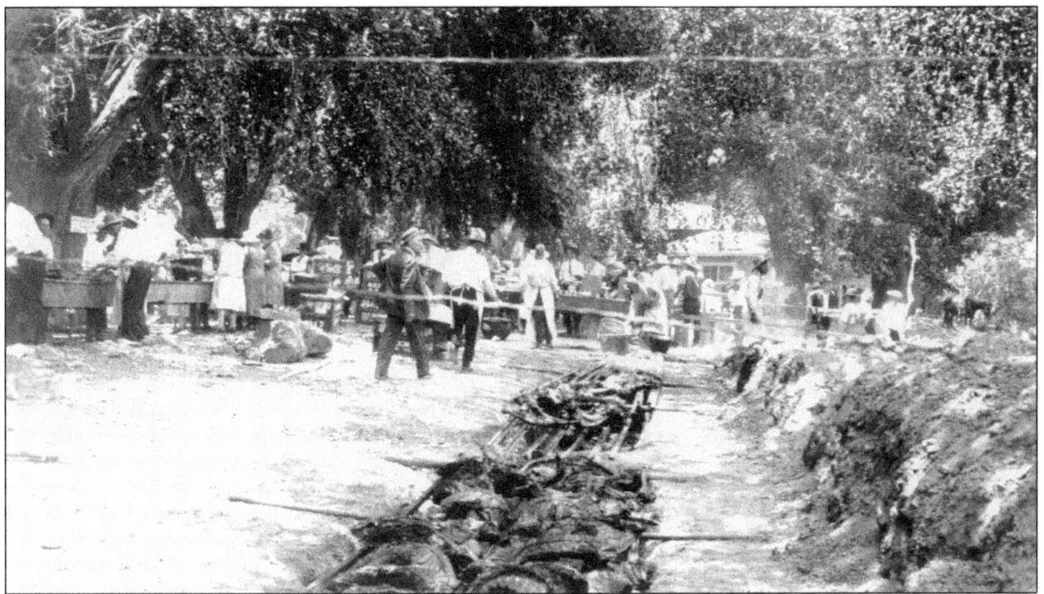

This is a Fourth of July celebration. The very large barbecue pit appears to have been dug right along one of the streets in town. Hillsboro still holds a celebration every July 4. (IHSF)

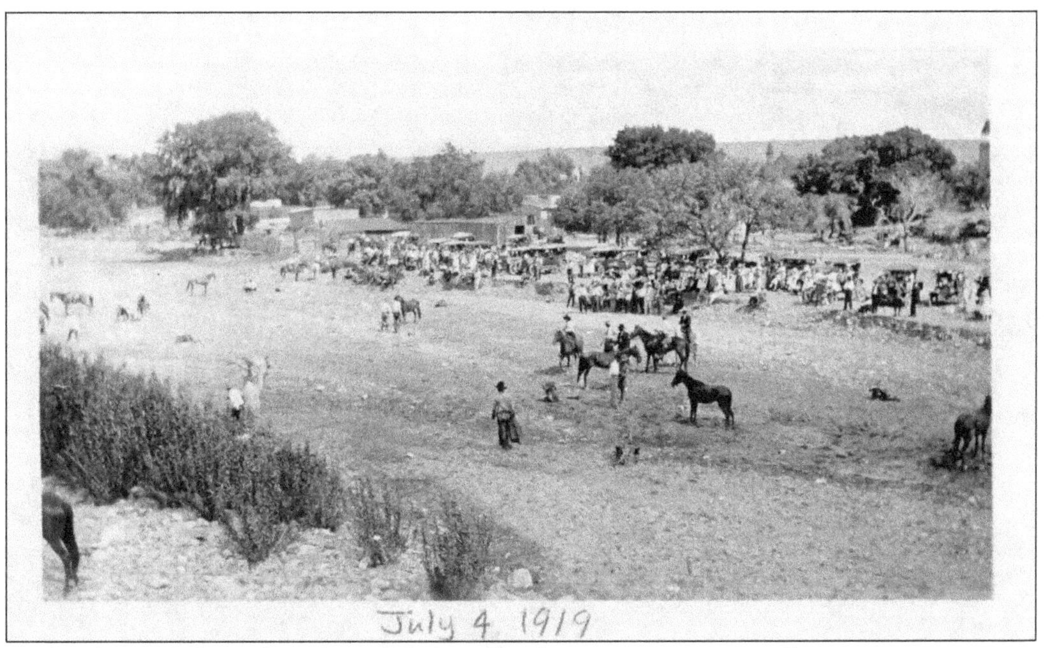

In the absence of grandstands, people brought their own seating, usually an auto or a wagon. Often, the cars were arranged around the selected "rodeo ground," thereby creating a sort of arena. The fact that the creek is running in this picture suggests that bronc riders might get a bath in addition to a spill when bucked off. (BRM)

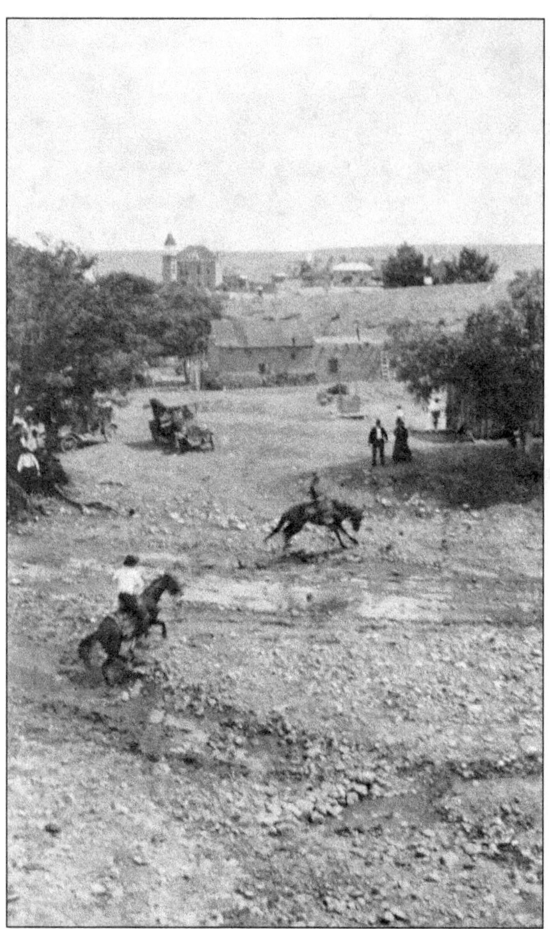

The saddle-bronc event was part of the 1919 rodeo. However, no arena was available to prevent the horse from heading for parts unknown. A pickup rider on a trained horse stayed close to help the successful broncobuster dismount when his ride was over, to give him a ride back if he bucked off, or to catch the bronc. (BRM)

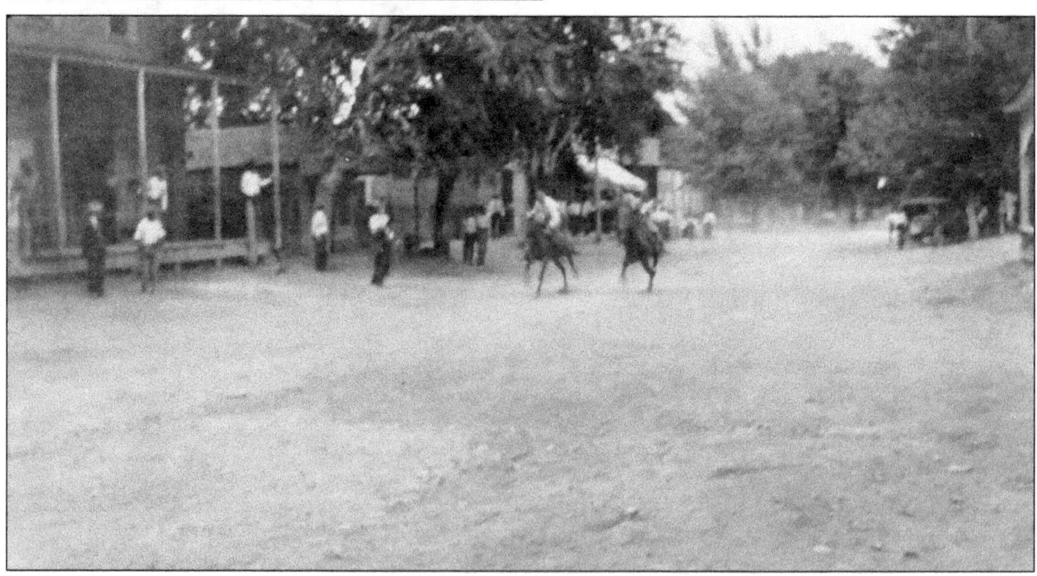

Another event that was part of the Fourth of July celebration was matched horse races down the middle of Main Street in Hillsboro. No doubt, there were a lot of bets made. (BRM)

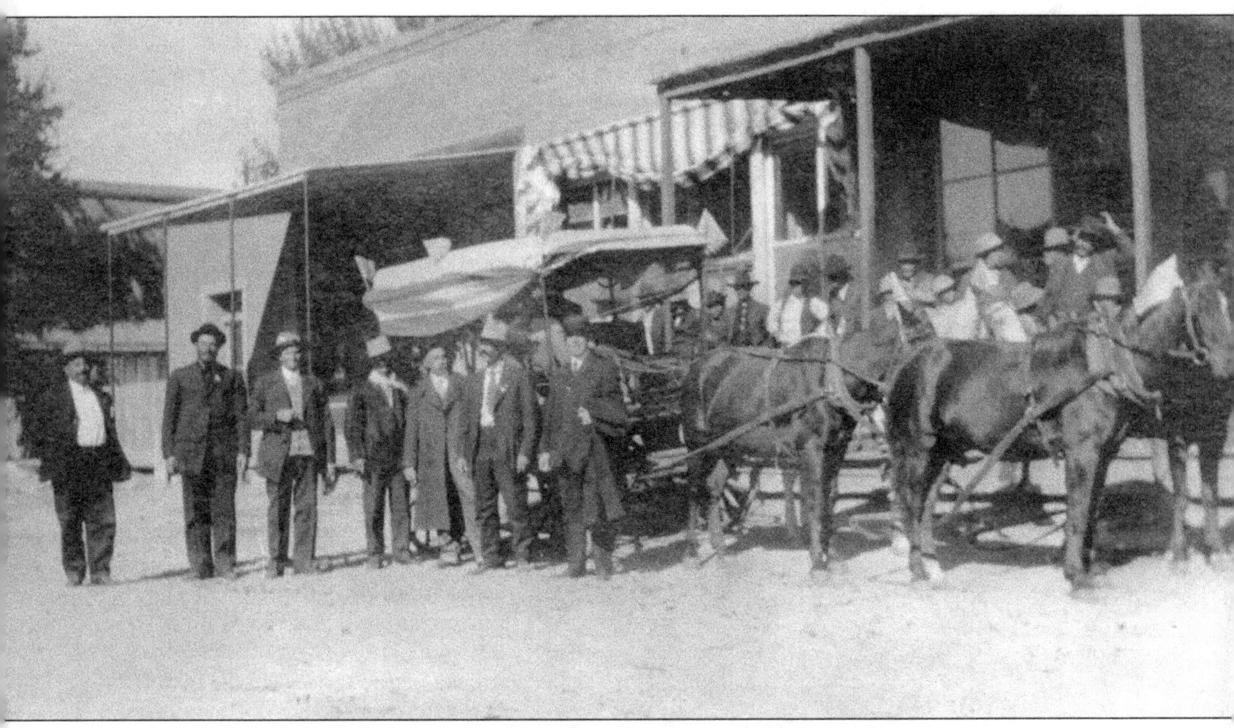

This photograph was labeled as a 1907 funeral in downtown Hillsboro. No information is given regarding the identity of the deceased. (IHSF)

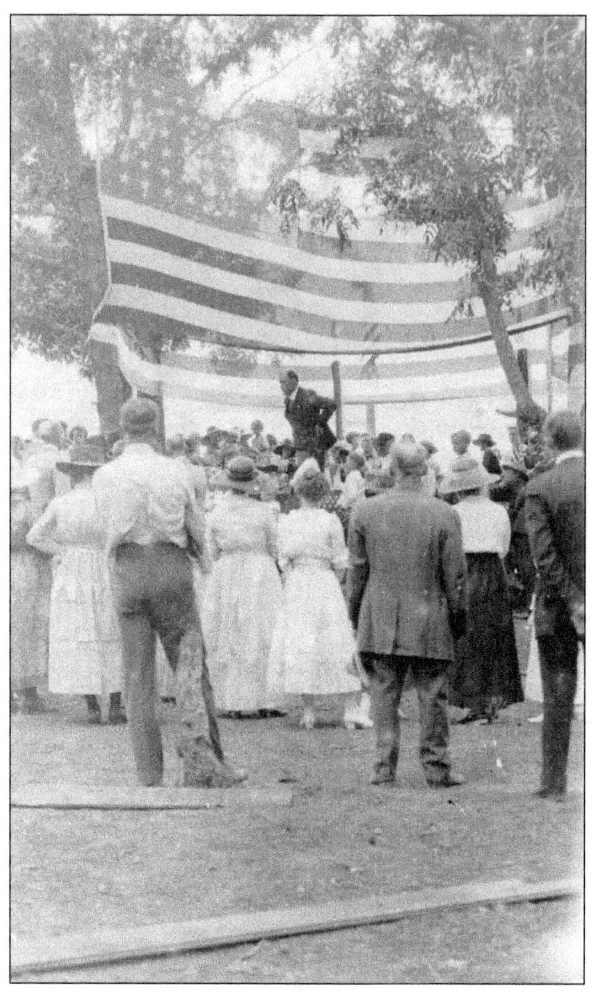

In 1921, a dam-to-dam road was built over the Black Range Mountains from the Berrenda to Mule Creek. It was meant to eventually connect Elephant Butte Dam to Roosevelt Dam in Arizona. These two photographs show a picnic that was held at the Parks ranch to dedicate the opening of the Black Range Scenic Highway. Speakers were Governor Mechem and other dignitaries. A short time after the opening, a hard rain hit, and the resulting floodwaters wiped out large portions of the road. It was never rebuilt. Today's State Highway 152 was not constructed until 1936 and not paved until 1968. (Both, GSM)

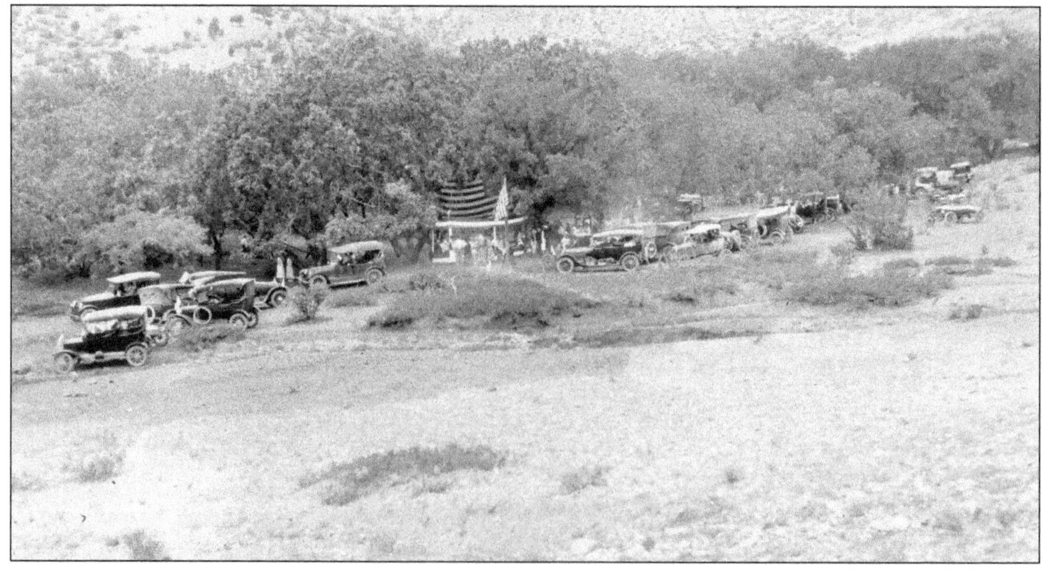

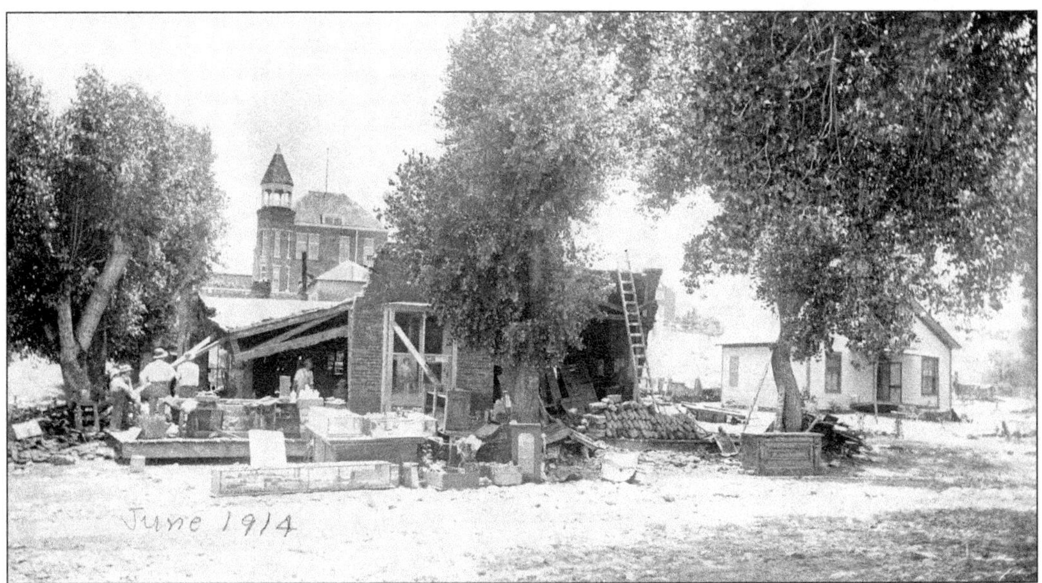

On June 10, 1914, a cloudburst sent a six-foot-high wall of water roaring through the town of Hillsboro that wiped out many buildings and damaged others. Thomas Murphy, a pioneer resident and Sierra County's first sheriff, lost his life. In an unpublished letter in the Hillsboro Historical Society Archives, Hattie Givens remarked about the flood: "From the bar-room across the way we could see the men standing in groups, then the door was closed, the lights went out. Then a terrible crash of falling timber and glass told us that the whole front of the drugstore had fallen out; still another crash and the back end where Dr. Givens office was falls; then farther down the street we could hear crash upon crash as the horrible waves demolished building after building." (Both, BRM)

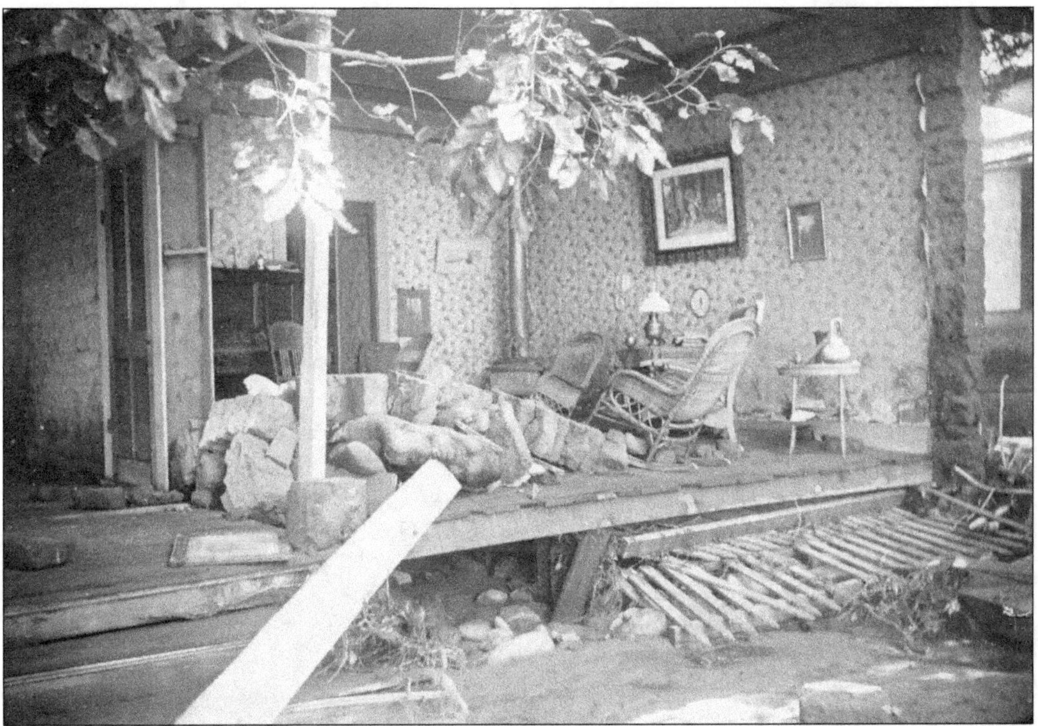

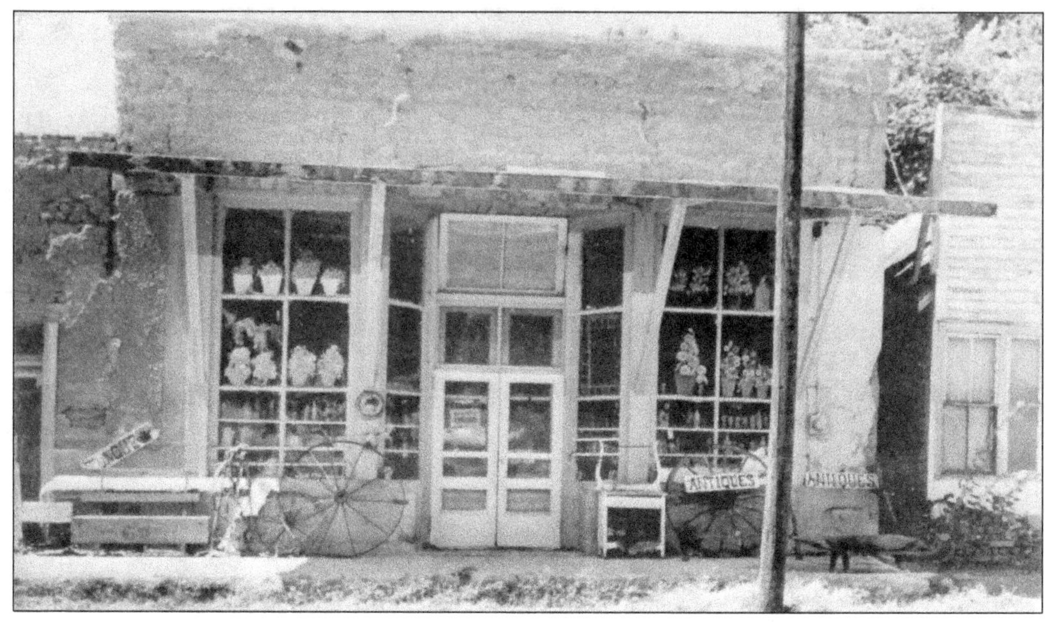

First known as the Keller Miller Store, this building became Andy Robinson's Meat Market and then Sue's Antiques. It barely survived the 1914 flood only to be destroyed in the 1972 flood. (Above, BRM; below, GSM)

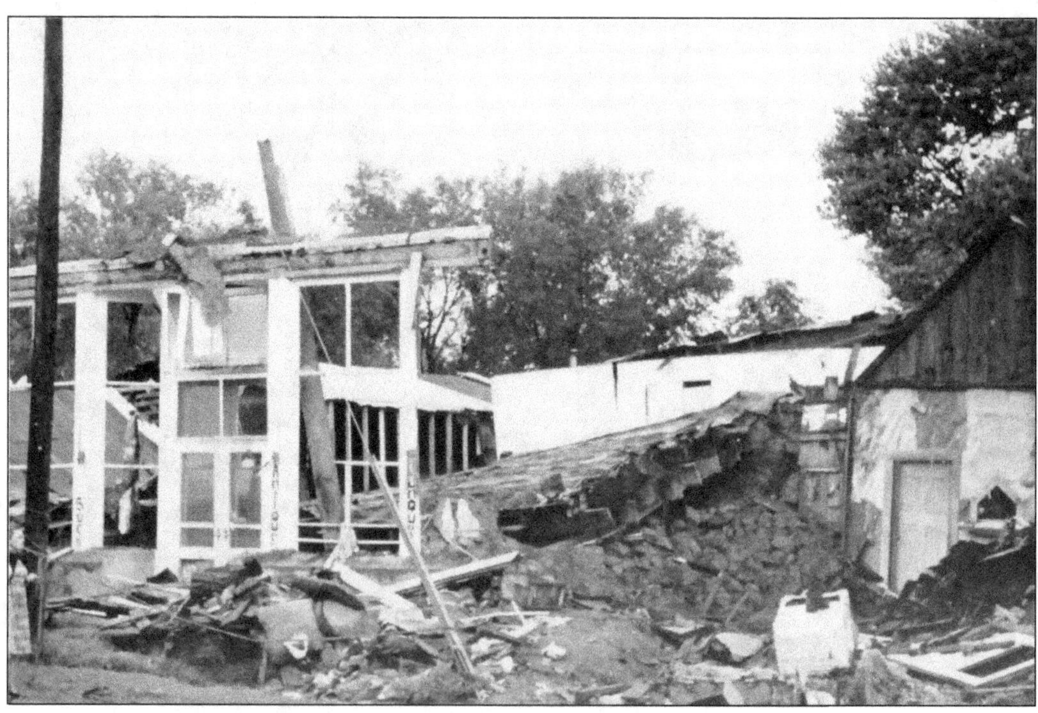

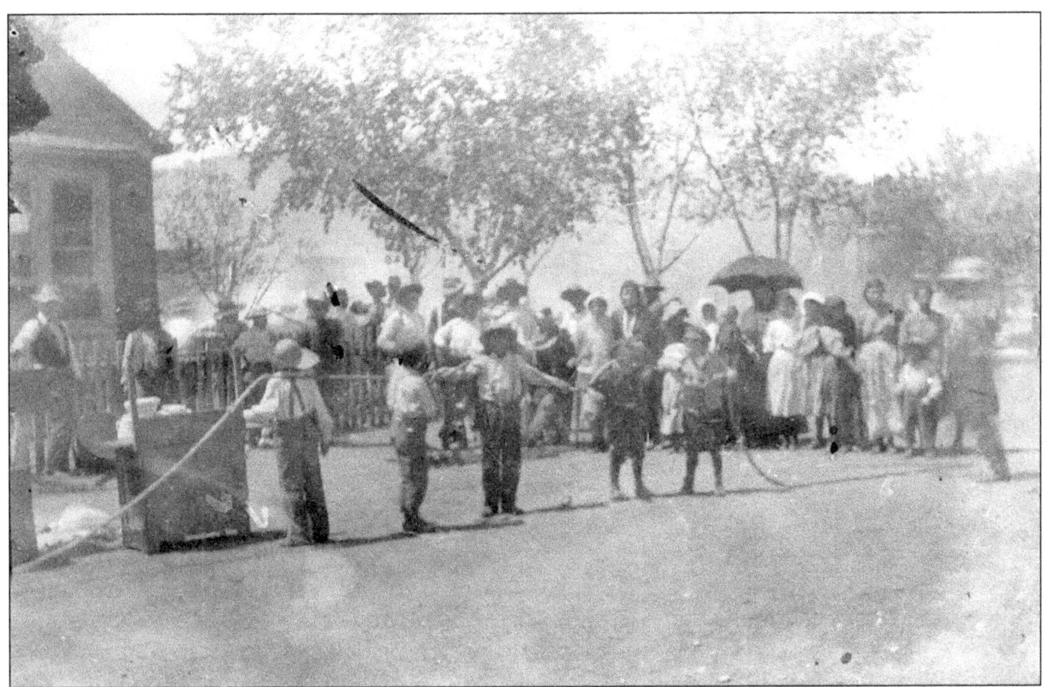

Fires were a big problem in Hillsboro, Lake Valley, and Kingston. There is no fire truck at this fire in 1910 (above). In 1949, four houses burning on Elenora Street (below) brought the fire truck from Hot Springs. Hillsboro Historical Society now owns that fire truck. (Above, BRM; below, SR)

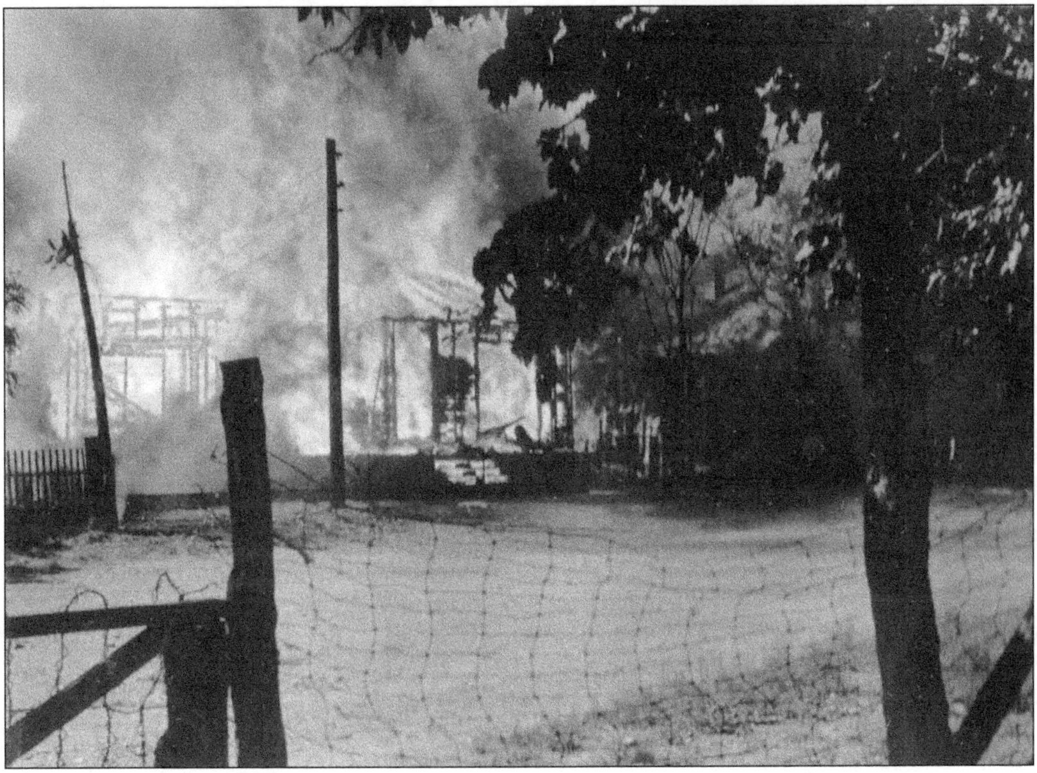

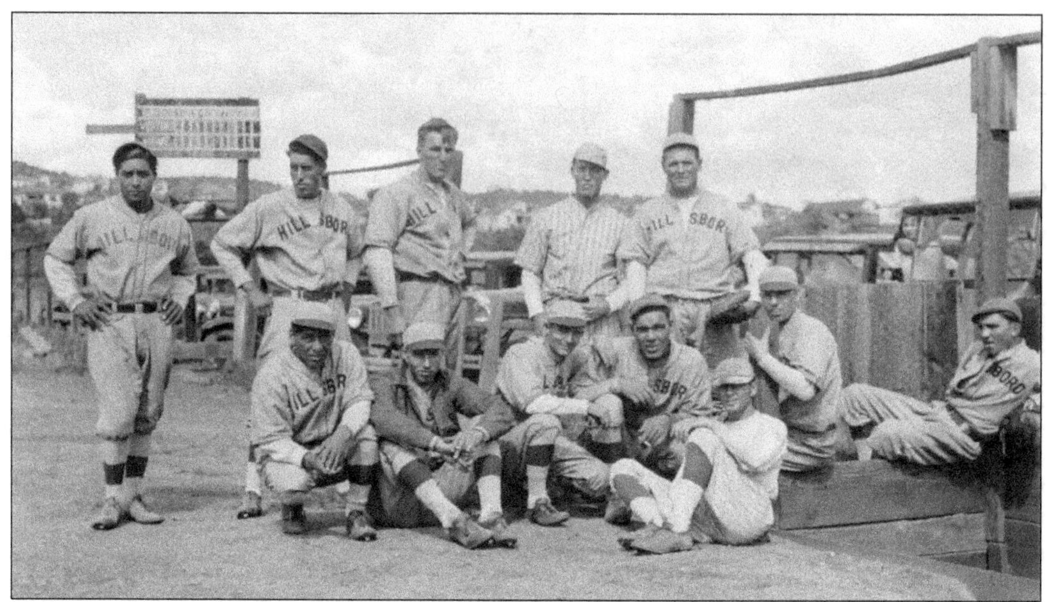

Hillsboro's baseball team, called the Sierra Browns and later the Hillsboro Grays, rode the stage to Lake Valley, and then took the train to Las Cruces to play State College in 1908. Shown here in 1931 from left to right are (seated) Pat Valencia, John Tittmann, Shorty McCurn, Herb Lett, Bingo Conner, Earl Lett, and Beningo Valencia; (standing) Tony Remeglio, Manuel Madrid, Bob Kinok, George Luna and Bill Sullivan. (BRM)

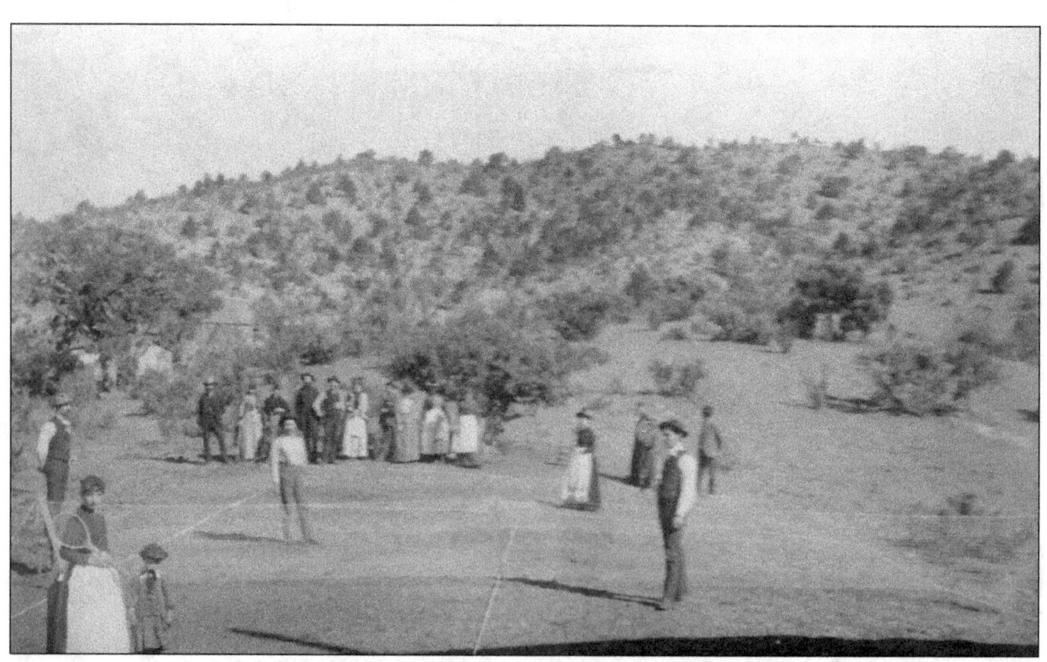

Mine managers brought their favorite forms of recreation to the area. Here, a tennis tournament is in progress in early-day Kingston. (PBM)

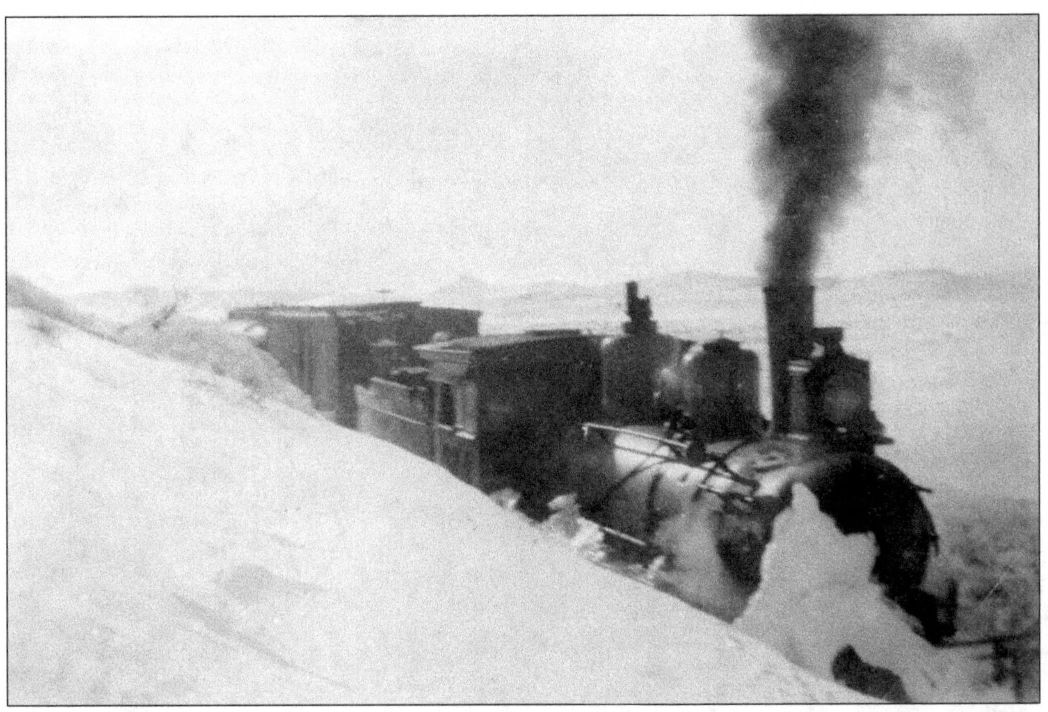

Even though southwestern New Mexico was known for its moderate climate, deep snow could come at times. Above, the train from Nutt to Lake Valley is bogged down in a snowdrift; below, a horse is rigged to pull the stuck mail wagon. (Both, BRM)

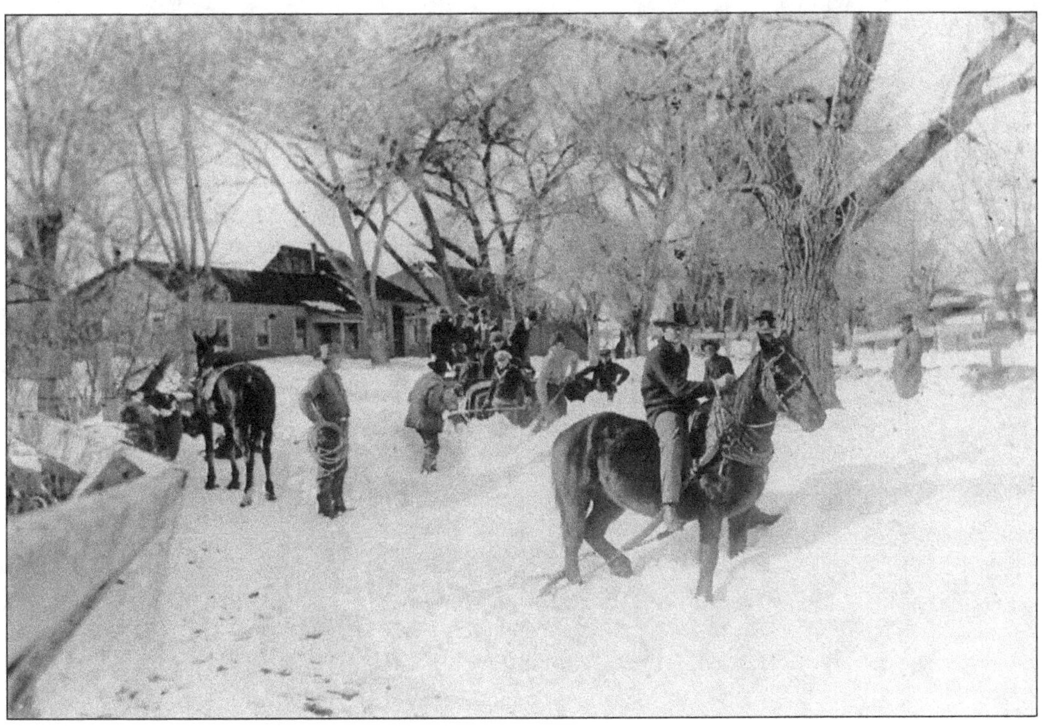

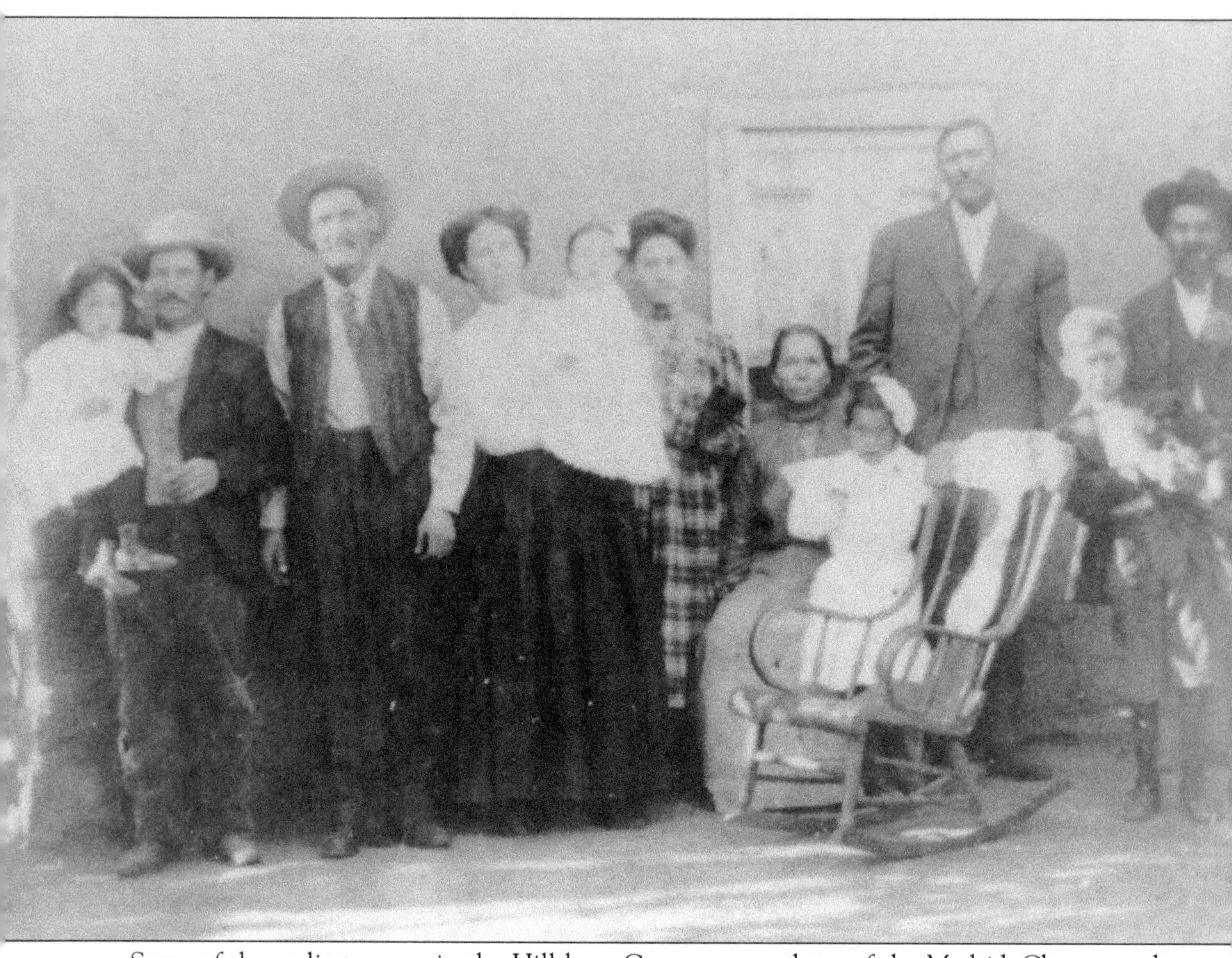

Some of the earliest graves in the Hillsboro Cemetery are those of the Madrid, Chavez, and Luna families. They were among Hillsboro's earliest pioneers. In this 1911 photograph, from left to right, are unidentified holding Max Luna, Adrian Luna, Elvira Chavez Luna holding George Luna, and Romelia Chavez. Seated is the family matriarch, Dolores Madrid Chavez, holding Alvina Luna. Standing is the family patriarch Abel V. Chavez (very large man), an unknown boy, and Alberto Baca. Their descendants are among the few remaining original families still living in Hillsboro.

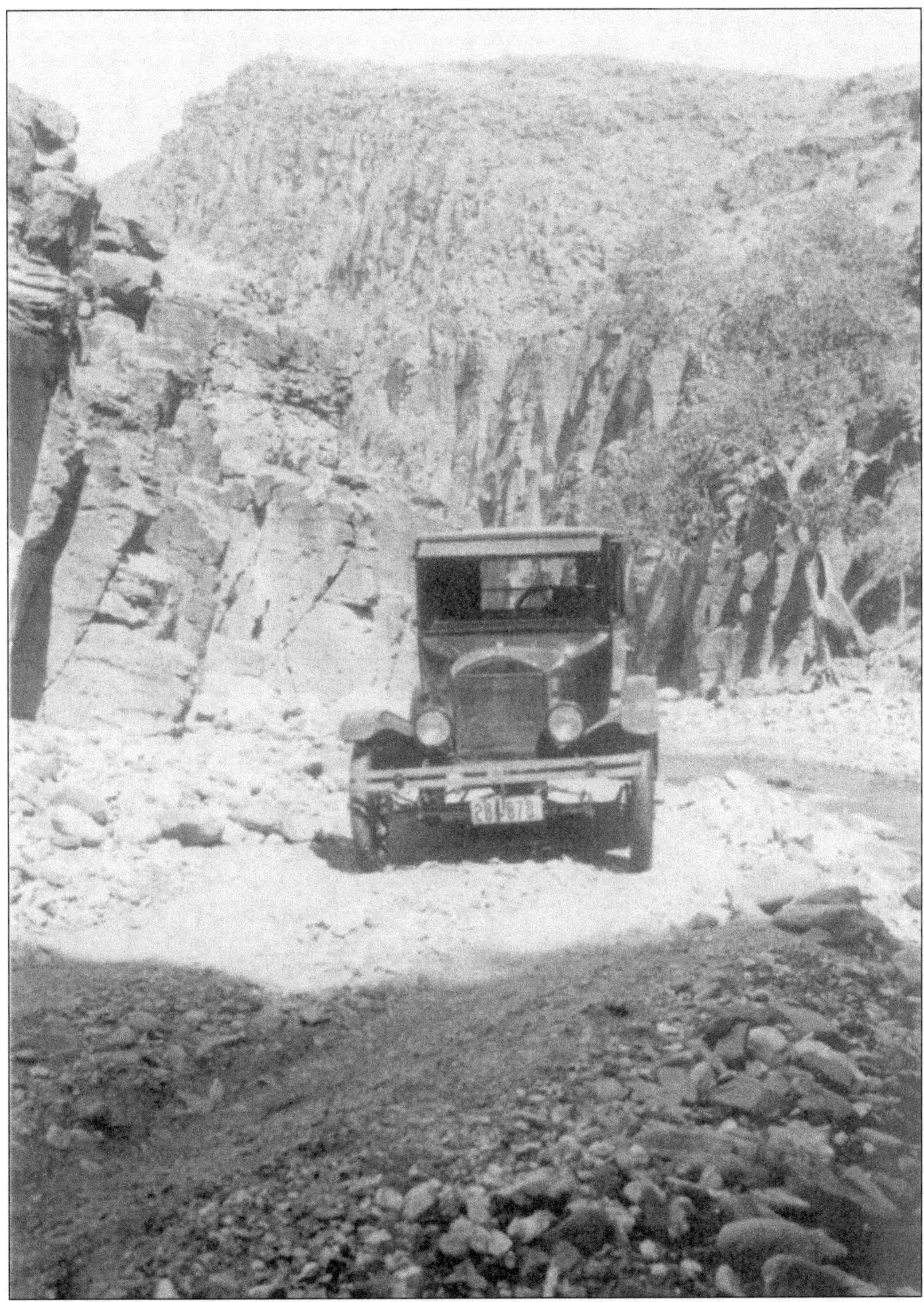

This is a c. 1935 view of the scenic Black Range Highway as it passes through the Upper Box, west of Hillsboro. Before a bridge was built, this road was not safe for stage or car traffic in the rainy season. (DW)

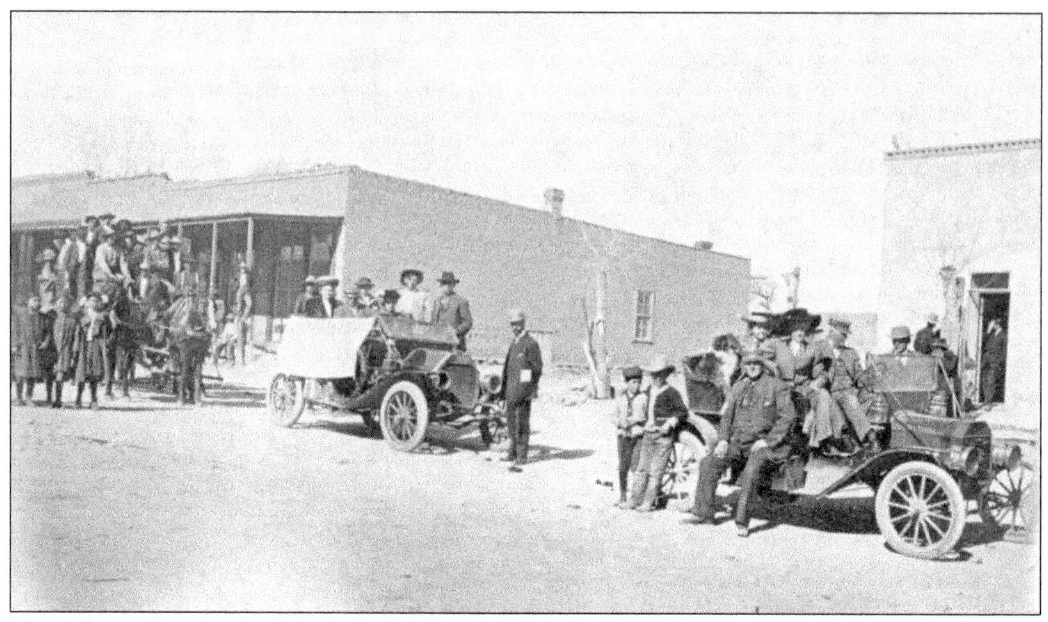

New Mexico become a territory on September 9, 1850, and did not become a state until January 6, 1912. A big statehood celebration was held in Hillsboro with a parade on Main Street. Here, the first two cars full of dignitaries lead the parade. Gus Hilton, the father of hotelier Conrad Hilton, is sitting on the running board. (BRM)

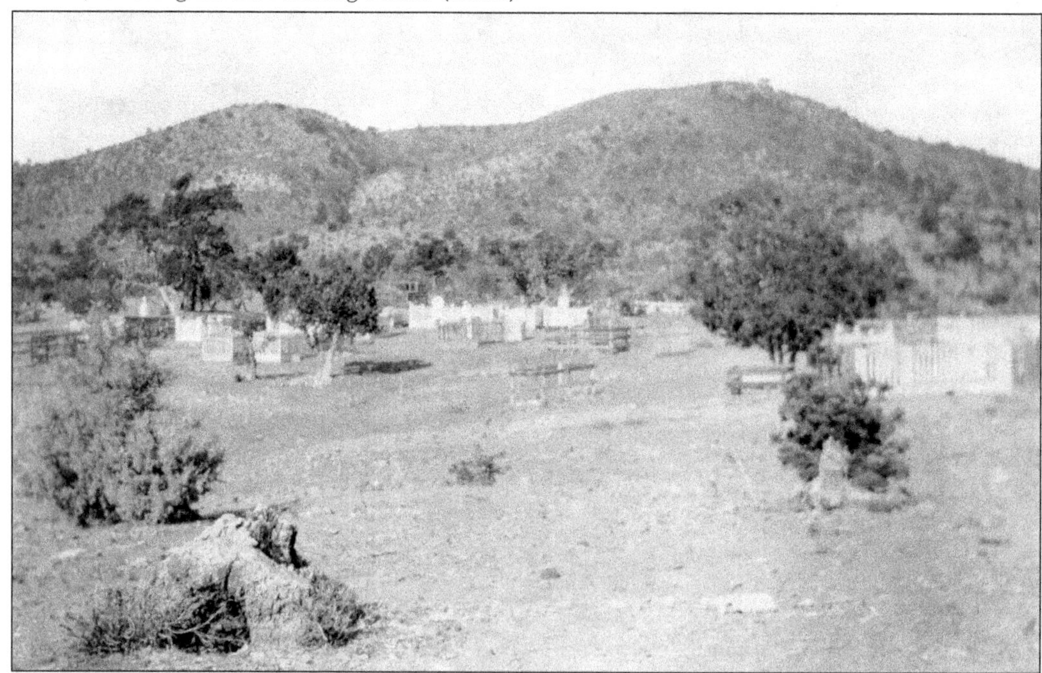

Some of Hillsboro's, Kingston's, and Lake Valley's early founders such as Daniel Dugan and David Stitzel are buried in the old graveyards. Also interred here are Indian fighters, Civil War soldiers, and veterans from both World War I and World War II. There are many unmarked graves in these cemeteries, such as those of the children who died in the flu epidemic of 1918. Many markers are simply rocks with initials or crosses chiseled on them. This is the Kingston cemetery.

Bibliography

Leckie, William H. *The Buffalo Soldiers: A Narrative of the Negro Cavalry in the West*. Norman, OK: University of Oklahoma Press, 1967.

McKenna, James A. *Black Range Tales*. New York: Wilson-Erickson, 1936.

Owen, Gordon R. *The Two Alberts: Fountain and Fall*. Las Cruces, NM: Yucca Tree Press, 1996.

Recko, Corey. *Murder on the White Sands: The Disappearance of Albert and Henry Fountain*. Denton, TX: University of North Texas Press, 2007.

Rhodes, Eugene Manlove. *The Proud Sheriff*. Boston: Houghton Mifflin, 1935.

Sierra County Historical Society. *History of Sierra County, New Mexico*. Mount Vernon, IN: Windmill Publications, 1979.

Sullivan, James B. *A New Mexican Family: Tafoya-Sullivan and the Origins of Sierra County*. San Antonio: Burke, 1994.

Sweeny, Edwin. *From Cochise to Geronimo: The Chiricahua Apaches, 1874–1886*. Norman, OK: University of Oklahoma Press, 2010.

www.ingramcontent.com/pod-product-compliance
Lightning Source LLC
LaVergne TN
LVHW081528100826
845153LV00004B/229
* 9 7 8 1 5 3 1 6 5 2 4 7 0 *

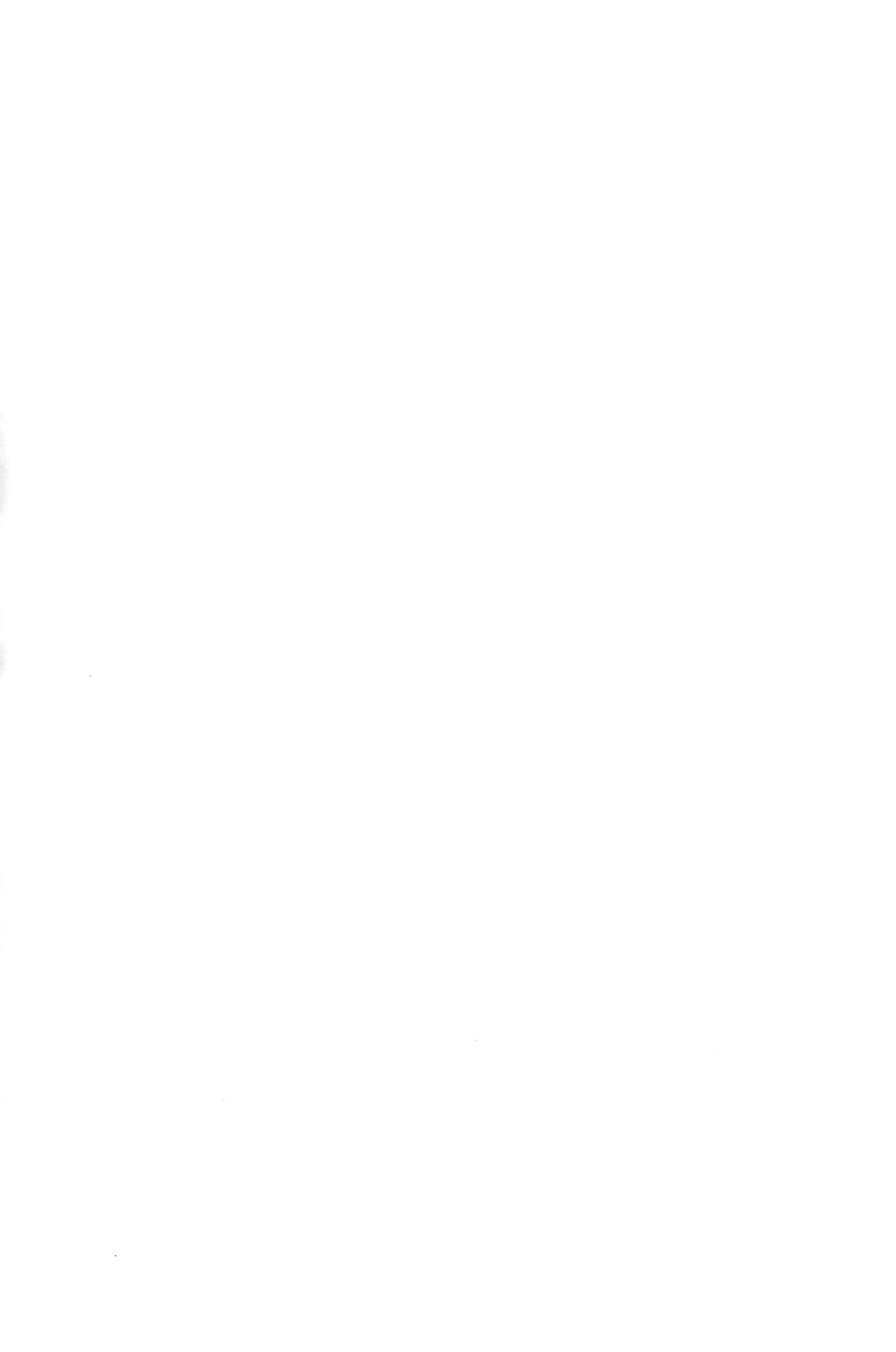

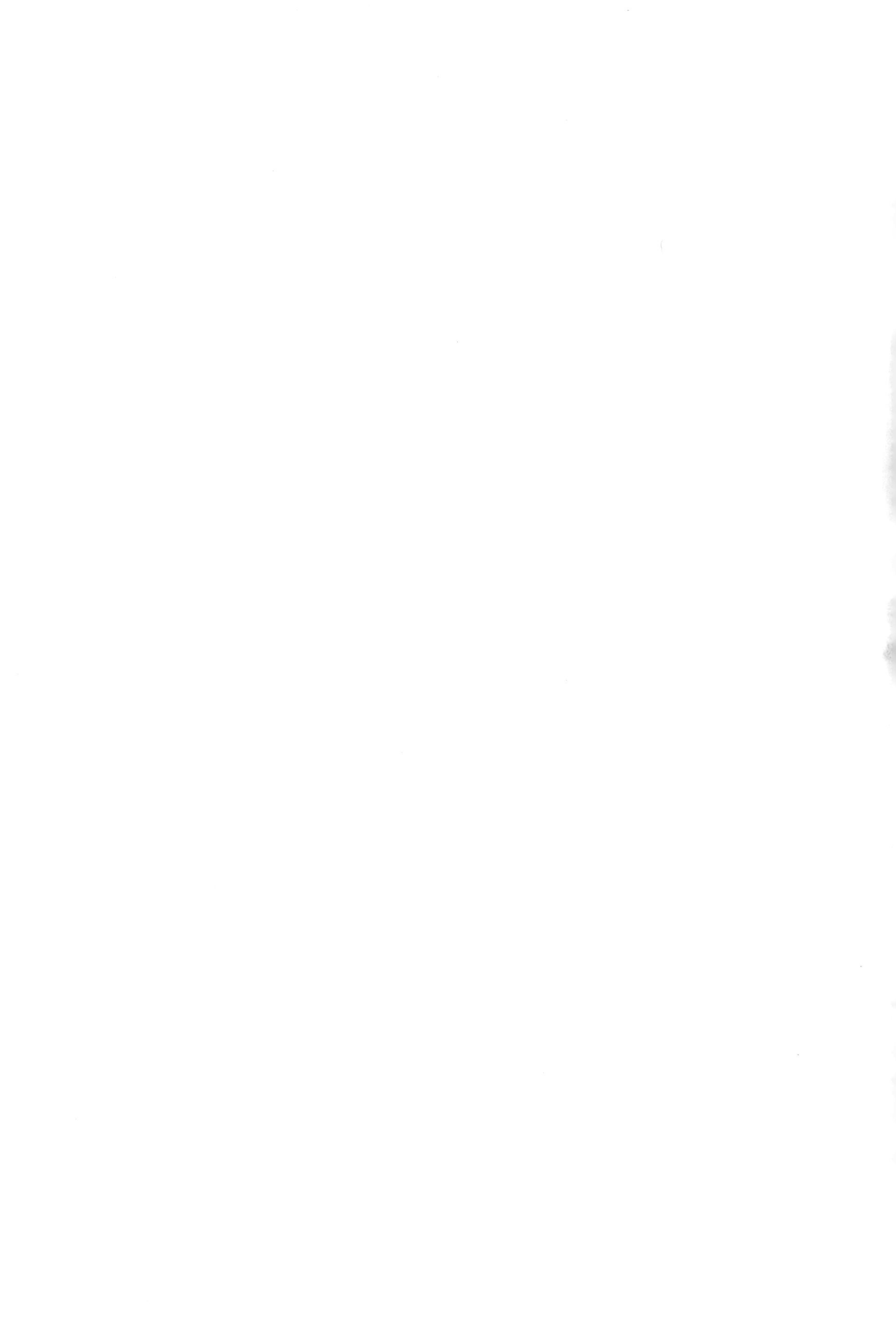